once a·day

DEVOTIONAL

{ for teens }

Kevin Johnson

ZONDERVAN®

ZONDERVAN.com/
AUTHORTRACKER
follow your favorite authors

ZONDERVAN

Once-a-Day Devotional for Teens

This title is also available as a Zondervan ebook.
Visit www.zondervan.com/ebooks.

Requests for information should be addressed to:

Zondervan, *Grand Rapids, Michigan 49530*

Library of Congress Cataloging-in-Publication Data

Johnson, Kevin (Kevin Walter)
Once-a-day devotional for teens / Kevin Johnson.
p. cm.
Includes bibliographical references and index.
ISBN 978-0-310-72995-2 (softcover : alk. paper)
1. Christian teenagers—Prayers and devotions. 2. Devotional calendars. I. Title.
BV4850.J638 2012
242'.63—dc23 2012009834

Cover design: Kristine Nelson
Interior design: Sherri Hoffman and Jamie DeBruyn
Interior composition: Greg Johnson/Textbook Perfect

Printed in the United States of America

---

13 14 15 16 17 18 /DCI/ 22 21 20 19 18 17 16 15 14 13 12 11 10 9 8 7 6 5 4 3

A NOTE ON THE DEVOTIONAL LAYOUT

As you begin using this book, you may notice the Scriptures for each devotion follow a unique pattern—somewhat chronological, but bouncing from the Old to New Testaments and Psalms and Proverbs, and then back. That's because this devotional is tied to the Once-A-Day reading plan, which takes a short, chronological selection from each of those "sections" of the Bible each day to help you read through the Bible in one year. We've tied each devotion to a key verse from the reading plan for that day—which may mean, for example, you're reading a devotional thought based around Genesis 1:1 one day, Proverbs 2 the next, and Matthew 3 the day after.

You can use this book on its own for your daily devotional time, of course. As an everyday devotional, this book will let you explore key ideas and verses from across Scripture and see how they apply to your life today. If you choose, you can also use this devotional alongside the full Once-A-Day reading plan, so the devotion for each day will correspond with your Bible reading for that day, deepening your understanding of God's Word and enhancing what you've read.

We've included the Once-A-Day reading plan alongside each devotion (under Read It) so you can follow along with the one-year plan if you desire. Or if you want a simple way to follow the reading plan, the *Once-A-Day Bible for Teens* works alongside this devotional by presenting the readings for the day in order, making tracking your progress and staying on track easy.

january 1 day1

READ IT

Genesis 1:1–2:17, Matthew 1:1–25, Psalm 1:1–6

"In the beginning God created the heavens and the earth."

GENESIS 1:1

LIVE IT

It's tough to wrap your head around the start of everything. But the Genesis account of the world's beginnings is more than a tale of distant history. It's more than a reason to debate with modern scientific theory. The first chapters of the Bible tell why you exist.

Suppose you make a clay sculpture in art class. Suddenly you hold in your hands an object that belongs uniquely to you. Because you made it, you own it. When God created the world, he instantly became master of all his handiwork. Psalm 24:1–2 says, "The earth is the LORD's, and everything in it, the world, and all who live in it; for he founded it on the seas and established it on the waters." The world belongs completely to God.

You might never be satisfied with what you shape from a lump of clay. But God was incredibly pleased when he made people. First he dreamed up our design. He determined our purpose. He thought of everything humans need for a happy existence. Then he went to work. He put us in the most perfect place ever. He made us partners with each other and gave us solid work to do. Because we belong to him, he expects us to follow his commands.

So why did God make you? He created you to enjoy life close to him—and to people.

PRAY IT

God, you made the world. So I belong to you now and forever. Teach me to live for you.

day2 january 2

READ IT

Genesis 2:18–4:16, Matthew 2:1–18, Psalm 2:1–12

> *"The kings of the earth rise up and the rulers band together against the* LORD *and against his anointed."*
>
> PSALM 2:2

LIVE IT

Everyone knows what it's like to make another person angry. But only God knows what it's like to have the whole human race up in arms against him.

Human rebellion started back with Adam and Eve in the garden of Eden (Genesis 3:1–24). But sin quickly spread to every person and place on earth. Psalm 2 shows the entire world rising up against the Lord. Nations scheme. Groups hatch useless plots. The earth's rulers want to break loose from God's control.

God studies this crowd of puny rebels and laughs because their might is nothing compared to his. And the Lord has a secret power: he has installed his Son as ruler over the earth. That's an astonishing Old Testament picture. Hundreds of years before Jesus showed up as a baby in Bethlehem, this Scripture reveals him reigning as king of everything. Even when human beings join together to fight God, they can't beat his "anointed," or chosen one. The whole world belongs to Jesus, and wise people everywhere submit to his authority. No one can stop the Lord's plan to save people, and he blesses everyone who runs to him for help.

Glance around and you'll see plenty of people living against God. But you can serve God with utter respect. You can celebrate his reign. You can bow to him with every part of who you are.

PRAY IT

God, you reign over everything. But people all around me rebel against you. I choose to serve you in awestruck respect.

READ IT

Genesis 4:17–6:22, Matthew 2:19–3:17, Psalm 3:1–8

> *"In those days John the Baptist came, preaching in the wilderness of Judea and saying, 'Repent, for the kingdom of heaven has come near.'"*
>
> Matthew 3:1–2

LIVE IT

Even before Jesus began to teach and do miracles, people knew someone amazing was on the way. That's because John the Baptist had come on the scene and prepared people to meet the Lord.

John's arrival was no surprise. Isaiah, the Old Testament prophet, once predicted a voice in the wilderness would clear a path for God (Isaiah 40:3). And an angel announced that Elizabeth, a relative of Mary the mother of Jesus, would give birth to the Lord's messenger.

John wore rough clothes and ate a plain diet. His grueling life in the desert reminded everyone of God's ancient messengers. When he commanded everyone to repent—to stop sinning and turn back to God—his challenging words drew crowds from every direction. John confronted not only the masses but Pharisees and Sadducees, religious rulekeepers who considered themselves too good to need cleansing from sin. He baptized everyone who accepted his message, dipping them in the Jordan River as a way of demonstrating remorse for doing wrong. His every word and action pointed to one fact: someone much greater was coming.

You would be startled if John the Baptist showed up shouting in your street. But his message hits home no matter where you live. You want to be prepared for Jesus. You need to recognize the awfulness of sin and be ready to meet your Savior.

PRAY IT

Lord, I'm tired of sin and the hurt it causes me, others, and you. I want to be done with doing wrong. I'm ready for your forgiveness.

day4 january 4

READ IT

Genesis 7:1–9:17, Matthew 4:1–22, Proverbs 1:1–7

> *"The fear of the LORD is the beginning of knowledge, but fools despise wisdom and instruction."*
>
> PROVERBS 1:7

LIVE IT

Fearing God might not sound fun. But again and again Scripture says it's your first step to getting the wisdom you need to survive real life.

The meaning of the word for "fear" ranges from feeling terror in the midst of a deadly storm (Jonah 1:10) to overflowing with awe in a king's presence (1 Kings 3:28). When you experience "the fear of the LORD" you simultaneously wonder about backing away in dread but can't help but draw close in amazement. This healthy reverence doesn't leave you quaking. It does remind you to honor God and not treat him casually, like some kind of heavenly buddy.

Proverbs says good things result when you choose to live for God with utter respect. You get insight, a grasp of what's sensible, right, and fair. Everyone will notice you're wise beyond your years, and your understanding will stay fresh until your final breath. You will gain an intelligence that guards you from acting recklessly or caving into evil peer pressure.

Proverbs is the Bible's most densely packed collection of wisdom. If you respect God, you will think hard about the instructions you find in these pages. And you won't hesitate to put your discoveries into action. After all, rejecting the Lord's choice wisdom will send you tripping down a fool's path. And nothing about that sounds enjoyable.

PRAY IT

God, I will live for you with complete respect. You fill me with awe and constantly amaze me. I need you to teach me through your wise words.

day5

READ IT

Genesis 9:18–11:9, Matthew 4:23–5:20, Psalm 4:1–8

> *"Answer me when I call to you, my righteous God. Give me relief from my distress; have mercy on me and hear my prayer."*
>
> Psalm 4:1

LIVE IT

Picture collapsing on your bed after your most unpleasant day ever. It's not hard to recall what pushed you into the misery zone. But you might wonder if God was around when you were hurting. He was. And he is.

Psalm 4 doesn't say why King David wrote these words, but the shape of his problem isn't hard to detect. He'd prayed but hadn't received an answer. He'd waited for compassionate relief from distress, after being humiliated by people who don't worship God. He trembled on his bed, trying to figure out where he went wrong. He was so tired of people doubting God's goodness that he just wanted to fall asleep and forget the day.

David's head was spinning with frustration. His heart was thick with sadness. But he fought back with true facts. He reminded himself that God watches over his followers and hears their cries. His own shaking wasn't an excuse to sin in what he thought, said, or did. His pain was a chance to trust, look for God's shining brilliance, and enjoy the Lord's simple gifts. He could sleep peacefully because the Lord kept him safe.

When you feel overwhelmed, you can be sure you're not praying to empty sky. God was listening when you felt deep pain. He's listening now.

PRAY IT

Lord, I trust that you're there for me when I feel pain. I trust you to answer my prayers and help me deal with my problems. I count on you to be completely good.

day6 january 6

READ IT

Genesis 11:10–13:18, Matthew 5:21–42, Psalm 5:1–12

> *"The LORD had said to Abram, 'Go from your country, your people and your father's household to the land I will show you.'"*
>
> GENESIS 12:1–2

LIVE IT

You know how it feels to have a plan where nothing turns out? When problems seem impossible, no one faults you for giving up.

Not long after Adam and Eve sinned back in the garden of Eden, God looked at the human race and concluded, "every inclination of the thoughts of the human heart was only evil all the time" (Genesis 6:5). Even after the Lord started over with Noah—the one good person he could find—everyone slid back into sin.

God had every reason to be done with the human race. Instead he picked Abram as the beginning of a new plan. When he told Abram to go to a distant, unnamed land, this faith-filled man heeded God's command. He immediately obeyed, packing up and moving his entire household without any idea where he was going.

God had an extraordinary future in store for Abram, but this blessing wouldn't stop with one man. The Lord would make him a powerful nation and use him to bless everyone on earth. Abram was the start of the plan that comes to completion in Christ.

Abram—later known as Abraham—is your spiritual ancestor (Romans 4:16). When God blessed that ancient nomad, he had you in mind. The Lord wanted so much for you to know him that he refused to give up. He dreamed up a plan to lead you to him.

PRAY IT

Lord, I'm amazed you were thinking of me when you gave Abram a new life. Thanks for including me in your plan.

READ IT

Genesis 14:1 – 16:16, Matthew 5:43 – 6:24, Psalm 6:1 – 10

> *"This, then, is how you should pray: 'Our Father in heaven, hallowed be your name.'"*
>
> MATTHEW 6:9

LIVE IT

You might have heard the Lord's Prayer a thousand times. It's the famous words Jesus gave his disciples when they said, "Lord, teach us to pray" (Luke 11:1).

Matthew showcases this prayer in the middle of the Sermon on the Mount, the longest message we have from the mouth of Jesus. The Lord tells us how to live for him in every part of life. But he's doing the opposite of trying to pile up religious rules. He aims to teach you how to have a real relationship with God. Jesus criticizes people who assume they have to pray loud and long to be heard, calling out hypocrites who make prayer a show or spew streams of babble to get to their point.

Then Jesus gives a model prayer. While there's nothing wrong with praying these exact words, they also give the gist of what prayer can be. Start by honoring God as your heavenly Father. Commit to fully obeying his will. Tell him about your daily needs, whether those requests are big or small. Ask for forgiveness, the same measure of mercy you show others. And ask him to guard you from overwhelming temptation.

When you pray like that, prayer doesn't have to feel scary. It's a simple conversation with the God who never stops caring for you.

PRAY IT

God, you're my Father in heaven. I want to honor you and do your will. Please give me everything I need today. Forgive my sins and keep me from letting evil draw me in.

day8 january 8

READ IT

Genesis 17:1 – 18:33, Matthew 6:25 – 7:23, Proverbs 1:8 – 19

> *"Do not judge, or you too will be judged. For in the same way you judge others, you will be judged, and with the measure you use, it will be measured to you."*
>
> Matthew 7:1 – 2

LIVE IT

It's tough to find a Bible verse more misused than Matthew 7:1. It's a phrase everyone knows but hardly anyone understands. Like it says in a classic version, "Judge not, that ye be not judged" (KJV).

Most people think those words mean you shouldn't criticize another person's decisions about right and wrong — that if a friend tells you she snuck out of the house without her parents knowing, you shouldn't tell her that's a bad idea. Or if you hear a friend planning to cheat on an exam, you shouldn't remind him cheating is wrong. Speaking up would be "judging" or "judgmental."

Keep reading in Matthew 7:1 – 4 to see what Jesus really means. He doesn't tell you to ignore the difference between good and evil but to be wise in how you respond to other people's failings. If you're arrogant in sizing up others, don't be surprised when they don't show you mercy. If you have a plank-sized sin of your own, get rid of it before you brush away the speck of sin you spot in someone else. Once you deal with your own problems, you can genuinely help others.

Offering unhypocritical help is what the Lord wants you to do. Like another Bible verse says, "If someone is caught in a sin, you who live by the Spirit should restore that person gently" (Galatians 6:1).

PRAY IT

Lord, teach me to deal with my own problems before I point out other people's sins. When a friend clearly needs my help, teach me to boldly speak up.

READ IT

Genesis 19:1–20:18, Matthew 7:24–8:22, Psalm 7:1–9

> *"LORD my God, I take refuge in you; save and deliver me from all who pursue me, or they will tear me apart like a lion and rip me to pieces with no one to rescue me."*
>
> PSALM 7:1–2

LIVE IT

You might shudder when you read some of King David's psalms. It doesn't take long for the man who writes poetic words like "The LORD is my shepherd" (Psalm 23:1) to break out in violent cries. He even sent up frequent prayers asking God to crush his enemies.

David wasn't exaggerating his situation. As leader of a nation often at war with neighboring lands, he faced constant threats. People inside and outside his kingdom wanted to tear him apart, and he didn't hesitate to ask the Lord for help.

You might never face an enemy who endangers your physical life. But the New Testament identifies the real opponents you face every day. Ephesians 6:12 says, "For our struggle is not against flesh and blood, but against the rulers, against the authorities, against the powers of this dark world and against the spiritual forces of evil in the heavenly realms." First Peter 5:8 says, "Your enemy the devil prowls around like a roaring lion looking for someone to devour."

People who get in your face aren't your real opponents. Your biggest nightmare isn't anyone you can fight with your fists. There are spiritual forces that want to put an end to your faith.

So ask God to protect you. Cry out for him to defend you. Invite him to make you strong.

PRAY IT

God, I have a world of enemies I can't see, dark spiritual forces that challenge my faith. Protect me as I count on you. Don't let them do me in.

day10 january 10

READ IT

Genesis 21:1 – 23:20, Matthew 8:23 – 9:13, Psalm 7:10 – 17

> *"Abraham answered, 'God himself will provide the lamb for the burnt offering, my son.' And the two of them went on together."*
>
> Genesis 22:8

LIVE IT

Abraham had waited years for his son Isaac to be born, and so must have been incredibly shocked when God said to him one day, "Take your son, your only son. [. . .] Sacrifice him there as a burnt offering on a mountain I will show you" (Genesis 22:2). And Abraham leaves with his son to do as God commands.

Bible critics point to this scene as an example of divine child abuse. But it's actually a picture of the sacrifice God would one day make by sending his only Son to die for the world's sins.

The Lord's command to Abraham challenged a father to obey an impossible instruction. Isaac was a miraculous gift from God, the first of a line that would outnumber the stars. God had promised to make Abraham the start of a great nation (12:1 – 3), and the Lord seemed to be going back on his word.

Abraham came face to face with the Lord's agonizing command. He led his beloved son up the mountain, carrying out his orders one tough step at a time. At some point Isaac realized *he* was the sacrifice, but Isaac trusted his father like Abraham trusted his Father in heaven.

Just at the moment when Abraham reached for the knife to end his son's life, the Lord provided the sacrifice he had planned all along: a ram caught in the thicket. Isaac was saved. And that's when you see a flash of Jesus. Even though human sin deserves the punishment of death (Romans 6:23), the Father provided another sacrifice, his beloved Son (John 3:16). His death on the cross is payment for your sins. When death looms, the Son willingly takes your place.

PRAY IT

Lord, help me understand you love me so deeply you sent your only Son to die for my sin. When I wonder if you care about me, I will remember your sacrifice.

READ IT

Genesis 24:1–67, Matthew 9:14–38, Psalm 8:1–9

> *"What is mankind that you are mindful of them, human beings that you care for them? You have made them a little lower than the angels and crowned them with glory and honor."*
>
> Psalm 8:4–5

LIVE IT

Teachers grade you, coaches score you, and parents seem to evaluate your every move. Bosses decide if you deserve to be hired or fired, and peers tell everyone whether or not you're hot. Some days you might feel like no one thinks much of you. But never assume the Lord concludes you don't measure up.

Psalm 8 starts out by describing God's stunning impressiveness. His majestic name ranks higher than any other on earth. Little children perceive him and worship. The skies shine with his glory. When you stare up at the heavens and study his handiwork—the moon and the stars he put in place—you can't help but wonder what God thinks of people. Why does he bother with human beings? How could he possibly care about a little speck like you?

That isn't how the Lord sees things. He made you and every person to be extraordinary. In the grand scheme of things, you rank just below his angels. He designed you to show off his own glory and honor. He put people in charge of the planet, and together with everyone else you have the weighty responsibility of ruling all of creation.

No matter how hard people might try to make you feel insignificant, they can't change the way the Lord made you. They can't undo your status. They can't take away the importance he built into you and every person on earth.

PRAY IT

Lord, when people look down on me I will remember that you made me uniquely worthwhile. You crown me with your own glory.

day12 january 12

READ IT

Genesis 25:1 – 26:35, Matthew 10:1 – 31, Proverbs 1:20 – 33

"As you go, proclaim this message: 'The kingdom of heaven has come near.'"

MATTHEW 10:7

LIVE IT

Jesus kept some of his most crucial words until his last moments on earth. Right before he went back to heaven, Jesus told his friends to go everywhere, tell everyone about him, make disciples, and teach those new followers to obey his commands (Matthew 28:18 – 20).

Jesus doesn't live on earth anymore, so people won't get true insight into God without hearing from his followers, including you. Matthew 10 shows Jesus sending out his first wave of messengers into the world. He tells his twelve closest followers to go straight to his own people, the ancient nation of Israel. You can pick up important lessons from what they did.

Jesus tells his followers to pack light, not getting tangled up in their possessions as they declare his message. They should be wise about knowing when to say more or when to move on. Not everyone will like their message, and they might even encounter violent opposition. But the most essential thing is to respect God enough to continue speaking his word.

Talking about your belief in Jesus might be one of the toughest things you ever do. But remember why it's worth speaking up. Not everyone will accept who Jesus is, but to everyone who trusts him, Jesus gives "the right to become children of God" (John 1:12).

PRAY IT

Lord, I need your help to boldly talk about you to my family, friends, and people I meet. I know that your love is real. Teach me how to share what I know.

day13

READ IT

Genesis 27:1–28:22, Matthew 10:32–11:15, Psalm 9:1–6

> *"Esau held a grudge against Jacob because of the blessing his father had given him. He said to himself, 'The days of mourning for my father are near; then I will kill my brother Jacob.'"*
>
> Genesis 27:41

LIVE IT

Siblings fight. They might clash more with each other than anyone else they ever meet. In fact, the feud between Isaac's sons Jacob and Esau grew so intense people still tell the story thousands of years later.

These twin boys start fighting back in Genesis 25, where they elbow inside their mother's womb. Esau is born first, and Jacob comes out grabbing his brother's heel. They grow up into complete opposites, and their parents do little to help the situation. Old Isaac favors Esau, while Rebekah likes Jacob better.

At the end of Genesis 25 Esau comes back famished from hunting. Jacob convinces Esau to swap all the benefits that belong to him as the oldest son for a pot of red stew. The scheming repeats when Jacob deceitfully steals his father's blessing. When Esau's anger grows into a murderous rage, Jacob has to flee for his life. It takes many years for the two grown brothers to call a truce and live at peace (Genesis 32–33). Even though they had their differences, they were still family. They had to find a way to get along.

If you have siblings at your house, you're setting patterns of getting along that will last a lifetime. So start by letting God be the Lord of your family. When you choose to live his way, there's far less to fight about.

PRAY IT

God, you're the real boss of my siblings and me. I want you to rule in my family. Teach me to make peace with my brothers and sisters.

day**14** january 14

READ IT

Genesis 29:1–30:43, Matthew 11:16–30, Psalm 9:7–12

> *"Come to me, all you who are weary and burdened, and I will give you rest. Take my yoke upon you and learn from me, for I am gentle and humble in heart."*
>
> Matthew 11:28–29

LIVE IT

People who hear that you live for Jesus might think you have the worst life ever. But they must have swallowed a lie about what being a Christian is actually like. They should check out how the Lord describes the experience of following him.

Jesus's words in Matthew 11:28–30 rank among his most encouraging ever. But look around at what leads up to his point. In Matthew 11:16–19 the Lord vents his frustration with people who complain he doesn't live up to their religious rules. In Matthew 11:20–25 he describes people who refuse to repent—to stop sinning and turn back to God.

Those words illustrate how most people live. Some get wrapped up in keeping petty religious rules, loving every opportunity to stifle everyone else's joy. Or others throw themselves into evil, constantly engaging in attitudes and actions that hurt themselves, others, and God.

But Jesus describes a better way. He invites everyone to come to him and unload their hopeless old ways. He asks you to put on his yoke. In farming terms, a yoke is a wood harness used to steer animals. But Jesus reminds you he's completely gentle—his yoke will not be used to harm you. If you learn from him and go his way, you discover rest. When you get to know the real Jesus, you discover his yoke is easy. Any burden he asks you to carry is light.

PRAY IT

Lord, I'm glad I follow you. You don't want me loaded down by empty religion or entrapped by evil. Show me your best way to live.

january 15 **day15**

READ IT

Genesis 31:1–55, Matthew 12:1–21, Psalm 9:13–20

"The Son of Man is Lord of the Sabbath."

MATTHEW 12:8

LIVE IT

Everyone expects Jesus to be down on people who do obvious evil. But he's a guy who makes friends with tax collectors, prostitutes, and other notorious sinners (Mark 2:16). Glance at his story and you see Jesus actually aims his toughest words at people who make rules the most important part of their religion.

The Pharisees were a group in ancient Israel famed for obeying any and all Old Testament regulations—and inventing new ones. While God himself gave these commands as a way for his people to demonstrate purity, the Pharisees forgot about the Lord and focused on rules, making laws even more strict than he intended. On the outside the Pharisees looked perfect, but inside they were full of filth (Matthew 23:27–28).

So the Pharisees weren't pleased when they saw the Lord's disciples pluck snacks from a wheat field on the Sabbath, God's appointed day of rest. And they thought it was wrong for Jesus to heal a handicapped man on the Sabbath. Jesus said the Pharisees completely missed the point: Doing good shouldn't wait another day. Love is more important than legalistic rules.

Jesus doesn't want you to put all your energy into outward spiritual habits. You can listen to the right music, wear Jesus shirts, and spend all your spare time at church, but what really matters is showing him and others true love. And spending our time with those who bring us closer to God, and taking one day to really focus and reflect on God—instead of distractions like homework—can give us the renewal and peace to go forward with the week.

PRAY IT

God, don't let me get so focused on keeping rules that I ignore people's urgent needs or forget all about you. Teach me true love for others and for you.

day16 january 16

READ IT

Genesis 32:1 – 33:20, Matthew 12:22 – 45, Proverbs 2:1 – 11

> *"If you call out for insight and cry aloud for understanding, and if you look for it as for silver and search for it as for hidden treasure, then you will understand the fear of the LORD and find the knowledge of God."*
>
> PROVERBS 2:3 – 5

LIVE IT

Proverbs 2 offers you a one-and-only chance to dig up buried treasure, but the wealth might not be what you expect. It's not a hoard of cash, gold, or precious jewels. This treasure is all about God.

The most valuable part of this fortune is "the fear of the LORD," an attitude of living for God with total respect. It's discovering "the knowledge of God," an authentic understanding of the Lord who made the universe.

The results of getting close to God are staggering. He gives you wisdom that leads to success. When you live with fairness and strive to be faithful to him, he protects you wherever you go. Instead of letting you wander through life, he helps you spot every good path and gives your heart satisfaction with everything he shows you.

That treasure matters more than anything else in the world. But it doesn't just show up in your backyard. These riches take more effort to find than all the energy you pour into school, sports, work, activities, and hobbies. You have to pay close attention to what God tries to teach you. You need to cry out for more wisdom. You have to hunt for it like silver. But when you go on this search, the Lord guarantees you will find what you're looking for (Jeremiah 29:13).

PRAY IT

God, I want to know you well. I want your wisdom to get me through today. I commit to searching with all my heart for you and your insight.

READ IT

Genesis 34:1 – 35:29, Matthew 12:46 – 13:17, Psalm 10:1 – 11

> *"Still other seed fell on good soil, where it produced a crop — a hundred, sixty or thirty times what was sown. Whoever has ears, let them hear."*
>
> Matthew 13:8 – 9

LIVE IT

You don't have to grow up on a farm to understand how seeds work. This "Parable of the Sower" is one of Jesus's most famous sayings, a small story with a major spiritual lesson. Make sure you read Jesus's own intriguing explanation of this parable in Matthew 13:18 – 23.

Jesus spoke to crowds who seemed unconcerned with understanding his message. They were so slow to process his words that he said they saw without perceiving and heard without understanding. They deliberately shut their eyes and plugged their ears, a sign of their hardness toward God.

The Lord wants his disciples to take his words to heart, so he compares human beings to various types of soil. Some are like a path where birds snatch up the message before it can grow. Others are like rocky ground where his words can't take root. Others act like a patch of life-choking weeds. Still others are like good soil. They hear his words and put them into action. Their life produces a bumper crop.

You have a choice today to be good ground. You can accept God's words, keeping them in mind all day long. If you make sure nothing steals them away or crowds them out of your life, you can be sure they will make you grow in ways no one will be able to miss.

PRAY IT

Lord, I want your words to sink deep into me and spring up like a healthy plant. Help me to listen to your words and apply them to my life.

day18 january 18

READ IT

Genesis 36:1–37:36, Matthew 13:18–35, Psalm 10:12–18

> *"Joseph had a dream, and when he told it to his brothers, they hated him all the more."*
>
> GENESIS 37:5

LIVE IT

Like the story of Jacob and Esau back in Genesis 25–33, the account of Joseph that spans from Genesis 37–47 shows off an ugly tale of violent sibling rivalry. This isn't a band of brothers whose relationships you want to imitate, but God had a plan bigger than any of them.

Joseph was exactly seventeen when he tattled about his older brothers' bad behavior. The brothers boiled with hatred as their father dressed Joseph in an ornate robe (made famous in the Broadway musical *Joseph and the Amazing Technicolor Dreamcoat*). And Joseph had an unhelpful habit of sharing dreams that elevated him at his brothers' expense. None of this helped Joseph get along at home, and it wasn't a surprise when his brothers plotted to kill him. When the opportunity arose, they spared his life and sold him as a slave. They told old Jacob that his favorite son was dead.

The saddest part of this story is watching it go from bad to worse. Jacob (who should have known better, having grown up in a family where his father preferred his brother) didn't treat his sons fairly. Joseph wouldn't shut his arrogant mouth. And ten adult brothers don't bother to find a better way to deal with their upstart sibling.

While God used Joseph's dire situation for his own purposes later, that doesn't excuse everyone's bad behavior. You might be able to slide by with mediocre relationships in your family, but the Lord wants you to aim higher than that.

PRAY IT

God, I can't fix anyone at home but me. But I choose to love my family like you love me. Help me be a better example of how to get along.

READ IT

Genesis 38:1–39:23, Matthew 13:36–58, Psalm 11:1–7

> *"The Son of Man will send out his angels, and they will weed out of his kingdom everything that causes sin and all who do evil."*
>
> Matthew 13:41

LIVE IT

No collection of Christians is perfect. Whether you're staring at peers in a youth group or random people in any church, you're sure to spot examples of sin. To be fair, others don't need to study you for long to notice your shortcomings.

Jesus has that fact in mind when he says the kingdom of heaven resembles weeds in a field. Look back to Matthew 13:24–30 for the parable. Here in Matthew 13:36–43 his disciples admit the Lord's story stumps them, and they ask for an explanation.

Jesus says God's kingdom is like a field full of good seeds. An enemy comes along and sows weeds. The specific word for "weed" is a plant that looks exactly like wheat but is poisonous to humans. Wheat and weeds grow together. They won't be sorted out until Jesus comes back.

That means real Christians and counterfeits will sit side by side in a pew, a prayer group, or Bible study. Some people are spiritually immature and need to grow up. Others might not be Christians at all. But it isn't your job to decide which is which, because trying too hard to sort real from fake damages everyone involved (v. 29).

You just have one job. When people claim to be your Christian brothers or sisters, your task is to help them grow up.

PRAY IT

God, teach me to love Christians I don't like. Make sure my faith in you is solid and real. Train me to use my gifts to help others grow.

day**20** january 20

READ IT

Genesis 40:1 – 41:40, Matthew 14:1 – 21, Proverbs 2:12 – 22

> *"I was forcibly carried off from the land of the Hebrews, and even here I have done nothing to deserve being put in a dungeon."*
>
> Genesis 40:15

LIVE IT

If you struggle to believe you can count on God to help you in a tough spot, think hard about these next scenes in Joseph's story.

Joseph annoyed his older brothers, but he did nothing to deserve being sold into slavery. Now he finds himself wrongly imprisoned, falsely accused of luring his powerful master's wife to bed (Genesis 39:1 – 20).

If anyone deserved to be rescued, it was Joseph. When he does everything he can to flee an easy opportunity to sin, his good behavior simply gets him tossed in another dark hole. Yet God doesn't hurry to spring him from prison. The one human being who could help Joseph — the royal cupbearer — forgets all about him. At least two years pass with no relief in sight.

God eventually moves Joseph from prison to a position of enormous power in the ancient kingdom of Egypt. But even before Joseph was set free, the Lord was at work. God granted him favor with the prison warden, who put Joseph in charge of the other prisoners. The Bible says that the Lord was with Joseph and gave him success in whatever he did (vv. 21 – 23).

Even when you get hit with undeserved pain, God has a bigger plan. He sees what's going on. He never leaves you. And in his time and his way, he will rescue you.

PRAY IT

God, help me trust you when I can't see your plan. I count on you to be with me when life is at its worst.

january 21

day21

READ IT

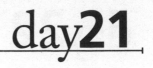

Genesis 41:41–42:38, Matthew 14:22–15:9, Psalm 12:1–8

> *"Then Peter got down out of the boat, walked on the water and came toward Jesus. But when he saw the wind, he was afraid and, beginning to sink, cried out, 'Lord, save me!'"*
>
> MATTHEW 14:29–30

LIVE IT

Waterwalking—the Bible's top extreme sport. Waterwalking—the miracle most Christians wish they could experience for themselves. Waterwalking—your great opportunity to show what your faith is made of.

While you might think walking across the waves of the Sea of Galilee is the Lord's best miracle ever, his disciples weren't so sure. In this story, winds have picked up and buffeted their fishing boat. In the dark of the night, a figure comes strolling across the sea. The disciples feel an adrenaline rush, but it's brought on by severe fright. They think they have seen a ghost, a foreboding presence of death.

The shadowy figure on the lake turns out to be Jesus, who invites Peter to stroll on the sea. But you know how that part ends: Peter doesn't stay on the surface for very long.

It would be easy to jab at Peter for his lack of trust. It's more informative to watch Jesus here. He comes to give courage to his wave-tossed disciples. When their faith fails, he still climbs in the boat and stops the wind. He gives his followers a fresh reason to worship him.

Sooner or later steep waves will rock your boat, and Jesus will invite you to step out on the water with him. That's your opportunity to put your faith into action. Remember not to quit believing in Jesus. He's not about to give up on you.

PRAY IT

Lord, don't leave me out on the waves alone. I want to trust you, but sometimes my faith comes up short. Thanks for never giving up on me.

day22 january 22

READ IT

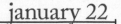

Genesis 43:1 – 44:34, Matthew 15:10 – 39, Psalm 13:1 – 6

> *"How long,* L*ORD? Will you forget me forever? How long will you hide your face from me?"*
>
> PSALM 13:1

LIVE IT

Lost. Forgotten. Friendless. Overlooked. Abandoned. When human beings put distance between you and them, those emotions leave you feeling like you're wrapped in shadows. When you worry it's God who has left you all alone, those feelings get even more gloomy.

David doesn't mask his emotions here. He spills all the contents of his heart, putting it in a song for God's people to sing. Here you catch David feeling forgotten, as if God has turned to look the other way. The king battles his thoughts. His heart can't stop feeling sad. His enemies rejoice, dreaming about his death.

Even the best believers have felt this aching loneliness. The prophet Elijah thought he was completely alone after clashing with a mob of pagan priests (1 Kings 19:10). Jeremiah was hated by all of his neighbors (Jeremiah 15:10). Even Jesus cried from the cross, "My God, my God, why have you forsaken me?" (Matthew 27:46).

But David shows what to do when you feel God has left you. As the king waits for the Lord to answer his prayers, he keeps telling God how badly he needs help. He keeps singing praises. He stays thankful for the rescue God always brings, and he keeps trusting that God's love never fails. That's a fact you can be sure of. The Lord's goodness never stops.

PRAY IT

God, I know you never leave me. Even when you feel far away, you're right here with me. I won't stop trusting you, because your love for me never ends.

january 23

day23

READ IT

Genesis 45:1–47:12, Matthew 16:1–20, Psalm 14:1–7

"'But what about you?' he asked. 'Who do you say I am?' Simon Peter answered, 'You are the Messiah, the Son of the living God.'"

Matthew 16:15–16

LIVE IT

Suppose someone asked you who Jesus is. What would you say? Now imagine you were the first person on earth ever to have been asked that question. How would you respond?

It's easy to think the disciples were instant spiritual geniuses when it comes to figuring out Jesus. But they actually understood him little by little. Sometimes they were puzzled. Once when Jesus calmed a deadly storm, they responded in sheer fright. Mark 4:41 says, "They were terrified and asked each other, 'Who is this? Even the wind and the waves obey him!'" They understood Jesus as he let them see more glimpses of his character and power.

When Jesus asked Peter, "Who do you say I am?" he was cutting through the confusion of crowds who didn't know him well. They all seemed to think he was a prophet back from the dead. But Peter had watched Jesus up close and concluded he was "the Messiah," the one sent by God to save the world. He was "the Son of the living God," God himself in human flesh.

But even with this knowledge, Peter was far from the perfect disciple: he later denies Jesus will ever die (Matthew 16:22–23), places limits on forgiveness (18:21), falls asleep when Jesus needs him for support (26:40, 43), and then denies Jesus three times because he's scared of what will happen to him once Jesus is arrested (26:69–75). Peter knew a very important fact, but he had to keep learning about Jesus and the Christian faith, even after Jesus ascended into heaven and Peter became the head of the Christian church.

You might still be figuring out Jesus. Or you might feel confident that Jesus is everything he claimed to be. But clarity doesn't happen overnight. No matter how well you know Jesus—or not—keep pressing in to know him better. There's always more to discover.

PRAY IT

Lord, you are the world's one-and-only Savior. You're God in human flesh, the one who shows me everything I need to know. Help me know you better.

day24 january 24

READ IT

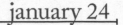

Genesis 47:13–48:22, Matthew 16:21–17:13, Proverbs 3:1–10

> *"Israel said to Joseph, 'I never expected to see your face again, and now God has allowed me to see your children too.'"*
>
> Genesis 48:11

LIVE IT

Sometimes you know you're headed for disaster. You're convinced you're going to flunk a test. Or hit a car. Or lose your spot on the team. Or face raging conflict with your parents. You're smart enough to read the signs and know what comes next, and it isn't good.

Joseph surely must have wondered where his life was headed when his brothers tossed him in a pit and then sold him into slavery. Life looked better when he rose to power within his master's household, but then he was wrongly jailed, where he was left to rot for years. But after many years God raised him to enormous responsibility, putting him in charge of one nation's critical food supplies. By the time he revealed his identity to his stunned brothers, and after his father died, Joseph has fresh insight into how the Lord works. He tells his brothers, "You intended to harm me, but God intended it for good to accomplish what is now being done, the saving of many lives" (Genesis 50:20).

You might feel like you're sure to crash and burn. Yet whether you can see it or not, the Lord has a different plan going on. Even when bad things happen, he works for your good and strives to fulfill his purposes (Romans 8:28). Like Joseph found out, with God on your side, the worst situations aren't as dire as they seem.

PRAY IT

Lord, I will trust you even when everything looks like it's falling apart. I know you watch over me no matter what happens.

READ IT

Genesis 49:1–50:26, Matthew 17:14–18:9, Psalm 15:1–5

> *"LORD, who may dwell in your sacred tent? Who may live on your holy mountain?"*
>
> PSALM 15:1

LIVE IT

David sounds like a sly teacher as he pens Psalm 15, asking a trick question even the smartest students might miss: "Who is good enough to get near God?"

David wonders aloud who can approach the "sacred tent" on the Lord's "holy mountain." Both phrases refer to the place set aside to worship the Lord—the tent-like tabernacle used in David's day and the beautiful temple his son Solomon built in its place.

David then lists all the qualifications of people good enough to get close to the Lord. They must live without fault. They must never lie or speak ill of a neighbor. They must honor God's friends, do right even when it hurts, and watch out for the poor.

The tricky part is that the question has two correct answers. One is that none of us meets those rigorous demands. Our sins make us spiritually unclean, unfit to enter the presence of a holy God (Psalm 14:1–3).

But there's another, even better, answer. When Jesus died on the cross for your sins, he made you righteous, as pure as if you never did wrong. If you trust in his death on your behalf, you can be sure God will welcome you near (Hebrews 10:19–23). He invites you to live close to him now, and one day he will usher you home to heaven.

PRAY IT

Lord, I trust in Jesus's death to make me right with you. Thanks for loving me enough to make a way for me to get close to you.

day26 january 26

READ IT

Exodus 1:1 – 3:22, Matthew 18:10 – 35, Psalm 16:1 – 11

> *"The Israelites groaned in their slavery and cried out, and their cry for help because of their slavery went up to God."*
>
> Exodus 2:23

LIVE IT

Blockbuster movies try hard to portray the drama that unfolds in the book of Exodus, from Cecil B. DeMille's *The Ten Commandments* to *The Prince of Egypt* from DreamWorks Animation. But no Hollywood film ever fully captures the spiritual point of this epic tale.

"Exodus" simply means "exit." It names not only this book but also the Old Testament's most important event, the rescue of God's people from slavery in Egypt. Many years after Joseph saved the Egyptian nation from famine (Genesis 41), a pharaoh rose to power who didn't remember Joseph. When the new Egyptian king grew fearful that Joseph's descendants would overrun the country, he made them all his slaves.

The start of this book recounts how God heard his people's cries and came up with a plan to send Moses to demand their freedom. Moses meets the Lord in a bush that burns but isn't consumed, where God shares his most important, sacred, and intimate name, I AM WHO I AM (Exodus 3:14). He's the God who has always existed, and he will always be present for his people.

Exodus is more than ancient history. This miraculous deliverance pictures how Jesus completely rescues you from bondage. It foreshadows your own escape from death and your newfound freedom from sin. This isn't just Israel's story; it's yours as well.

PRAY IT

God, thank you for this old story. Remind me what slavery feels like and why I need saving from sin. Show me how you powerfully rescue me and all your people.

day27

READ IT

Exodus 4:1 – 6:12, Matthew 19:1 – 15, Psalm 17:1 – 5

> *"So they are no longer two, but one flesh. Therefore what God has joined together, let no one separate."*
>
> MATTHEW 19:6

LIVE IT

The Bible is the most straight-forward book you will ever read. There's not a tough issue it doesn't discuss, either directly or through principles you can reach through tough-minded reasoning. It reaches into the pain of life's most agonizing situations.

The Pharisees tried to use a question about divorce to test Jesus. These religious hypocrites were more concerned about tricking the Lord into saying something foolish or immoral than caring about real husbands and wives. But their question gave Jesus an occasion to speak up about the right and wrong of divorce.

The Pharisees noted that Moses allowed a husband to simply divorce his wife and send her away. Jesus dodges their interpretations of ancient law and goes straight to Scripture, reminding everyone of God's original intent. The Lord had a plan from the very beginning. He designed husbands and wives to be united in body and every part of their being. What God boldly joins together, no human should dare separate.

You don't have to look far to see broken marriages. You might see one as near as your own family. It isn't your job to rub Jesus's teaching in the faces of people you know who choose to divorce. But it is your job to learn and to practice the kind of sacrificial love you need to stay permanently bonded to a future mate.

PRAY IT

God, help me work through the pain I feel when divorce strikes near me or my friends. Teach me to love in a way that will last for a lifetime.

day28 january 28

READ IT

Exodus 6:13–8:32, Matthew 19:16–30, Proverbs 3:11–20

> *"Blessed are those who find wisdom, those who gain understanding, for she is more profitable than silver and yields better returns than gold."*
>
> Proverbs 3:13–14

LIVE IT

You wouldn't start building a house without first learning to swing a hammer. And rather than struggling to teach yourself, you would be wise to connect with an experienced craftsperson who can train you in the basics of working with things like wood, pipe, and wire.

If you want to get the essential wisdom you need to build a real life, check out the awe-inspiring knowledge God offers. Proverbs 3 says he poured the earth's foundations. With powerful understanding he put the heavens in place. He parts the seas and shows the clouds how to rain. And this passage adds a few of the highly-prized results of getting the Lord's insights. His wisdom yields bigger profits than investing in silver or gold. It's worth more than a bag of rubies. It's better than anything else you could ever want.

Here's the twist. Wisdom doesn't just happen. Just as you inevitably bang your thumb a few times when you learn how to pound nails, you gain expertise and endurance when you push through difficult times. And God's plan to make you capable goes even beyond getting through random difficulties. When you need correction, he speaks up. When you do wrong, he disciplines you.

That might feel like the Lord is being excessively tough on you, but it's all a sign of his love. His correction proves you belong to him.

PRAY IT

Lord, I can't begin to imagine all the wisdom you can teach me. The next time you choose to correct me, I will try to remember you care.

READ IT

Exodus 9:1 – 10:29, Matthew 20:1 – 19, Psalm 17:6 – 12

"Keep me as the apple of your eye; hide me in the shadow of your wings."

Psalm 17:8

LIVE IT

There's a phrase in Psalm 17 that should leap off the page at you. And it might sound sickly sweet until you catch its meaning.

Psalm 17 details David's familiar problems and his usual pleas for God's help. Deadly enemies surround the king and there's a wicked plot to take him down. He cries loudly to God for help. He voices unshakable trust that the Lord will hear his prayers and show off his enormous love. All of that sounds like many other psalms.

But then a phrase pops up that seems out of place, as if it were clipped from an old greeting card or your great-grandmother's poetry. David begs God to keep him as the apple of his eye.

That metaphor doesn't ooze with as much sentimentality as you might think. David the fierce warrior knows his fighting skills are worthless without his sight. He would prefer that an enemy lop off his arm or leg than put a stick in his eye. So David pleads with God to guard him like the apple … the center … the pupil of his eye. David is saying, "God, cherish me above anything else. Protect me at all costs."

God doesn't include pretty phrases in Scripture for nothing. All his words are true (Psalm 119:160). So believe that you're the apple of his eye. He will do everything in his power to protect you.

PRAY IT

God, you treasure me more than I know. Guard me from every harm. Thank you for your powerful protection.

day30 january 30

READ IT

Exodus 11:1 – 12:51, Matthew 20:20 – 34, Psalm 17:13 – 15

> *"When the LORD goes through the land to strike down the Egyptians, he will see the blood on the top and sides of the doorframe and will pass over that doorway."*
>
> Exodus 12:23

LIVE IT

God had heard the Israelites groan in their slavery, and he knew it was time to rescue his people (Exodus 2:23 – 25). He sent Moses to command Pharaoh to let his people go, reinforcing his demand with increasingly ominous plagues. But Pharaoh stubbornly refused to set God's people free.

That's when the Lord announced a chilling final act. He would send an angel of death throughout Egypt, killing every firstborn son. He would provoke deafening wails of grief and force Pharaoh to emancipate hundreds of thousands of slaves.

Most significantly, the Lord made a way for his people to escape death. He told each family to slaughter a lamb and paint the doorframes of their home with blood. The angel of death would see the blood and pass over that household, sparing everyone who trusted the Lord's promise.

That "Passover lamb" is an Old Testament picture of Jesus. John the Baptist called the Lord "the Lamb of God, who takes away the sin of the world" (John 1:29). In Revelation he's "the Lamb, who was slain" (5:12).

You take shelter under the blood of the Lamb when you trust that Jesus died for your sins on the cross. Death passes over you and the Lord breaks you loose from slavery to sin. Because of this Lamb's blood, you have already passed from death to life (v. 24).

PRAY IT

Lord, you sent Jesus to die in my place. His blood covers the doorframes of my life. I take shelter in your protection.

READ IT

Exodus 13:1 – 14:31, Matthew 21:1 – 17, Psalm 18:1 – 6

> *"A very large crowd spread their cloaks on the road, while others cut branches from the trees and spread them on the road. The crowds that went ahead of him and those that followed shouted, 'Hosanna to the Son of David!'"*
>
> MATTHEW 21:8 – 9

LIVE IT

Maybe you're one of the Sunday school hordes who have reenacted the first Palm Sunday by waving palm branches and tramping through church shouting "Hosanna!" But there's more to this passage than a little kids' story.

First, Jesus's ride into Jerusalem on the back of a donkey fulfills a precise prophecy made hundreds of years earlier in Zechariah 9:9. Second, the scene shows that the crowds recognize Jesus as an important dignitary, with their spreading clothes and branches on the road as the ancient equivalent of rolling out a red carpet. Third, Jesus makes a loud statement about his kingship by entering the city not on a braying war horse but on a peaceful donkey. He's not coming into Jerusalem to lead a physical rebellion against the Romans, as many Jews had hoped the Messiah would do. And fourth, when the crowd greets Jesus with shouts of "Hosanna!" ("Save now!"), he accepts their eager worship and their plea for salvation.

All of this adds up to nothing less than a royal entry by Jesus. He arrives in Jerusalem right before his death on the cross not as a common person or an ordinary teacher, but as the King of kings.

Those ancient crowds recognized Jesus as the King whose reign is bursting into this world. So go ahead and wave palm fronds to Jesus on Palm Sunday as proof of your enthusiasm. But make sure you also submit to him every other day of the year. While the worship on Palm Sunday was wonderful, some of the people shouting "Hosanna!" that day yelled "Crucify him!" several days later. Be someone who gives him true worship every day. He rules the world and all of you.

PRAY IT

Lord, you are King of everything and King of me. I count on you to save me, and I promise you my complete loyalty.

day32 february 1

READ IT

Exodus 15:1 – 16:36, Matthew 21:18 – 32, Proverbs 3:21 – 35

"The LORD said to Moses, 'I have heard the grumbling of the Israelites. Tell them, "At twilight you will eat meat, and in the morning you will be filled with bread. Then you will know that I am the LORD your God."'"

EXODUS 16:11 – 12

LIVE IT

You would feel stabs of hunger if God roused you in the middle of the night and told you to flee to the desert with all of your farm animals and family members. That's what the Hebrew slaves did, hundreds of thousands of them exiting slavery in Egypt (Exodus 12:31 – 42).

It didn't take long for the Israelites to start complaining about the lack of food. They wished they had died back in Egypt. They were clearly delirious, recalling their years of slavery as a never-ending party of abundant food and meat.

Yet the Lord had a patient response to their groaning. Each morning he would miraculously rain bread from heaven. Every night he would send birds to cover their camp. Then everyone would remember that the Lord is God. He gave his people just enough food for the moment. If anyone lacked trust and gathered too much, it grew maggots and start to smell.

That's how God takes care of your needs — little by little, day by day, as predictable as dawn and dusk. You can be doubly sure he will meet your needs as you track with him and go where he sends you — even if your shoes keep filling up with sand as you obediently follow to places that feel like a desert. Like the pioneer missionary Hudson Taylor once said, "God's work, done God's way, will never lack God's supply."

PRAY IT

God, provide for my needs — from shelter and food to clothing and care. I trust you to be the source of everything I need today and every day.

february 2 **day33**

READ IT

Exodus 17:1 – 18:27, Matthew 21:33 – 22:14, Psalm 18:7 – 15

> *"Smoke rose from his nostrils; consuming fire came from his mouth, burning coals blazed out of it."*
>
> PSALM 18:8

LIVE IT

When you pray you don't likely envision the Lord with smoke billowing from his nostrils and blazing fire filling his mouth. But that's how plenty of the Bible's writers pictured God. And if you want to be an honest reader of the Bible, you can't skip the scary parts. You have to discern what they tell you about your Lord.

The start of Psalm 18 tells the upside of worshiping the omnipotent God. "I love you, LORD, my strength," says David. The Lord is his rock, fortress, and salvation. But David needs a fortress as protection from something, and that something is an onslaught of evildoers.

David didn't just pray for help. He saw God arise and come to his rescue. God split the heavens and came down, arriving wrapped in dark clouds. In fact, God becomes so angry while coming to David's aid that smoke spewed from his nose, and his sharp voice exposed the ocean floors.

It's an undeniable biblical truth that God is angered by sin. From front to back the Bible shows wrongdoing earns his mighty wrath, and God protects the righteous (Psalm 22:20 – 24). But anger is a small part of an accurate portrait of God. Psalm 30:5 says the Lord's anger "lasts only a moment, but his favor lasts a lifetime." Through Jesus, you and everyone else can experience God's mercy, forgiveness, and safety. When you quit sin, trust him, and believe in him, you choose to be on his side.

PRAY IT

God, I know that you will put an end to evil. And I would rather submit to you now than suffer later. Thanks for letting me call you my fortress.

day34 february 3

READ IT

Exodus 19:1–20:26, Matthew 22:15–46, Psalm 18:16–24

> *"I am the LORD your God, who brought you out of Egypt, out of the land of slavery. You shall have no other gods before me."*
>
> EXODUS 20:2–3

LIVE IT

The only thing worse than teachers with high expectations are those who don't spell out what they want. You can't tell if you're passing or failing. You never know if you're hitting the mark or headed for failure.

In Exodus 20 the Lord makes his requirements absolutely clear, laying out his top Ten Commandments. Remember when and where he gave these familiar laws. For hundreds of years Pharaoh and his underlings had controlled every facet of life. Now the Lord tells the newly freed slaves his way to live. As they follow God in the desert, they pause and hear these major laws and more.

The Lord starts with commands that explain how people should get along with him. They should worship him alone, never bowing to other gods. They should reverence his name, including setting aside a day each week for him. The Lord continues with commands that explain how people should relate to each other. Children should honor parents. Everyone should stay away from murder, sexual sin, theft, lying, and plotting to take what their neighbors possess.

God spoke those laws long ago and far away, but they still matter now. They declare that the Lord always comes first. They inform you that people come a close second. And they teach you that God expects obedience. He couldn't be more clear.

PRAY IT

Lord, I need to know and understand your commands big and small. I promise to put you first and treat everyone around me with respect.

READ IT

Exodus 21:1–22:31, Matthew 23:1–39, Psalm 18:25–36

> *"You clean the outside of the cup and dish, but inside they are full of greed and self-indulgence. Blind Pharisee! First clean the inside of the cup and dish, and then the outside also will be clean."*
>
> Matthew 23:25–26

LIVE IT

You can learn a lot from hypocrites—if you carefully study what they do and pursue the opposite.

Scripture shows Jesus speaking harsh words to the Pharisees almost every time they meet. These religious rulekeepers focused so intently on the smallest of God's laws that they forgot about the Lord himself. They constantly called out the failings of ordinary "sinners," anyone who didn't fit in their exclusive group.

Jesus faults the Pharisees for loving applause and grabbing the most visible seats in their synagogues, local places of worship. He picks apart how they pile rules upon rules, as if their misguided devotion would get them closer to God. They carefully measure out offerings from their spice jars, but they forget to show mercy.

Yet there's one habit of the Pharisees you truly want to watch—and do differently. Jesus condemns the Pharisees for putting all their effort into looking spotless on the outside. Jesus knows that inside they're still full of sin and death.

True followers of God get clean from the inside out. It's like scrubbing the grime from the inside of a dirty glass. By the time you get to the outside, the whole cup sparkles.

You can wash your insides by letting the Lord wash you with forgiveness. Then let him scrub your thoughts and attitudes. By the time he's done, your actions will be pure as well.

PRAY IT

God, cleanse me from the inside out. Forgive my sinful heart. Change how I think and feel. Then teach me to live well for you.

day36 february 5

READ IT

Exodus 23:1–24:18, Matthew 24:1–31, Proverbs 4:1–9

"I too was a son to my father, still tender, and cherished by my mother. Then he taught me, and he said to me, 'Take hold of my words with all your heart.'"

PROVERBS 4:3–4

LIVE IT

Your parents have been around the block more than once. And not just in a literal four-wheeled vehicle. They know your world well. And they drive through neighborhoods you don't know exist.

Little kids accept their parents' words as total truth. They assume their parents' actions are always right. Sooner or later you realize moms and dads don't know everything. Like the rest of humankind, they sometimes make selfish or sinful choices. But that doesn't mean you should stop counting on them to be an essential source of wisdom. All parents but abusive ones can help teach and guide you.

The Lord lists respecting your parents as one of his top Ten Commandments. His decree comes with a promise, "Honor your father and your mother, so that you may live long in the land the LORD your God is giving you" (Exodus 20:12). The Lord reminds you of the same point in the New Testament when he says, "Children, obey your parents in everything, for this pleases the Lord" (Colossians 3:20).

One crucial way you can honor your parents is by respecting their experience, especially lessons they learned through life's hardest knocks. Proverbs promises that when you grab hold of your mother's or father's teaching, you experience life. When you take their words to heart, you get protection and honor for yourself that top your head like a shiny crown.

PRAY IT

God, you know the times I struggle to listen to my parents — to hear their wisdom or obey their rules. Help me show them honor.

READ IT

Exodus 25:1–26:37, Matthew 24:32–25:13, Psalm 18:37–42

> *"But about that day or hour no one knows, not even the angels in heaven, nor the Son, but only the Father."*
>
> Matthew 24:36

LIVE IT

Don't get wound up with worry when people claim they know when Jesus will return to earth. Whether you're listening to a preacher or your closest friend, Jesus himself says they have no idea what they're talking about.

In the scene at the start of Matthew 24, Jesus converses with his disciples about the end of time. He details alarming events that will precede his "second coming," when life will go from bad to worse. His arrival will be unmistakable. Everyone on earth will see him "coming on the clouds of heaven, with power and great glory" (v. 30).

Then Jesus makes a crucial point that seems to slip past a wild-eyed preacher or two every few years. He says that no one knows the "day or hour" of his coming. The angels in heaven aren't in on the secret. They don't know the year, month, day, or minute of his arrival. Even Jesus is unaware. Only the Father knows.

You can be sure no human being understands what Jesus can't. But you can still be certain you're ready for his arrival. Because you don't know when he will show up, you keep watch. You continue to do what he expects you to do. You obey him in every way you know how—every year, month, day, and minute until he arrives.

PRAY IT

Lord, your second coming is exciting and scary all at the same time. I want to obey your commands and be ready for your arrival today and every day.

day38 february 7

READ IT

Exodus 27:1–28:43, Matthew 25:14–46, Psalm 18:43–50

> *"His master replied, 'Well done, good and faithful servant! You have been faithful with a few things; I will put you in charge of many things. Come and share your master's happiness!'"*
>
> MATTHEW 25:21

LIVE IT

Suppose someone asked you to invest a sack of gold that was worth something just short of a million dollars. Or maybe two bags. Or five. What wise thing would you do with the money?

That's an important question, because that's roughly the value of the significant sums Jesus describes in Matthew 25. He tells a story of three men. Two wisely invest their master's cash and make more. One buries his master's money in the ground, the equivalent of stashing it in a super-safe vault. When the master returns, the third man earns nothing but condemnation.

While Jesus spins an intriguing story about big money, he isn't giving a lecture on Wall Street investing. His topic is investing your life, as part of a longer teaching about being ready for his return.

Jesus had said that your key task from now until his return is to get busy doing what the Father wants (Matthew 24:46). The lesson of the Parable of the Bags of Gold is that God has entrusted you with something of enormous value—everything that adds up to you. Each person gets a different mix of resources—talent, money, energy—but each should put it all to work for the Lord.

When you do that, you can count on the Lord being happy with your work. He will give you even more ways to do well for him.

PRAY IT

God, I want to faithfully put to work everything you give me. My talents, money, and energy all belong to you. Show me how to use them to honor you.

READ IT

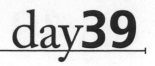

Exodus 29:1–30:38, Matthew 26:1–30, Psalm 19:1–6

> *"The heavens declare the glory of God; the skies proclaim the work of his hands."*
>
> Psalm 19:1

LIVE IT

Watch the bumpers of cars and soon you'll spot faith-challenging slogans. Or listen to your peers' conversations and you hear pronouncements by people who are done with the idea of God.

Psalm 19 points you to the deep truth that you live in a world that bears the marks of a powerful and loving creator. The heavens shine with his greatness. The skies tell his story without speaking a word. Like the apostle Paul once wrote, "Since the creation of the world, God's invisible qualities—his eternal power and divine nature—have been clearly seen, being understood from what has been made, so that people are without excuse" (Romans 1:20).

Everything you see reveals God. But pointing to creation might not persuade a friend or stranger who doesn't believe. What humans can see with our eyes hasn't changed since David composed this song. But some people now think everything exists without the Lord's help.

When the apostle Paul met people struggling to wrap their minds around God, he led them to the source of everything good. He said God has shown undeniable kindness, "giving you rain from heaven and crops in their seasons; he provides you with plenty of food and fills your hearts with joy" (Acts 14:17).

It's tough to argue someone into faith, but keep passing along the truth and love you have experienced from the Lord. Prove where real care comes from.

PRAY IT

Lord, I believe you're real. You made the world and everything I see. Help me show your love and talk wisely with friends who aren't sure about you.

day40 february 9

READ IT

Exodus 31:1 – 33:6, Matthew 26:31 – 46, Proverbs 4:10 – 19

> *"He took what they handed him and made it into an idol cast in the shape of a calf, fashioning it with a tool. Then they said, 'These are your gods, Israel, who brought you up out of Egypt.' "*
>
> Exodus 32:4

LIVE IT

If the spectacular escape from slavery in Egypt had happened with a fleet of cars transporting hundreds of thousands of Israelites to freedom, this would be the scene where everyone takes a very wrong turn.

The Lord couldn't have been more clear that he alone was the Israelites' God. His bold rescue of the slaves proved his Lordship to everyone (Exodus 7:5). He began his Ten Commandments with the words "I am the Lord your God, who brought you out of Egypt, out of the land of slavery" (20:2), then he immediately declared, "You shall have no other gods before me" (v. 3).

Yet suddenly the Israelites were demanding Aaron mold them new gods to lead them through the desert. The people figured Moses had gone missing talking with the Lord atop Mount Sinai, and they were tired of waiting for him to return. Aaron was eager to make a golden calf and present it as the people's god and savior, and only Moses' fervent prayer kept God from destroying the people.

Idols aren't just an issue for ancient followers of God. We craft new gods whenever we let anything become more important than the Lord. Our idol isn't likely a chunk of gold or wood. It's a thing, a person, an activity, or whatever we treasure too highly — be it getting the right grades or making the team, having a certain item, having the right clothes, being friends with certain people, etc. Whatever your false god is, don't let it rule you. Only God deserves to be your Lord.

PRAY IT

Lord, forgive me when I make anything more important than you. You're my one-and-only God.

READ IT

Exodus 33:7–34:35, Matthew 26:47–68, Psalm 19:7–14

> *"The law of the LORD is perfect, refreshing the soul. The statutes of the LORD are trustworthy, making wise the simple."*
>
> PSALM 19:7

LIVE IT

Some people believe in God because of the Lord's awesome work in crafting the universe, everything they see in the sky, the sea, and on land. That's the gist of the start of Psalm 19.

But there's another solid reason to believe the Lord is real. Psalm 19 goes on to praise the perfection of God's Word, everything he reveals in the Bible. What the Lord says is perfect, trustworthy, right, radiant, pure, and firm. His words refresh, make wise, give joy, light the way, endure forever, and display his perfect goodness.

Believers in all times and places have heard and read Scripture and noticed it matches up with their observations of life. It makes sense of tough puzzles and answers difficult questions.

God's Word is at its most persuasive when it details what Jesus said and did, from his birth to his ministry, death, and resurrection. Like the apostle John said at the end of the book that bears his name, "But these are written that you may believe that Jesus is the Messiah, the Son of God, and that by believing you may have life in his name" (John 20:31).

God designed everything in the Bible to lead you to faith in Jesus and show you how to live. If you want a deep faith in God, dig deeply in his Word.

PRAY IT

Lord, you teach me about yourself through the Bible. It shows me who Jesus is and everything he did for me. Thank you for solid reasons I can believe in you.

day42 february 11

READ IT

Exodus 35:1–36:38, Matthew 26:69–27:10, Psalm 20:1–9

> *"So Bezalel, Oholiab and every skilled person to whom the LORD has given skill and ability to know how to carry out all the work of constructing the sanctuary are to do the work just as the LORD has commanded."*
>
> Exodus 36:1

LIVE IT

Your artwork might hang on the refrigerator at home or in a showcase at school. The more you practice your craft, the more likely your art will land in a contest or exhibition. A handful of gifted artists even show up in the pages of Scripture.

Moses and the Israelites set out to build an elaborate tent according to God's design, a place set aside for worshiping God. Detailed instructions for this "tabernacle" or "dwelling" fill the book of Exodus. The tent was a special place of God's presence, and at the end of Exodus his shining glory moves into the tent (Exodus 40:34).

God gave artists like Bezalel every gift they needed to fill his tent with beautiful designs. The Spirit gave them wisdom, knowledge, and every kind of skill "to make artistic designs for work in gold, silver and bronze, to cut and set stones, to work in wood and to engage in all kinds of artistic crafts" (35:32–33).

The Lord has loaded you up with a unique mix of gifts (1 Corinthians 12:7). You can't choose what you're good at—that's up to God—but you can choose to practice the skills he builds into you. Whatever your skill, he intends for you to put it to use for your growth, others' good, and his glory.

PRAY IT

God, sometimes I feel talented. Other times I'm not sure I'm good at anything. Help me search for the gifts you have put in me. I want to use them for you.

READ IT

Exodus 37:1–38:31, Matthew 27:11–44, Psalm 21:1–7

> *"'What shall I do, then, with Jesus who is called the Messiah?' Pilate asked. They all answered, 'Crucify him!'"*
>
> Matthew 27:22

LIVE IT

Nobody will track you down and charge you with murder. But you and every human being are guilty of Jesus's death on the cross.

Right after Peter spoke up and acknowledged Jesus as the Messiah sent to save the world (Matthew 16:16), the Lord began telling his disciples he would suffer terrible harm at the hands of the chief priests and religious teachers, ending in his death (v. 21).

Some time later, Jesus appeared before Pilate, a Roman governor who could decide whether a subject lived or died. Although Pilate declared Jesus innocent of any crime, he did nothing to save him. Then there were crowds who shouted for Jesus to be crucified and mocked him as he died. And a particular company of Roman soldiers did the deed of nailing him to the cross.

It seems like plenty of people share blame for the Lord's death. But Jesus didn't go the cross because of a sequence of cruel people. He wasn't killed just because there was a deadly conspiracy between religious authorities and Roman rulers. Jesus gladly went to the cross to take the punishment for our sins. As the apostle Paul wrote, "God made him who had no sin to be sin for us, so that in him we might become the righteousness of God" (2 Corinthians 5:21).

Ancient people were the ones who nailed Jesus to the cross. But our sins were the reason he had to die.

PRAY IT

Lord, you died because of the sins I have committed. I'm as responsible for your death as everyone else. Thanks for willingly dying to save me.

day44 february 13

READ IT

Exodus 39:1–40:38, Matthew 27:45–66, Proverbs 4:20–27

"Above all else, guard your heart, for everything you do flows from it."

Proverbs 4:23

LIVE IT

You're not thinking of a blood-pumping muscle in your chest when you say your heart feels "wounded" or "broken." The "heart" is a quick tag for the place you experience emotions like love, sadness, or joy. That's the same imagery you can spot in the Bible's ancient culture. The heart, for example, is where you feel Christ's peace (Colossians 3:15). It's the home of deep love (1 Peter 1:22).

But to the ancients, "heart" signified more than that. It's also the place you think, what we call "mind." The heart follows (Jeremiah 9:14), reasons (Esther 6:6), and holds knowledge (Proverbs 2:10).

"Heart" as it's used in the Bible is also the source of your character. According to Jesus, actions that flow from your heart prove whether you're inwardly good or evil (Matthew 15:19). God knows what goes on in every human heart (1 Samuel 16:7), and "hardening" your heart means ignoring and turning away from him (Hebrews 3:8). Purifying your heart should be one of your top goals.

In Bible terms, the heart sums up the core of who you really are. When you "guard your heart" like it says in Proverbs 4:23, you make sure your feelings, thoughts, and will are all fully dedicated to God. You don't let anything harm that commitment or pull you away to less important things.

PRAY IT

God, you rule my heart. Alert me when my heart comes under attack. I don't want anything to pull me away from you.

READ IT

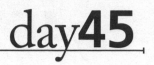

Leviticus 1:1 – 3:17, Matthew 28:1 – 20, Psalm 21:8 – 13

> *"Therefore go and make disciples of all nations, baptizing them in the name of the Father and of the Son and of the Holy Spirit, and teaching them to obey everything I have commanded you."*
>
> MATTHEW 28:19 – 20

LIVE IT

Missionaries once stood on ship decks and waved good-bye to family and friends before sailing to far parts of the globe, often never to return. Giving their lives so distant strangers could meet Jesus was a price they willingly paid. As one group expressed it, "may the Lamb that was slain receive the reward of his suffering!"

Missionaries still go to exotic lands, even places where no one has heard Jesus's name. And you're part of that process. The Lord didn't utter his command to "go and make disciples" to a select few, but to all Christians.

When the task is taking the news to far-off places, you can join in through prayer, financial donations, and even going yourself. Yet the world is also all around you right at this moment, whether it's the neighbor who looks exactly like you or a classmate who doesn't speak your language. You have the privilege of going and telling.

You might wonder what gives you the right to tell others they need to meet the Savior. But you get to declare the truth about the Lord who died on the cross for their sins and leaped from the grave. And like Jesus said, "All authority in heaven and on earth has been given to me" (Matthew 28:18). He invites the entire world to follow him, and you're one of his messengers.

PRAY IT

Lord, talking about you doesn't always come easily. Help me to find the people who will be receptive to your message. People need to know you.

day46 february 15

READ IT

Leviticus 4:1–5:13, Mark 1:1–28, Psalm 22:1–11

> *"In this way the priest will make atonement for them for any of these sins they have committed, and they will be forgiven."*
>
> Leviticus 5:13

LIVE IT

The New Testament clarifies a fact you may have already figured out. All the Old Testament animal sacrifices you read about in Leviticus couldn't fix the problem of human sin. Hebrews 10:4 says, "It is impossible for the blood of bulls and goats to take away sins." So what was God thinking when he gave his people these detailed instructions about animal sacrifice?

The New Testament explains that the blood of those animals made people "outwardly clean" (Hebrews 9:13), offering a temporary solution to humankind's long-term problem of sin. They also taught God's people the high price of wrongdoing, serving as an "annual reminder of sins" (10:3). Every time an animal bled and died, people saw with their own eyes the horrors of evil.

And those sacrifices were a foreshadowing of what lay ahead. At God's right time, Jesus came and offered himself as a complete and permanent payment for every human sin. Hebrews 9:26 says, "He has appeared once for all at the culmination of the ages to do away with sin by the sacrifice of himself."

It's easy to think sin can't possibly be as bad as the Bible says. But the only real way to understand the true awfulness of evil is to measure it the way God does. Sin is so bad Jesus had to die for it.

PRAY IT

Lord, I have a hard time picturing animals getting killed for something I did wrong. But you came and died in my place for my sins. I know how bad sin must be.

february 16 **day47**

READ IT

Leviticus 5:14–7:10, Mark 1:28–2:17, Psalm 22:12–21

> *"It is not the healthy who need a doctor, but the sick. I have not come to call the righteous, but sinners."*
>
> MARK 2:17

LIVE IT

Suppose you were a doctor dropped into the rubble of a natural catastrophe. As you survey countless injured and dying, you stumble on a group that eyes you suspiciously. They're as badly wounded as everyone else, but they claim they don't need your care. When they reject your treatment, you wouldn't hesitate to move on to others begging for help.

That's the scene in Mark 2. Jesus had just called a follower named Levi, better known as Matthew. He was a despised tax collector, hated not only for cheating fellow citizens but also for collaborating with the Romans who occupied Israel. Everyone regarded Levi as one of the worst sinners of his day, yet Jesus didn't shy away from dining with him. It flashed a powerful sign of acceptance and fellowship.

The Pharisees couldn't understand why Jesus ate with sinners. They didn't want to join up with Jesus as friends. And they certainly weren't eager to obey his teachings. Jesus didn't get hung up on their criticisms. Those religious rule keepers were like dying people living in denial of their condition. They could pretend to be well, but they were as needy as everyone else.

The Lord comes to people who recognize they have problems. If you're honest, you realize that's all of us. But you have to want his help.

PRAY IT

God, I admit that I need you. I need not only your forgiveness but your help to act in a way that honors you. I won't refuse your help.

day48 february 17

READ IT

Leviticus 7:11–8:36, Mark 2:18–3:30, Proverbs 5:1–14

> *"For the lips of the adulterous woman drip honey, and her speech is smoother than oil; but in the end she is bitter as gall, sharp as a double-edged sword."*
>
> Proverbs 5:3–4

LIVE IT

To be "adulterous" means you're a married person sexually involved with someone other than your spouse. Since you're not married, this passage doesn't apply to you, right? Think again.

There's no end to excuses that try to dodge God's commands about sex. But you can't get off the hook on a technicality. Starting with the story of Adam and Eve back in the garden of Eden, the Bible consistently teaches that sexual intimacy is designed solely for a husband and wife. The Lord's commands apply to you from now until forever.

The Bible declares God made sex great, a point that's obvious in the second half of Proverbs 5. It also reveals the downside of misusing God's gift. The experience promises to be as sweet as honey, an ancient treat and a symbol of abundant goodness. Misused, it turns out as bitter as gall, a poisonous herb. It's a two-edged sword. Or a path to the grave.

Sexual temptation isn't something you can ignore and hope it goes away. You have to actively distance yourself from the opportunity for sinful choices, staying far from anyone or anything that lures you into wrong. Sometimes that might mean distancing yourself from movies, TV shows, magazines, and other things in our culture. That's how you hang on to a part of you that isn't yours to give away. It's how you prevent cruel people from stealing your dignity and harming your body. Otherwise you end up wishing you had listened to God.

PRAY IT

God, I commit myself to purity, keeping your commands about sex. Teach me to run fast and far from temptation. I want to keep my honor.

READ IT

Leviticus 9:1 – 10:20, Mark 3:31 – 4:29, Psalm 22:22 – 31

> *"They offered unauthorized fire before the LORD, contrary to his command. So fire came out from the presence of the LORD and consumed them."*
>
> Leviticus 10:1 – 2

LIVE IT

The book of Leviticus need only two sentences to recount the story of Nadab and Abihu. They took shovels made for carrying hot coals, scooped them full of fire and incense, and offered it all to God. Fire licked at them from the Lord's presence, and they died.

The Bible doesn't say precisely what the men did wrong, except that their fire was "strange," unauthorized by God. The fire might have come from a source other than the altar, or it might have been offered to false gods. Either way you get the same point. God demands to be treated as holy, honored with reverent obedience.

You also see here that God holds leaders to high standards. Nadab and Abihu weren't random individuals but rather sons of Aaron, high priest and second only to Moses in leading Israel. The Lord didn't let these boys off easy because they were born to a notable family. Thankfully, we don't have to have a fear of being instantly burned for disobeying God's rules today — Jesus's death on the cross gave us the gift of grace. But the idea of worshiping God with respect still holds true. Even if you've been going to church since you were a baby, God still expects reverence.

In addition, God gives you everything you need to be a leader — some time, some way, in the venue he designs for you. Whatever he has planned, take the advice the apostle Paul offered his friend Timothy: "Don't let anyone look down on you because you are young, but set an example for the believers in speech, in conduct, in love, in faith and in purity" (1 Timothy 4:12). Show others the way to follow God with their whole heart.

PRAY IT

God, you take obedience more seriously than I know how. But I want to treat you as holy and live up to your standards. Use me to lead however you think is best.

day50 february 19

READ IT

Leviticus 11:1 – 12:8, Mark 4:30 – 5:20, Psalm 23:1 – 6

> *"The LORD is my shepherd, I lack nothing. He makes me lie down in green pastures, he leads me beside quiet waters, he refreshes my soul."*
>
> PSALM 23:1 – 3

LIVE IT

There's a good chance someone will read the cherished words of Psalm 23 at your funeral, beginning with "The Lord is my shepherd, I shall not want...." But God doesn't reserve those words for a moment you're no longer around to hear them. They're encouragement to live by right now.

Long before David became king of Israel he watched his father's flocks (1 Samuel 16:11), even killing a lion and bear to protect the family's sheep (17:36). So David knew shepherding up close. He pictured the Lord as the best shepherd ever.

You don't have to know much about sheep to catch this imagery. With the Lord as your shepherd, there's nothing you need. He shows you safe places to rest and leads you to drink at waters that won't spook your timid soul. He stakes his honor on leading you to good places and protecting you from death. Evil doesn't scare you when you're under God's care. His protection is fierce. He blesses you in front of your enemies, giving you luxurious provisions and honoring you with perfumed oils. He lavishes you with gifts you don't deserve.

When the Lord is your shepherd, you will experience his loyal love every day of your life. And one day he will bring you home to heaven to live even closer to him.

PRAY IT

Lord, you are my shepherd. You give me everything I need. Lead me along peaceful paths today. Protect me from my enemies. Don't ever stop loving me.

READ IT

Leviticus 13:1 – 59, Mark 5:21 – 6:6a, Psalm 24:1 – 10

> *"They took offense at him. Jesus said to them, 'A prophet is not without honor except in his own town, among his relatives and in his own home.'"*
>
> Mark 6:3 – 4

LIVE IT

Winning a worldwide talent competition could score you friends in your hometown. But don't count on them to cheer you on if you show up and speak for the Lord. Expect no love at all if you suddenly inform everyone you're God.

Mark 5:21 puts Jesus in Capernaum, a detail hinted at in Matthew 9:1. That's a city where the Lord based much of his ministry. There he not only healed a chronically ill woman but also raised a dead girl to life. So when Jesus arrived in his boyhood town Nazareth in Mark 6 with at least a dozen disciples in tow, he must have made a scene. Indeed, people who heard him preach were amazed.

The thrill old neighbors felt about Jesus quickly faded. They questioned his wisdom and wondered about his miracles. They remembered he was a carpenter, the kid who grew up in a family they knew. Instead of welcoming Jesus, people rejected their hometown prophet.

As tough as it is to hear, the people closest to you might be the least enthusiastic about seeing you follow God. They might be hostile when you break out of bad habits. So if you feel their love, be grateful. If they're less than impressed, don't take it personally. God's people often are honored everywhere except their hometown.

PRAY IT

God, help me live in a way that honors you among the people who know me best. I don't want to be the center of attention. I want everyone to notice you.

day52 february 21

READ IT

Leviticus 14:1–57, Mark 6:6b–29, Proverbs 5:15–23

"Should your springs overflow in the streets, your streams of water in the public squares? Let them be yours alone, never to be shared with strangers."

PROVERBS 5:16–17

LIVE IT

Anyone who thinks God dislikes sex obviously hasn't read Proverbs 5. While the chapter starts with stern warnings about misusing one of the Lord's maximum gifts, that portion merely sets up a song of love.

This voice in this passage assumes the person benefiting from this wisdom is a young man, but every point here matters just as much to a young woman. You might be startled to read these words in your Bible, but there they are. God lays it all out. His design for sex is satisfying. His plan is intoxicating.

God's main point in this honest passage is that sexual intimacy is so outstanding that it shouldn't be wasted. It's anything but casual. It's a treasure a husband and wife can enjoy for life, and it's for them alone.

Sex with anyone other than your mate for life is like spilling your most valuable possession in the streets. It's like letting strangers splash in your priceless fountain. So sex is "never to be shared with strangers." It isn't a recreational activity with someone who wanders into your life and tries to lead you astray. It isn't a gulp of water you grab wherever you can.

God examines everywhere you go and sees everything you do. He's pointing you down the path to real life, challenging you to wait for his very best.

PRAY IT

God, I give you points for saying what you think about sex. You made it, and I want to stick with your plan for it. Teach me to guard my mind, heart, and body.

READ IT

Leviticus 15:1 – 16:34, Mark 6:30 – 56, Psalm 25:1 – 7

> *"On this day atonement will be made for you, to cleanse you. Then, before the LORD, you will be clean from all your sins."*
>
> LEVITICUS 16:30

LIVE IT

Of all the sacrifices detailed in Leviticus, the Day of Atonement is the most profound. This once-a-year ceremony foreshadowed Jesus's sacrificial death on the cross, illustrating his payment for sin and the removal of sin.

The Bible says that "without the shedding of blood there is no forgiveness" (Hebrews 9:22). God instituted Old Testament sacrifices to show the awfulness of sin and temporarily cleanse the people.

The Day of Atonement was Israel's most sacred moment. On that day, the head priest chose two goats. He sacrificed the first as an offering for sins, sprinkling the blood in the Most Holy Place, a small room of the Lord's strong presence entered only by the high priest once a year on this day. The priest then placed his hands on the second goat's head, symbolically transferring the nation's sins to the goat. This "scapegoat" was led into the desert, taking the people's sins far away as a sign of the removal of sin.

Jesus fulfilled this divine drama. Because of his death on the cross, God welcomes you into his presence. Hebrews 10:19 – 20 says, "We have confidence to enter the Most Holy Place by the blood of Jesus, by a new and living way opened for us through the curtain, that is, his body." Because of Jesus, you can boldly get close to God wherever and whenever you want.

PRAY IT

God, I won't be afraid to get close to you, because Jesus forever opened the way into your presence. Thanks for pulling me near.

day54 february 23

READ IT

Leviticus 17:1 – 18:30, Mark 7:1 – 30, Psalm 25:8 – 15

> *"Nothing outside a person can defile them by going into them. Rather, it is what comes out of a person that defiles them."*
>
> Mark 7:15

LIVE IT

Old Testament rules can sound odd, especially laws detailed in Leviticus, a book named after Israel's priestly tribe, Levi. Yet each of God's commands had a purpose. As the Lord revealed himself and his character to his people, his laws taught them to obey and made them distinct from the people around them.

Jesus came along in the New Testament and clarified God's intentions. He reinforced rules about right and wrong, like the great command to love the Lord with all your strength and to love people as much as you love yourself (Mark 12:29 – 31). He freed people from reliance on the old laws, like the ban on wearing clothes made of mixed fibers (Deuteronomy 22:11).

Jesus aimed to help everyone see the law's real purpose. When he noticed the Pharisees' strictness in keeping rules about foods, for example, he declared that nothing people ate could make them "unclean" or "defiled" in God's sight. The Lord cares far more about evil that starts in people's hearts and comes out in their actions. Sins like sexual sin, envy, and arrogance are what make people truly unclean.

We act like those hypocritical Pharisees whenever we care more about looking good on the outside than getting rid of the sin that lurks inside us. We resemble those religious rule keepers whenever we put our ideas and traditions ahead of God and his commands.

PRAY IT

God, I want to live up to your expectations. Don't let me get stuck in my own made-up rules. Make me pure inside and out.

READ IT

Leviticus 19:1–20:27, Mark 7:31–8:13, Psalm 25:16–22

"Be holy because I, the LORD your God, am holy."

Leviticus 19:2

LIVE IT

As you press on through the Old Testament, you might find yourself feeling like an ancient Israelite, forever wandering through the desert on the hunt for a cool drink. Suddenly Leviticus 19:2 rises on the horizon. It's like an oasis, a refreshing spot of green in the midst of endless hot sand.

That verse repeats a statement God first made in Leviticus 11:44. He intends for you and the rest of his people to be just like him, and the quality he chooses for you to imitate is his holiness. That awesome trait is the heart of who God is. The root of the Hebrew word for "holy" wraps together "separation" and "brightness," and it adds up to the Lord's one-of-a-kind distinctiveness and glory. To be holy is to be completely pure and without fault.

Being like God is impossible, at least if you try to be good without the Lord's help. But later in Scripture the apostle Peter explains how holiness happens. He quotes this passage, then reminds you how Jesus rescued you from an empty way of life. He bought your life with his own precious blood. Because he came back from the dead, you have faith and hope in God. His Word causes you to be born again (1 Peter 1:14–2:3).

And the result? Now you can grow up and rid your life of every kind of evil.

PRAY IT

Lord, purify me so I'm holy like you. I can't do that on my own. But I trust you to teach me and change me.

day56 february 25

READ IT

Leviticus 21:1–22:33, Mark 8:14–9:1, Proverbs 6:1–11

> *"He then began to teach them that the Son of Man must suffer many things and be rejected by the elders, the chief priests and the teachers of the law, and that he must be killed and after three days rise again."*
>
> Mark 8:31

LIVE IT

Suppose you volunteer to tutor young kids. Instead of bringing about breakthrough educational moments, you end up babysitting a crew of little monsters. When you sign up to do something noble, you might get more than you bargained for.

Jesus knew exactly what lay ahead as he journeyed toward the cross. He told his disciples straight up that he would suffer, die, and come back to life. When Peter pulled him aside to protest that terrible thought, the Lord became angry. He accused his friend of forgetting God's perspective. In Peter's harsh words Jesus heard Satan attempting to stop him from saving the world.

Jesus thought hard about the cost of dying for sin. As he prayed in the garden of Gethsemane hours before his crucifixion, he asked his Father if there was a way he could avoid the cross. Yet Jesus embraced his Father's plan (Luke 22:42). He "humbled himself by becoming obedient to death—even death on a cross!" (Philippians 2:8). He endured the cross for "the joy set before him," the good result that would come from his pain (Hebrews 12:2).

The cross didn't catch Jesus by surprise. Don't be shocked when showing love feels like more trouble than it's worth, or if it causes you true agony. Look hard at what love will cost you, then do what you know Jesus would do.

PRAY IT

Lord, it's easier to simply think about my own needs instead of loving others. Toughen me up and help me see the good results of my sacrifice.

READ IT

Leviticus 23:1 – 24:23, Mark 9:2 – 32, Psalm 26:1 – 12

> *"When Jesus saw that a crowd was running to the scene, he rebuked the impure spirit. 'You deaf and mute spirit,' he said, 'I command you, come out of him and never enter him again.'"*
>
> MARK 9:25

LIVE IT

You probably haven't spotted demons hanging around in your world. Maybe you were also astounded to read about your Lord shining with heavenly glory. Supernatural spiritual happenings might not seem real life, but Jesus's coming to earth as God in the flesh provoked intense activity by dark forces.

Mark gives an account of a boy who brought his parents sadness and terror from birth onward. They watched him violently tossed around, sometimes nearly killed in fire or water. The boy foamed at the mouth and gnashed his teeth. These parents were desperate for help, but this wasn't an ordinary physical or psychological problem. It had a spiritual source.

This episode is one of many in the Gospels — the first four books of the New Testament — that show Jesus exerting power over demons. In the story, his disciples attempted to drive out the spirit possessing the boy, but couldn't. Jesus speaks sharply to the impure spirit, commanding it to come out. The spirit shrieks and leaves the boy.

The Lord challenged his disciples — and the boy's father — to believe in his power. And that dad offered a prayer to Jesus that's worth repeating every time you encounter a challenge you can't understand or defeat: "I do believe; help me overcome my unbelief!" (Mark 9:24). God wants you to trust in him. He also wants to help grow your faith.

PRAY IT

Lord, I do believe in your power and unstoppable love for me. When I question your power or anything about you, help me overcome my unbelief!

day58 february 27

READ IT

Leviticus 25:1 – 26:13, Mark 9:33 – 10:12, Psalm 27:1 – 6

> *"One thing I ask from the LORD, this only do I seek: that I may dwell in the house of the LORD all the days of my life, to gaze on the beauty of the LORD and to seek him in his temple."*
>
> PSALM 27:4

LIVE IT

There's only one thing that will keep you obeying the Lord, learning from Scripture, and staying on task to grow together with Christian friends. You have to want to live close to God.

That passion consumed David. As king of all Israel he expected to get whatever he wanted. There were few limits on his power, which sometimes got him into trouble, like when he stole the wife of a loyal soldier (2 Samuel 11). Like every other human being, David was flawed. Yet Psalm 27 captures his pure heart. The only thing he wants is more of God.

David starts this song by pointing out God's greatness. The Lord is his light — the one who shines in the darkness. The Lord is his salvation — the one who comes to his rescue. With God on his side he has nothing to fear, even when an army marches against him.

Here's where David gets down to discussing his one desire. He uses surprisingly flowery language, saying his goal is to dwell near God every day of life and gaze on his beauty. Then he goes back to reciting God's greatness. The Lord lifts him above his enemies and makes him sing.

David wasn't too self-sufficient or hard-shelled to write a love song to God. Are you ready to make those words your own?

PRAY IT

God, you light up my life and rescue me. The only thing I want is more of you. Show me more of yourself and let me stay close to you.

READ IT

Leviticus 26:14–27:34, Mark 10:13–31, Psalm 27:7–14

"My heart says of you, 'Seek his face!' Your face, LORD, I will seek."

PSALM 27:8

LIVE IT

Back at the start of Psalm 27 David wants nothing more than to get close to God. That sounds like a wish the Lord should instantly answer, as if he will leap from heaven and grab hold of your hand. But a life close to God takes time to develop. It doesn't come to pass without effort from you, and the rest of Psalm 27 shows how it happens.

David's tight friendship with God starts and ends with one thing—prayer. He calls out to the Lord, pleading for mercy and begging for answers. Along the way he discovers God doesn't want him lazing around looking for God to make the next move. He expects people to pursue him. So David has a conversation with himself. He says, "David, it's time to seek God!"

David understands the agony of feeling cut off from God. He asks the Lord to let go of his anger and never reject him. While David has no right to expect God to accept him after he sins, he appeals to God as the one who forgives. Then this powerful king humbles himself and invites God to teach him the right path for life.

You can't help but experience closeness to God when you make a habit of talking with him ... seeking him ... asking forgiveness ... looking for his wisdom. And there's one more thing to do. Count on him to show you his goodness.

PRAY IT

Lord, alert me when I do anything that makes you feel far away. Show me how I can live closer to you.

day60 march 1

READ IT

Numbers 1:1–2:9, Mark 10:32–52, Proverbs 6:12–19

> *"Whoever wants to be first must be slave of all. For even the Son of Man did not come to be served, but to serve, and to give his life as a ransom for many."*
>
> Mark 10:44–45

LIVE IT

James and John, two of the disciples, had heard Jesus say his kingdom was coming soon, so they plotted to secure heaven's two best seats. When Jesus began to reign, one would sit in the place of highest honor—the king's right hand. The other would rank second—the king's left.

The book of Matthew adds a juicy detail to this story. Not only do James and John come to the Lord with their self-centered request, but their mom tags along and kneels before Jesus to make her case (Matthew 20:20–28). This is a family anxious to grab power.

The other disciples weren't happy when they heard about this scheme, only because they hadn't thought of it first. Jesus gave them all the same lesson. The world is full of leaders who abuse power, but Jesus's kingdom doesn't work like that. Anyone who wants to be great must willingly serve others, waiting on their needs.

That humble approach sounds absurd until you realize it's exactly what Jesus did. This king came to serve his subjects. This ruler gives his life as a ransom to save all of humankind.

You can choose to act like everyone else, expecting others to fulfill your wishes and bend to your whims. Or you can serve others like your Lord did, looking out not only for your own interests but also for theirs (Philippians 2:4).

PRAY IT

Lord, it's astonishing that you don't rub your power and authority in my face. You chose to serve me. I will choose to serve others.

READ IT

Numbers 2:10–3:51, Mark 11:1–25, Psalm 28:1–9

"These are the Israelites, counted according to their families. All the men in the camps, by their divisions, number 603,550. [...] The total number of Levites counted at the LORD's command by Moses and Aaron according to their clans, including every male a month old or more, was 22,000."

NUMBERS 2:32, 3:39

LIVE IT

If you set out to write a blockbuster book meant to sell millions of copies and play on the big screen, you wouldn't fill your work with numbers and long family lists. But God had a different purpose when he included raw data in the pages of Scripture.

Numbers isn't all about numbers. Much of the book records the tragic failure of God's people to conquer the land promised to their ancestor Abraham. Instead of enjoying a land of plenty, most of the slaves who left Egypt died wandering in the desert.

The book gets its name from two censuses. The first one begins the book, a count of God's people after leaving Egypt. The second concludes the book, a numbering of the people as they again prepare to enter the promised land. If you do the math—or check Numbers 1:46—you learn there were 603,550 men of fighting age at the time of the first census, implying a total population of two or three million.

Learn a couple lessons as you ponder that overwhelming crowd. First, the Lord knew every one of the individuals he counted. To him, not a single one was just a number. Second, that enormous tally shows the Lord's amazing power. You serve a God who thinks big. He reached out to rescue a crowd we can hardly imagine.

PRAY IT

God, I'm not a number to you. Even when I'm in a crowd you know who I am. You notice me and reach out to save me. Thank you.

day62 march 3

READ IT

Numbers 4:1–5:10, Mark 11:27–12:12, Psalm 29:1–11

> *"Ascribe to the LORD, you heavenly beings, ascribe to the LORD glory and strength.... The LORD is enthroned as King forever."*
>
> PSALM 29:1, 10

LIVE IT

It's not every day you get to order angels around. Yet that's what David dares to do in Psalm 29. He begins his song by telling heavenly beings to give the Lord all the worship he deserves. Yet that command doesn't just apply to angels. David wraps up his song by instructing everyone in the Lord's temple to cry, "Glory!"

Worship isn't worship if it has to be dragged from your mouth. Authentic praise is a natural response to understanding God's unsurpassed worth. It doesn't invent warm feelings about the Lord. It simply reflects on who he is. So David spells out why the Lord deserves your worship.

Start where David ends. God rules as King forever. He isn't Lord of a little corner of earth but of the entire universe. He isn't a temporary ruler to be replaced in the next election, but the only being who will reign for all eternity.

This eternal king is full of brilliant glory and matchless strength. He is holy, absolutely pure. And the Lord is incredibly powerful. His voice thunders louder than the roar of an ocean. It strips bark from tall cedars and twists strong oaks. No wonder everyone should cry, "Glory!"

This mighty Lord is enthroned forever. But he doesn't reside in a distant castle—he's enthroned in our hearts as well. Count on him today to give you strength. He will give you his peace.

PRAY IT

Lord, teach me to study your greatness. I want to understand your power and perfection. I plan to praise you for what I see.

READ IT

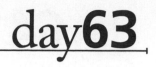

Numbers 5:11–6:27, Mark 12:13–27, Psalm 30:1–7

> *"The LORD bless you and keep you; the LORD make his face shine on you and be gracious to you; the LORD turn his face toward you and give you peace."*
>
> NUMBERS 6:24–26

LIVE IT

This section of Numbers might leave you flipping through emotions ranging from a wry smile to deep thoughtfulness to puzzled concern. Who knew a skin disease would make someone unfit to live with God's people? How can the principles of restitution be applied today? And what's up with that test of an unfaithful wife?

Not every portion of God's Word is easy to understand or apply. Every honest Bible reader needs a plan to deal with difficult parts.

You can start by coming to the Bible to learn. Some people read this book looking for points to correct instead of letting it alter how they think and act. Or when you can't understand the details, look for the main point. A puzzling passage like the test for unfaithful wives shows that God cares about sexual purity. Or keep digging for answers. Ask your pastor or look for Bible helps online that deal with everything from language to archaeology. Or admit you don't know everything. You don't need answers for every minor issue.

No matter where you read in the Bible, one truth comes through. The Lord has a plan to bless you. He will keep you safe and smile at you. He will grant you favor you don't deserve. He will look your way and fill you with peace.

PRAY IT

God, help me keep digging when I can't understand everything in the Bible. Teach me what I need to know and help me find a safe place to ask all my questions.

day64 march 5

READ IT

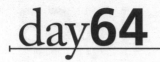

Numbers 7:1–65, Mark 12:28–44, Proverbs 6:20–29

> *"'Love the Lord your God with all your heart and with all your soul and with all your mind and with all your strength.' The second is this: 'Love your neighbor as yourself.'"*
>
> Mark 12:30–31

LIVE IT

Your day might go a lot easier if you could unclutter your to-do list, cutting it down to essentials. But unless you plan to drop out of life, that isn't likely to happen anytime soon. You can count on everyone in your world to eagerly pile on bigger and higher expectations. At least Jesus keeps his commandments simple.

In this scene the Lord answers a question from a "teacher of the law," a student and interpreter of Old Testament regulations. Unlike many people who quizzed Jesus, this scholar sounds sincere. Impressed by the Lord's response to a complex question tossed at him by other religious experts, the man asks which of God's commands ranks as most important of all.

Here's where Jesus simplifies what you need to do. He declares that the greatest commandment is to love God with every part of yourself—heart, soul, mind, and strength. Another commandment comes a close second—loving your neighbor as much as you love yourself.

Studying all the commands and instructions of the Bible shows you exactly what it means to live out those words. But you can be sure you're on track with God as long as you obey those all-important instructions: Love God first, and love people second. If you pin those commands to the top of your to-do list, everything else falls into place.

PRAY IT

Lord, I'm overwhelmed by all the things I have to get done, and I don't want to lose track of what you want me to do. I will love you and love others.

READ IT

Numbers 7:66–9:14, Mark 13:1–31, Psalm 30:8–12

"Tell us, when will these things happen? And what will be the sign that they are all about to be fulfilled?"

Mark 13:4

LIVE IT

Have no doubt: Jesus intends to come back to earth with fireworks impossible to miss. Expect him to soar on the clouds and send his angels to gather his own to heaven. But when will all that action go down?

Jesus declares no one knows exactly when he will show up and end the world (Mark 13:32). But he does describe signs that will precede his coming, including increased war, earthquakes, and famine. Those pains are like a woman going into labor, but they aren't the end.

The real trouble hits after that. Although the good news about Jesus will spread to every nation on earth, believers will suffer brutal persecution. False messiahs will show up to perform deceptive miracles. After a time of suffering unlike anything humankind has ever seen, the sun and moon will go dark and Jesus will return.

There's only one difficulty with those signs. Believers in many times and places have read them as a description of the events of their own era. Even though the Lord's words are perfect and won't ever fail (v. 31), our understanding is limited. Yet while you wait for the Lord's return, you have an important task. Make every effort to grow in your faith and not let anything steal you away from him. Like Jesus said, "Be on your guard; I have told you everything ahead of time" (v. 23).

PRAY IT

Lord, I believe you're coming back to earth. I don't know when, but I do know why. You're coming to bring me home to heaven.

day**66** march 7

READ IT

Numbers 9:15–11:3, Mark 13:32–14:16, Psalm 31:1–8

> *"In you, LORD, I have taken refuge; let me never be put to shame; deliver me in your righteousness."*
>
> PSALM 31:1

LIVE IT

You're sure to have days that make you want to crawl in a hole. When you feel like hiding from everything and everyone, you're wise to head toward God.

A hiding spot can't help you if it isn't strong and safe, and the Lord offers you indestructible protection. He's your rock of refuge and a strong fort. He comes quickly to your rescue, spares you from shame, and keeps you away from traps set by your enemies. But exactly how do you take refuge in God?

You wouldn't have to wonder if the Lord were a literal large rock. You would look for a crack and climb inside. But there's more to taking shelter in God than that.

Starting with prayer is an obvious first step. You can tell God you hurt, asking him for whatever specific help you need. But don't stop there. Study what David does in Psalm 31. He asks the Lord to lead and guide him, eager to go wherever he directs. David entrusts his spirit to the Lord, relying on God and not dashing away to cook up his own problem-solving schemes. He rejects worthless idols, refusing to look for help from false gods or sinful choices. And he reminds himself of God's love.

The Lord always stands ready to protect you. Make sure you make the most of his care.

PRAY IT

God, you are my sheltering rock. Teach me how to run to you and climb inside your protection. I count on you to care for me.

march 8 **day67**

READ IT

Numbers 11:4–13:25, Mark 14:17–42, Psalm 31:9–18

> *"The rabble with them began to crave other food, and again the Israelites started wailing and said, 'If only we had meat to eat!'"*
>
> NUMBERS 11:4

LIVE IT

Every morning in the desert the Lord rained down miraculous bread from heaven. The Israelites called it "manna" ("what is it?") because it looked like nothing they had ever seen (Exodus 16:14).

But now their taste buds were bored. Back in Egypt there was more on the menu, and even as slaves the people ate free fish garnished with vegetables and garlic. While their complaining began with "the rabble," unbelievers who had joined the escape from Egypt, soon every family wailed in their tents. Moses wondered why he had to put up with their complaints. The people were God's children, not his.

The Lord became exceedingly angry and decided to give his people the meat they craved, not just for a single meal but until it came out of their nostrils. Like manna, this meat would arrive miraculously from God. Soon birds blew in from the sea and piled up six feet deep in every direction. While the people picked meat from their teeth, the Lord struck some of them dead.

God happily listens to human problems, but that day the Israelites' complaining crossed a line. They despised what God had kindly provided. They not only demanded a different menu but questioned the Lord's care, daring to think they were better off without him. When you whine at the loving God of the universe, be careful what you pray for.

PRAY IT

God, I'm grateful for everything you give me. Teach me the difference between telling you about my problems and doubting your love.

day68 march 9

READ IT

Numbers 13:26–14:45, Mark 14:43–72, Proverbs 6:30–35

> *"And they spread among the Israelites a bad report about the land they had explored. They said, 'The land we explored devours those living in it. All the people we saw there are of great size.'"*
>
> Numbers 13:32

LIVE IT

The trip from Egypt to the Promised Land hadn't gone as smoothly as planned. There were peak moments, like when God's people bolted across the Red Sea (Exodus 13:17–14:31) and heard the Lord speak his Ten Commandments (20:1–21). But then the people bowed to a false god (32:1–35) and complained about the Lord's care (Numbers 11:4–35).

Now those escaped slaves had camped on the edge of the land the Lord had sworn to their ancestor Abraham. A series of battles loomed near, so Moses sent a dozen spies to scout the land. These men returned carrying a giant cluster of grapes and reported that the land was as full of milk and honey as the Lord had promised. But there was a catch: the land was also occupied by strong people and well-fortified cities.

Only Caleb and Joshua believed the Lord was mighty enough to fulfill his promise to give the land to the Israelites. When the people rebelled and refused to enter, the Lord sent them to wander in the desert. None of the adults except Joshua and Caleb would survive to enter the land—not even Moses.

The Lord expects you to take him at his word. His commands might seem unattainable and his promises unreal. But when you refuse to believe and act on his word, you risk missing out on his very best. Trust is the only way you can grab hold of his amazing promises.

PRAY IT

Lord, point me in the direction you want me to go, and give me the courage to follow. I choose to believe every one of your promises to me.

READ IT

Numbers 15:1–16:35, Mark 15:1–32, Psalm 31:19–24

> *"Love the LORD, all his faithful people! The LORD preserves those who are true to him, but the proud he pays back in full."*
>
> PSALM 31:23

LIVE IT

Santa Claus is famed for keeping a list of everyone who's nice and naughty. He checks his records then spans the globe to bestow presents and chunks of coal. While God also can tell the difference between good people and bad—and he also gives superb gifts—don't mistake the Lord for a red-suited myth.

Every human being aches for justice. God himself builds a sense of fairness into us, so we cheer when good wins and evil loses. We applaud when evil gets what it deserves, as when the Lord pays back the proud for their arrogance. We're glad when the Lord grants good people blessings like shelter, safety, wondrous love, and answered prayers.

David's words might make it sound like being good can earn you God's gifts. But this song hints at the real reason the Lord showers his goodness: it's a sign of his mercy. This mercy comes to all who count on his kind care. The New Testament makes clear that no one will ever be good enough to earn God's favor (Ephesians 2:8–9). If Jesus hadn't gone to the cross for our sins, we would all get the payback our sins deserve.

God exists. His presents are real. But only he makes us good. So go to the Lord and get forgiveness. Be glad for his kindness you don't deserve. And then enjoy everything good he sends your way.

PRAY IT

Lord, I understand that everything good I experience in life comes as a gift of your grace, pure mercy I don't deserve. Thanks for your nonstop kindness.

day70 march 11

READ IT

Numbers 16:36–18:32, Mark 15:33–47, Psalm 32:1–11

> *"So Joseph bought some linen cloth, took down the body, wrapped it in the linen, and placed it in a tomb cut out of rock. Then he rolled a stone against the entrance of the tomb."*
>
> MARK 15:46

LIVE IT

Jesus died by one of the cruelest forms of execution ever devised, but physical pain was only a fraction of his spiritual agony.

Jesus went to the cross carrying every sin—every wrongdoing ever committed in every time and place. Like the Old Testament foretold, "the LORD has laid on him the iniquity of us all" (Isaiah 53:6). Our sin caused Jesus to be cut off from his absolutely holy Father, a separation heard in the cry, "My God, my God, why have you forsaken me?" (Mark 15:34).

Not long after that mournful scream, Jesus died. His death marks the darkest moment in human history.

But don't miss an intriguing event that happens in the shadows. Joseph of Arimathea was a prominent leader of the Jewish ruling council. He was so fearful of his peers that he followed Jesus secretly (John 19:38). Yet now he boldly asks for the Lord's body, carefully placing it in a stone tomb carved for a rich man. Along with Joseph comes Nicodemus (v. 39), another leader who had slipped in to speak with Jesus under cover of darkness (3:2).

You might begin as a secret follower of Jesus, but you can become like Joseph and Nicodemus. Look hard at what the Lord did for you on the cross as he suffered agony beyond imagination. Maybe that's the nudge you need to let everyone know you follow the Lord.

PRAY IT

Lord, I don't want to hide that I'm your follower. Because of what you did in the darkness the night you died on the cross, I choose to step into the light.

READ IT

Numbers 19:1 – 21:3, Mark 16:1 – 20, Psalm 33:1 – 11

> *"Praise the LORD with the harp; make music to him on the ten-stringed lyre. Sing to him a new song; play skillfully, and shout for joy."*
>
> PSALM 33:2 – 3

LIVE IT

Worship should flow from your mouth as an awe-filled response to perceiving the one real God. Yet that doesn't mean worship shouldn't be planned and practiced.

Psalm 33 says worship is the right thing to do. While you don't want to turn worship into pure duty — something you dislike but do anyway — the psalm does imply you can decide to praise God. If you feel like sleeping in rather than heading to a worship service, you can choose to do the appropriate thing.

This song tells you to grab an instrument and play it to God. The "harp" and "ten-stringed" lyre are likely different-sized versions of the same thing. The larger harp was an aristocratic instrument and varied from three to twelve strings. It could be plucked with fingers or stroked with a pick.

Don't miss the other instructions easy to spot in this passage. Praising God isn't an excuse to play badly, so practice. You might not have a dazzling voice, but you can still shout with joy. And everyone gets bored with the same old songs, so sing something fresh.

Psalm 33 doesn't leave you wondering why you should worship. After telling you to sing and play to God, the little word "for" in verse 4 signals the beginning of a list of reasons to worship. Start by thanking the Lord for his true words. Then praise him for his unfailing love.

PRAY IT

Lord, you are worth worshiping. Teach me to make a habit of praising you on my own and with others. I want to worship you well.

day72 march 13

READ IT

Numbers 21:4–22:20, Luke 1:1–25, Proverbs 7:1–5

> *"Since I myself have carefully investigated everything from the beginning, I too decided to write an orderly account for you, most excellent Theophilus, so that you may know the certainty of the things you have been taught."*
>
> Luke 1:3–4

LIVE IT

Bible critics suggest the Bible is a collection of made-up stories. But that isn't the picture that emerges from the pages of Scripture. Luke, for example, purposely set out to write trustworthy history.

Luke begins his book about Jesus by acknowledging that others had already written about events everyone had seen and heard. These writers didn't invent stories about the Lord but relied on the reports of eyewitnesses. As someone who has "carefully investigated everything from the beginning" (Luke 1:3), Luke decides to write an orderly history for someone he calls Theophilus, or "lover of wisdom." This person might have been a new believer or someone especially interested in testing the claims of Christianity. Luke presents facts to help his reader be convinced of the truth about the Lord.

When you read about Jesus in Scripture, you can be sure you aren't reading a tale slapped together by a writer careless with facts. Luke penned both this gospel and the book of Acts, works that contain details that can be checked against archaeology and ancient documents. Luke's accuracy astounds historians, not only intelligent believers but also scholars hostile to the idea of God.

When Luke tells you about Jesus, he begins with key details surrounding his birth. What Luke writes is valuable history. But he has a bigger point. He wants to assure you that your Savior is on his way.

PRAY IT

Lord, thanks for the accuracy of the accounts I read about you in the Bible. They teach me facts about you and convince me to believe.

READ IT

Numbers 22:21–23:26, Luke 1:26–38, Psalm 33:12–22

> *"Then the LORD opened the donkey's mouth, and it said to Balaam, 'What have I done to you to make you beat me these three times?'"*
>
> NUMBERS 22:28

LIVE IT

You know people who insist on learning everything the hard way—a friend, a family member, maybe even you. Balaam took that sort of stubbornness to the extreme.

Balaam speaks for God in this scene, but he isn't one of the Lord's prophets or spokespersons. Joshua 13:22 calls him a practitioner of the ancient dark art of divination, a side of witchcraft that attempts to get guidance from a pagan god. When Balak the king of Moab calls for Balaam to curse the Israelites, the Lord intervenes, commanding Balaam not to curse his people (Numbers 22:12).

You see Balaam at his best when he turns down a large financial reward for cursing the Israelites and promises to say only what the Lord commands him (vv. 18–20). But you see him at his worst as he deals with his donkey. Balaam must have intended to go back on his promise, because an angel of the Lord blocks his path. His donkey sees the angel and refuses to go further. After Balaam beats the poor beast three times, God lets the animal speak up.

The point for you? Being stubborn isn't smart, so pay attention to God before he gets tough. Like the Lord says elsewhere, "Do not be like the horse or the mule, which have no understanding but must be controlled by bit and bridle or they will not come to you" (Psalm 32:9)

PRAY IT

God, forgive me when I need tough knocks before I stop doing something less than smart. Help me not be stubborn when you speak.

day74 march 15

READ IT

Numbers 23:27–26:11, Luke 1:39–56, Psalm 34:1–10

> *"From now on all generations will call me blessed, for the Mighty One has done great things for me—holy is his name."*
>
> Luke 1:48–49

LIVE IT

The details of the first Christmas get retold every December, but don't rush past this reminder to trust the Lord no matter what.

Even though the angel Gabriel brought Mary a friendly greeting that the Lord was with her, she was confused and disturbed. Her head didn't likely clear when the angel declared she was chosen to give birth to God's son.

Jewish marriage customs of the day meant Mary was likely only fourteen or fifteen when the Lord sent this news. Pregnancy would be proof of her sexual immorality, a sin that could be punished by stoning. As Gabriel detailed the Lord's plan, Mary posed a straightforward question. When she asked how a virgin could bear a child, the angel explained that the Lord was able to do the impossible (Luke 1:26–37).

That's when you catch Mary's true heart: "I am the Lord's servant. . . . May your word to me be fulfilled (v. 38). And she expands on that thought in song. She trusts the merciful and mighty God has chosen her for a special purpose. He scatters the proud and cares for the poor. Because she trusts God, she isn't afraid of the future.

The Lord won't ever ask you to bear his Son. Yet he challenges you to obey his every call and command. When he asks you to do something unusual or uncomfortable, how will you respond?

PRAY IT

God, I'm willing to obey you no matter what. Help me to trust you enough to do difficult things for you.

READ IT

Numbers 26:12–27:11, Luke 1:57–80, Psalm 34:11–22

"The eyes of the LORD are on the righteous, and his ears are attentive to their cry."

Psalm 34:15

LIVE IT

God knows more about you than you know about yourself. While being under the watchful gaze of the all-knowing God can sound spooky or worse, it's a good thing to be noticed by the Lord.

The entire Bible unfolds God's knowledge of you. He knows when you sit or stand, what goes on in your heart, and what you're about to say (Psalm 139:1–4). He counts the hairs on your head (Luke 12:7). He foresees every day of your life (Psalm 139:16). He understands all the plans he crafts for you (Jeremiah 29:11). He sees you at your worst and still loves you (Romans 5:8).

Psalm 34 isn't about a mythic god with actual eyeballs or ears. It assures you the Lord looks out for your every need and tunes in to your every prayer. He isn't too busy with world problems to pay attention to you. He isn't more interested in people with life-threatening issues. He doesn't care more about your peers.

When the ancient Israelites faced brutal enemies, they wondered if God cared about their plight. A foolish king turned to a foreign power for help instead of looking to God. The prophet Hanani corrected him with words you can still count on today: "The eyes of the LORD range throughout the earth to strengthen those whose hearts are fully committed to him" (2 Chronicles 16:9).

PRAY IT

God, I'm not sure I always want you to see what I do or know what I think. But I trust you to watch over me and look after my needs.

day76 march 17

READ IT

Numbers 27:12–29:11, Luke 2:1–20, Proverbs 7:6–20

> *"While they were there, the time came for the baby to be born, and she gave birth to her firstborn, a son. She wrapped him in cloths and placed him in a manger, because there was no guest room available for them."*
>
> Luke 2:6–7

LIVE IT

The four gospels are all very different in what they have to say about Jesus's nativity. The book of Matthew tells about magi arriving from the east to worship the young Jesus (Matthew 2:1–12). Mark says nothing at all about the Savior's birth. John zooms wide with a cosmic introduction of Jesus as God come in the flesh (John 1:1–18). Luke is where you find the most familiar facts of the Christmas story.

There's nothing here about an obnoxious innkeeper's rejection of a desperate man and his pregnant wife, just that they could find no lodging. This story doesn't mention a stable, simply noting that the baby boy was placed in an animal feedbox. And there are no details about lowing cattle waking the poor baby. In the Bible account, there are no animals at all.

Except for sheep. Dirty, underpaid shepherds are guarding their flocks in a nearby field when an angel shines with God's glory. He announces the birth of a Savior, the Messiah, the Lord. Then a vast army of angels praises God.

The shepherds run to look for the baby. They say, "Let's go to Bethlehem and see this thing that has happened, which the Lord has told us about" (Luke 2:15).

That eager hunt for Jesus should challenge all of us who think we have heard this Christmas story too much. The news was fresh, and the shepherds ran fast. Jesus wasn't born yesterday, but he still has new things to teach you today.

PRAY IT

Lord, I will search your Word and seek you out in prayer. Surprise me by teaching me new things about yourself each day.

READ IT

Numbers 29:12–31:24, Luke 2:21–40, Psalm 35:1–10

> *"Contend, LORD, with those who contend with me; fight against those who fight against me."*
>
> PSALM 35:1

LIVE IT

Sometimes it might feel like you're up against enemies that seem impossible to get past. But your God is mightier than anyone you might ever face.

Psalm 35 shows David asking the Lord to take his side in a deadly clash. He isn't vague about what he wants. He asks the Lord to unleash an arsenal against his enemies. He begs God to reassure him of his rescue. And there are a couple of reasons David feels justified asking for help.

First, David says he's done nothing to deserve this violence. "They hid their net for me without cause," he complains, "and without cause dug a pit for me" (v. 7). David knows God doesn't run to the rescue of people who wrong others. But he asks the Lord to nudge evildoers into the exact hole they dug for him.

Second, David understands that God stands on the side of the "poor and needy" (v. 10). The poor appear about two dozen times in the psalms. Wicked people oppress them, and God strives to help them. The Lord always sides with people who have little instead of the powerful people who hurt them.

You too have someone on your side when you're in dire need. When the Lord rescues you, don't forget to say thanks. Tell others what he did. There's no one like your God.

PRAY IT

God, I rely on you to rescue me from my enemies. I won't expect your help when I feed the problem, but I count on you when I have done nothing wrong.

day78 march 19

READ IT

Numbers 31:25–32:42, Luke 2:41–52, Psalm 35:11–18

> *"'Why were you searching for me?' he asked. 'Didn't you know I had to be in my Father's house?' But they did not understand what he was saying to them."*
>
> LUKE 2:49–50

LIVE IT

While it may seem funny that Mary and Joseph lost young Jesus on a road trip to Jerusalem, don't laugh—unless you find humor in your parents forgetting you at a desolate rest stop. But that's not exactly what happened.

Luke ends his story of Jesus's birth with the Lord growing up in Nazareth (Luke 2:39–40). The next time you spot him, he's turned twelve. He travels to the Lord's holy city to celebrate the Passover, not just with parents and siblings, but in an extended family group. After the festival, the family heads home. Assuming Jesus is elsewhere in the caravan, his parents travel a day before they realize he's missing. It takes a second day to retrace their steps and a third to find him.

The Bible doesn't say how Joseph reacted to finding his son. Mary sounds like any mother who locates a lost child. When Jesus claims he was exactly where he should be, his parents don't track with his logic. They don't realize he felt drawn to his Father's house, where he amazed the religious experts with his deep insights into God.

That's an intriguing scene. Jesus was on the loose, but he didn't run wild. He was twelve, but he was wise beyond his years. He was God in the flesh, but he obediently went home with his parents. He had to grow up the same way you did, and he had to make the same everyday choices you do as well.

PRAY IT

Lord, I'm not you. But I know you were born as a human being and lived in a real family. Help me imitate your choices.

READ IT

Numbers 33:1–34:29, Luke 3:1–22, Psalm 35:19–28

> *"Here are the stages in the journey of the Israelites when they came out of Egypt by divisions under the leadership of Moses and Aaron."*
>
> NUMBERS 33:1

LIVE IT

Forty years spent wandering in the scorching desert. The Lord didn't intend for the time span between his people's escape from Egypt and their enjoyment of the Promised Land to last so long. Yet that's how it played out after God's people were too timid to enter the land he swore to their ancestor Abraham. Of all the adults who left Egypt, none except Joshua and Caleb survived to make a home in the Lord's amazing new place (Numbers 14:30).

Numbers 33 lists every step on the people's extended journey, from Rameses in Egypt to the plains of Moab just east of the Jordan River. While the sites of many of these temporary camps can't be pinpointed on the ground today, they were sites of the Lord's astonishing care. For forty years, God fed his people with manna (Exodus 16:35). During that time the people's clothes and sandals didn't wear out (Deuteronomy 29:5).

Even though God's people had sinned terribly, he nevertheless showed them mercy. He used their years of walking to discipline them, teaching them to follow him without question. Like Moses described their experience, "Know then in your heart that as a man disciplines his son, so the LORD your God disciplines you" (8:5). As God leads you step by step through life, he's training you to walk with him no matter where he sends you.

PRAY IT

God, I'm not always sure where you're leading me or what my next step should be. So guide me. Remind me you're with me. I will stay close to you wherever we go.

day80 march 21

READ IT

Numbers 35:1–36:13, Luke 3:23–4:13, Proverbs 7:21–27

> *"Jesus, full of the Holy Spirit, left the Jordan and was led by the Spirit into the wilderness, where for forty days he was tempted by the devil."*
>
> Luke 4:1–2

LIVE IT

Don't believe that Jesus was nothing like you. Or that you have nothing to learn from him. Or that you can't live up to his example. As a human being, Jesus faced the same temptations you do and then some. He had to fight back the same way you can.

Facing temptation was part of the Father's training plan for his one-and-only Son. The Spirit led Jesus into the Desert of Judea, a real place between Jerusalem and the Dead Sea. For forty days Jesus encountered more than your everyday enticement to do wrong. The devil himself attempted to lure him into evil.

The devil told Jesus to use his power to fill his empty stomach, but the Lord answered that he needed more than bread, he needed to fill up on God's Word (Deuteronomy 8:3). When the devil offered Jesus instant authority over the world, the Lord reminded himself that God alone deserves worship (6:13). And when the devil dared Jesus to prove the Father's care, the Lord refused to test God (v. 16).

Each time Jesus faced potent temptation, he fought back with indisputable facts. He trusted God's words more than the devil's empty promises.

When you feel lured into evil, you can respond in the same ways. Remind yourself of God's goodness. Recall his trustworthy promises to you in the Bible. Resist the devil and he will flee from you (James 4:7).

PRAY IT

Lord, because you were born as a human being, you understand temptation. You know how to beat it. When I feel tempted, I will fight back with your Word.

march 22 **day81**

READ IT

Deuteronomy 1:1 – 2:23, Luke 4:14 – 37, Psalm 36:1 – 12

> *"The Spirit of the* L*ORD is on me, because he has anointed me to proclaim good news to the poor."*
>
> LUKE 4:18

LIVE IT

Jesus knew he was arriving in a troubled world. That's the reason he came. But opposition came at him fast and furious. After Jesus survived forty days of grueling tests in the desert, the devil gave up "until an opportune time" (Luke 4:13). But when Jesus went to his hometown and preached, he almost got thrown off a cliff.

Luke says that the Lord made a habit of worshiping in the synagogue each Sabbath, the day set aside as God's own. On one occasion Jesus was handed a scroll, and he read from Isaiah 61. The passage relates big news about what God is up to in the world — bringing good news to the poor, freedom to prisoners, sight to the blind, and freedom for the oppressed.

Then Jesus added a twist: He claimed the passage is talking about *him*. That's the gist of "Today this scripture is fulfilled in your hearing" (Luke 4:21). He's the one ushering all those good things to earth. The hometown people were in awe, and then they realized Jesus had accused them of shutting their hearts to God. Because Jesus is not just telling his friends and neighbors he's the Messiah — he also tells them that he is a Messiah not just for the Jews, God's chosen people, but the non-Jews as well, since many Jews are closing their ears to Jesus's preaching. The last part is what *really* sends him to the edge of a craggy outcrop.

If you want to be part of what the Lord is doing in your world, pay attention to what Jesus proclaimed that day. Make his causes part of your everyday life. Just don't expect everyone to applaud.

PRAY IT

Lord, I want to be involved in your work. Help me dream big about what you aim to do in my world.

day**82** march 23

READ IT

Deuteronomy 2:24–4:14, Luke 4:38–5:16, Psalm 37:1–9

> *"Trust in the* LORD *and do good; dwell in the land and enjoy safe pasture. Take delight in the* LORD*, and he will give you the desires of your heart."*
>
> PSALM 37:3–4

LIVE IT

There's no trick to the promise God makes in Psalm 37:4. He will "give you the desires of your heart." But don't miss the crucial condition. That promise comes true when you "take delight in the LORD."

There's a nagging difficulty in the background of this passage. Evil people surround David, crafting wicked schemes and carrying them out. Life goes well for these people. They do wrong, yet they win. Watching sinful people succeed makes even the best believers fret. They feel a jittery worry that gnaws from the inside out. Envy can swell in their hearts. Their inner frustration can explode in outward anger.

David lists reasons not to surrender to those feelings. Evil people will wither like dying grass, yet if you trust the Lord and choose to do right, he will certainly lead you to green pastures. If you dedicate your life to him, he will sooner or later make your goodness shine. Sometimes he even proves you correct so everyone else can see.

Then comes the most intriguing promise of all. When you delight in God, he gives you exactly what you're looking for. That isn't a promise to fulfill a random wish for a sweet car or soaring popularity. When you want God more than anything else, he can't help but give you more of himself.

PRAY IT

Lord, I want more of you. I want to be your friend and follower more than anything else. Please give me what my heart wants more than anything.

march 24 **day83**

READ IT

Deuteronomy 4:15–5:33, Luke 5:17–32, Psalm 37:10–20

> *"You were shown these things so that you might know that the LORD is God; besides him there is no other."*
>
> DEUTERONOMY 4:35

LIVE IT

At the start of Deuteronomy, Moses sounds like a coach drilling his team with a motivating talk before a championship game. But the stakes here are higher than any sports contest. This wise leader is getting God's people ready to enter the land promised to them hundreds of years before.

Moses begins by recapping highlights of the forty years since the Lord freed his people from slavery from Egypt. Three chapters later, he finally gets around to the reason for his speech. He plans to outline everything God's people need to know to conquer the land and live well (Deuteronomy 4:1).

Moses reminds the people of a truth they can't afford to forget: "The LORD is God; besides him there is no other" (v. 35). Moses proves that fact from the people's own history. From the day of creation until then, no one has ever seen anything as great as the birth of that nation. No other people have heard God's voice and lived. No other god has ever done such awesome miracles as when the Lord's presence and strength brought the Israelites out of Egypt.

God accomplished all these things to prove he's the one-and-only God. He worked mighty wonders to demonstrate his love. When the Lord acts in your life, he wants you to know that his love for you will never stop. And when he does amazing deeds, he's reminding you that he alone is God.

PRAY IT

Lord, you show me your love all the time. Your powerful actions prove to me that you're the one-and-only God.

day84 march 25

READ IT

Deuteronomy 6:1 – 8:20, Luke 5:33 – 6:11, Proverbs 8:1 – 11

> *"When the* Lord *your God has delivered them over to you and you have defeated them, then you must destroy them totally."*
>
> Deuteronomy 7:2

LIVE IT

Your parents could promise you a new room, but the sibling you push out of that space wouldn't be happy. When God swore he would give a spectacular land to his people, there was one major problem. The land was already occupied by other people, and they weren't about to leave without a fight. Why would God eject one group from the land, and basically destroy them, simply to give that land to another?

Bible critics claim this predicament exposes the God of the Bible as completely unjust, yet Scripture offers a bigger picture. The inhabitants of Canaan were known for their blatant sin as far back as the days of Abraham. Leviticus offers ghastly details about their involvement in adultery, incest, homosexuality, and child sacrifice (Leviticus 18:3, 24). Rather than immediately drive these peoples from the land, God waited to judge them until their sins were so serious they deserved to be wiped out (Genesis 15:16). God warned that if these inhabitants were allowed to remain in the land, they would lure his people into the same terrible sins.

The Lord's Old Testament command isn't an order for you to physically do battle with sinful people today. Jesus won the battle against sin for us. But it's still a warning against letting sin remain in your life after you come to believe in God. You're wise if you get rid of anything that pulls you away from the Lord.

PRAY IT

God, I commit my life completely to you. I want to rid my life of anything that lures me into sin. Show me what needs to go.

READ IT

Deuteronomy 9:1 – 10:22, Luke 6:12 – 36, Psalm 37:21 – 31

> *"Blessed are you who are poor, for yours is the kingdom of God. Blessed are you who hunger now, for you will be satisfied."*
>
> Luke 6:20 – 21

LIVE IT

When Jesus says he's handing out blessings, you're smart if you grab as many as you can. Yet you might be surprised exactly who gets his happiness — and how they get it.

Jesus had just finished teaching a large crowd of followers, along with others who converged from every direction to hear him. These were hurting people who found help simply by getting close to the Lord. His power healed their physical diseases and freed them from demonic oppression.

Then Jesus looked straight at his followers and said that poor people are blessed. So are the hungry, the weeping, and the hated. The word for "blessed" can also be translated as "happy," a deep joy you can only get from the Lord. Jesus's unique happiness arrives in the form of membership in his kingdom, real physical fullness, solid laughter, and a connection with Jesus himself. His rewards are so exceptional they make you leap for joy.

Jesus also lists ways you're sure to miss out on his happiness, like when you count on money to make you happy, laugh at other people's expense, or arrange your life around trying to impress people.

Right at this moment, you might not feel poor, hungry, sad, or persecuted. But whenever you help hurting people like Jesus does, you're also sure to experience his joy.

PRAY IT

Lord, I want the joy only you can give. I won't settle for the cheap happiness I get from shallow things. Teach me to help the people you bless most.

day**86** march 27

READ IT

Deuteronomy 11:1 – 12:32, Luke 6:37 – 7:10, Psalm 37:32 – 40

> *"Consider the blameless, observe the upright; a future awaits those who seek peace."*
>
> Psalm 37:37

LIVE IT

A hundred times a day you stand at a fork in the road, faced with a decision to go God's way or down some other path. You might hear that either choice is as good as the other. But one leads to a future. The other doesn't.

In this psalm David describes an evil and ruthless person who flourishes like a native green tree. Even if you're underwhelmed by a nearby stand of oaks or pines, a tree thriving in Israel's arid climate makes an impressive sight. But this prosperous man soon dies. Not only that, he disappears. He's nowhere in sight. No matter how hard everyone looks, a guy who looked successful and safe is gone.

That destiny awaits everyone who lives against God. In God's time and way, they vanish. But a real future lies ahead for people who "hope in the Lord and keep his way" (Psalm 37:34). These are the people who try hard to do right and consistently seek peace. The Lord won't let them be overpowered by evil, and in the end, they will inherit everything good.

You probably don't plan to go chasing down a path of all-out evil. But whenever you compromise any of the Lord's commands, you take a step away from him. Small steps can add up to big leaps until you find yourself distant from God. And there's no future in that.

PRAY IT

God, train me to walk close to you, making every small choice a step in the right direction. I have a future when I stick with you.

march 28

day87

READ IT

Deuteronomy 13:1 – 14:29, Luke 7:11 – 35, Psalm 38:1 – 12

"If your very own brother ... or your closest friend secretly entices you, saying, 'Let us go and worship other gods' ... do not yield to them or listen to them."

DEUTERONOMY 13:6, 8

LIVE IT

Make a mental list of the five or six people you hang out with most. Then answer this. Who pushes you closer to God? Who pulls you away?

You're wise if you think hard about what the Lord says in this passage about people who hurt your relationship with him. He describes a "prophet" or "dreamer" who offers persuasive reasons you should follow a different god. The Lord warns you to shut your ears to that person. He urges you to "purge the evil from among you" (Deuteronomy 13:5).

In the Old Testament laws of the nation of Israel, that meant the person should be put to death. The Lord's rule applied not just to strangers but to anyone who taught others to disobey God's commands or worship other gods, even family and close friends. Today, talking against God isn't a crime. It's not punishable by death or anything else. It isn't your job to silence followers of other religions. And if you never get close to unbelievers, you'll never have opportunities to tell others about Jesus.

Yet this scene shows how seriously God treats anything that tears you away from him. So watch out for relationships that encourage you to live against God (2 Corinthians 6:14). Search out friendships that help you flee evil and pursue the Lord (2 Timothy 2:22). God doesn't want anything coming between you and him.

PRAY IT

Lord, I don't always notice when others lead me away from you. Alert me when I stop influencing people who don't know you and they start influencing me.

day**88** march 29

READ IT

Deuteronomy 15:1–16:20, Luke 7:36–50, Proverbs 8:12–21

> *"Therefore, I tell you, her many sins have been forgiven—as her great love has shown. But whoever has been forgiven little loves little."*
>
> Luke 7:47

LIVE IT

By dining at the home of a Pharisee, Jesus scored points with the religious rule keepers of his day. Sharing a meal with someone signaled deep agreement and approval, even more than it does in our culture. The Lord's host would have been proud to have a famous spiritual teacher in his home.

Then a sinful woman interrupted that pleasant dining experience. Everyone in town knew her sins, although the Bible doesn't say what they were. After wetting the Lord's feet with her tears and wiping them with her hair, she splashed him with precious and expensive perfume. The Pharisee was appalled, mumbling to himself that Jesus couldn't possibly be a prophet. A real man of God would know the woman's character and never allow such a display.

But Jesus had a lesson for Simon, a story about two men who owed money—one more than a year of wages, the other about a month. Like someone forgiven an enormous debt, the sinful woman was simply showing thanks. Because Simon didn't think he needed forgiveness, he didn't show the Lord such affection.

Love for God isn't something you have to force yourself to feel. It grows whenever you comprehend what the Lord has done for you. The more you realize how much he has forgiven you, the more love you feel for him.

PRAY IT

Lord, I won't brush off my sins, as if they didn't really need to be forgiven. I want to be washed clean. I want to grow even more grateful to you.

march 30 **day89**

READ IT

Deuteronomy 16:21–18:22, Luke 8:1–18, Psalm 38:13–22

> *"Let no one be found among you ... who practices divination or sorcery, interprets omens, engages in witchcraft, or casts spells, or who is a medium or spiritist or who consults the dead."*
>
> DEUTERONOMY 18:10–11

LIVE IT

Reckless people think it's safe to climb all over an electrical tower, but smart people hear the wires buzz with high voltage. That's how it is with dark arts. Others might think they're harmless, but wise people recognize their dangerous spiritual powers.

God warned his people about the occult ("hidden") practices of nations inhabiting the Promised Land. These people attempted to gain supernatural power and secret information from sources other than God. They cast spells. They sought to contact the dead. They interpreted omens. They even sacrificed their children to win favors from their pagan gods.

The Lord absolutely forbade these practices, promising to speak to his people through prophets whose truthfulness could be tested. New Testament believers confessed their involvement in the occult and publicly burned their magic scrolls. God's word spread widely and grew in power as a result (Acts 19:17–20).

Those forbidden arts haven't gone away. While some people dismiss dark arts as harmless, nothing about them is safe. If you look to horoscopes, tarot cards, and Ouija boards for guidance, you are attempting to tap into evil powers. If you engage in séances and spells, you tangle with dangerous forces. All of these dark arts take you far from God. Don't give them the smallest place in your life.

PRAY IT

Lord, don't let me be tempted by dark ways of getting power and knowledge. I choose to rely on you for all the strength and wisdom I need.

day90 march 31

READ IT

Deuteronomy 19:1–20:20, Luke 8:19–39, Psalm 39:1–13

"He got up and rebuked the wind and the raging waters; the storm subsided, and all was calm. 'Where is your faith?' he asked his disciples."

Luke 8:24–25

LIVE IT

You're aboard a sinking boat, taking on water in a furious sea. Your best friend has the ability to save you from certain death. But he sleeps soundly, unmoved by the foaming waves. You're in a panic. Evidently he's not.

Luke didn't exaggerate this scene for dramatic effect. While the Sea of Galilee is only eight miles wide, this oversized lake in northern Israel is surrounded on three sides by mountains rising thousands of feet above water level. When tropical lake air collides with cool mountain air, sudden winds create fatal waves. It's a phenomenon you can still witness today.

Remember that several of Jesus's disciples were professional fishermen, and they weren't mistaken about this real danger. They woke Jesus, hoping for some sort of help from the teacher who had healed a paralyzed man (Luke 5:24–25) and raised a dead boy (7:14–15). The gospel of Mark records that the disciples wondered aloud if the Lord cared that they drowned (Mark 4:38).

Jesus calmed the raging waters and saved his closest friends from death. But he called out their lack of trust. Even after this miraculous demonstration of his power over nature, they still weren't sure what to think about him.

The Lord invites you to put your complete faith in him. You can trust not only his might but also his care.

PRAY IT

Lord, I trust you to help me through the turbulence I will face today. You might not choose to fix all my problems, but you won't ever stop showing me your care.

april 1

day91

READ IT

Deuteronomy 21:1–22:30, Luke 8:40–9:9, Psalm 40:1–8

> *"He lifted me out of the slimy pit, out of the mud and mire; he set my feet on a rock and gave me a firm place to stand."*
>
> Psalm 40:2

LIVE IT

The "slimy pit" in Psalm 40 sounds like an amusing obstacle in a race course meant to prove your toughness, a place to slip and slide in mud and mire.

But David isn't having fun as he writes this song. He faces people who would love to see him ruined and plot to take his life (v. 14). They taunt him mercilessly (v. 15). David is either headed for the throne of Israel or already a powerful king, yet calls himself poor and needy (v. 17). David needs serious help, and he credits the Lord for giving it. God lifts him from the pit and props him up on a rock-solid place. David hopes everyone who sees this dramatic rescue will respect and trust God.

You can't help but celebrate with David, but this song also tells you what to do while you wait for your own rescue: you keep humbly trusting the Lord. You don't turn to false gods for help. You worship God's wonderful works and believe he has a plan for your life.

Most of all, you keep doing what God wants. Like David said, "I desire to do your will, my God; your law is within my heart" (v. 8). That's a verse Jesus echoed as the cross loomed near (Matthew 26:39). According to the book of Hebrews, Jesus uttered those very words (10:4–7).

PRAY IT

God, I trust you to save me from this pit and put my feet on a rock. I plan to act on your will as I wait for you to rescue me.

day92 april 2

READ IT

Deuteronomy 23:1 – 25:19, Luke 9:10 – 27, Proverbs 8:22 – 31

"The Lord brought me forth as the first of his works, before his deeds of old; I was formed long ages ago, at the very beginning, when the world came to be."

Proverbs 8:22 – 23

LIVE IT

The Bible presents God as one being in three persons, a "trinity" or "tri-unity" of the Father, Son, and Holy Spirit. Someone speaks in this passage, but it isn't a member of the trinity. It's the personified voice of the Lord's wisdom, employing a literary form you likely recognize from school. Check Proverbs 8:1 – 4 and 8:12 to hear wisdom introduce herself.

In this poetic passage, wisdom says, "the Lord brought me forth as the first of his works" (v. 22), informing you that God's intelligence and practical knowledge flow from his very core. Always knowing the right thing to do is the essence of who God is.

Wisdom filled the Lord when he raised up vast mountains and put the starry heavens in place. It was present when he marked the horizon and set boundaries for the ocean waves. Then the all-knowing God looked at his creation and overflowed with joy. He examined human beings and felt delight. You can be sure that long ago he foresaw your birth, and he couldn't have been happier at the thought of you.

God's wisdom calls out to you through every page of Scripture. And you truly thrive when you let even more wise voices into your life, people who echo the Lord's thoughts and teach you to live well. The world is full of people who say unwise things. You're smart if you answer wisdom's call.

PRAY IT

God, I can't get enough of your wisdom. Please put wise people in my life to teach me everything I need to know about living for you.

april 3 **day93**

READ IT

Deuteronomy 26:1 – 28:14, Luke 9:28 – 56, Psalm 40:9 – 17

> *"As he was praying, the appearance of his face changed, and his clothes became as bright as a flash of lightning."*
>
> Luke 9:29

LIVE IT

When a friend asks you about God you might feel stumped, unable to string together words to adequately describe what you have learned about the Lord through the Bible or experienced in real life.

That's how Peter, James, and John must have felt after they saw Jesus shine with heavenly glory. After this scene the disciples "kept this to themselves and did not tell anyone at that time what they had seen" (Luke 9:36).

When Jesus was born as a human baby, he gave up much of the brilliance that was his before the world began (John 17:5). Even so, his life revealed the glory of God (1:14). But this "Transfiguration" is the one spot in the Gospels where you begin to glimpse Jesus as he really is. His face radiates brightness, his clothes flash like lightning, and two of the greatest Old Testament leaders show up to share in his splendor.

Peter, James, and John awoke to see this phenomenal display. Peter was so dumbfounded that he offered to set up tents so Jesus, Moses, and Elijah could stick around for awhile. Then, the Father spoke from heaven and affirmed his Son.

The Transfiguration was a one-of-a-kind event, yet someday you and all the Lord's followers will see Jesus glow with every bit of his mind-blowing glory. You might not have words to explain that, but don't give up trying.

PRAY IT

Lord, show me your glory. You lived as a human like me, but you were so much more. I look forward to seeing you shine in heaven.

day94 april 4

READ IT

Deuteronomy 28:15–68, Luke 9:57–10:24, Psalm 41:1–6

> *"Then the LORD will scatter you among all nations, from one end of the earth to the other. There you will worship other gods—gods of wood and stone, which neither you nor your ancestors have known."*
>
> DEUTERONOMY 28:64

LIVE IT

You might feel uneasy hearing God order the Israelites to storm the Promised Land and drive out the people who already live there (Deuteronomy 7:2). Yet the Lord's judgment was the result of the persistent sin of the Amorites and other nations (Genesis 15:16).

This section of Deuteronomy gives you more insight into God's justice. As the Lord prepares his people to enter the land, he utters amazing promises. If they obey him fully, he will bless them in every imaginable way. He will root them in the land as his holy people, causing all the nations to see and show them appropriate respect (Deuteronomy 28:1–14). Yet if the people ignore the Lord's commands, they will face all kinds of disasters as individuals and as a nation.

That's where you spot God's ultimate fairness. If the people fail to follow the Lord, he will remove them from the land he gave them, scattering them to distant nations for worshiping other gods. The Lord gave them a home as a free gift, but they won't get to stick around and enjoy the gift if they don't obey.

God has the same high expectations of everyone on earth. He alone deserves worship, and he wants everyone to quit sinning and turn to him. And the Lord is fair. When it comes to judgment, he doesn't play favorites.

PRAY IT

God, teach me to live with respect for you. You love me, forgive me, and work to change me. Yet you don't play favorites.

READ IT

Deuteronomy 29:1–30:10, Luke 10:25–11:4, Psalm 41:7–13

> *"He went to him and bandaged his wounds, pouring on oil and wine. Then he put the man on his own donkey, brought him to an inn and took care of him."*
>
> Luke 10:34

LIVE IT

Adults taught you not to talk to strangers, and that wise tactic indeed keeps you from harm. But our world is increasingly packed with people who look, talk, and act nothing like us. And they need our care.

In Luke 10 Jesus tells a parable of a wounded man helped by a complete stranger, the famous "Good Samaritan." Jesus tells this tale as a response to a test from one of the religious rule keepers. The Lord describes a man traveling from Jerusalem to Jericho, a seventeen-mile route marked with caves where thugs easily hid. The man is attacked by robbers and left for dead. A couple of religious people cross the road to avoid dealing with the man's wounds. The man who boldly rescues the man is a Samaritan, a guy hated for his race and "incorrect" religion. He pays for a month of care at the inn.

Jesus makes the point that organized religion got in the way of helping someone in obvious need, with representatives of the religious code failing to show real love or do anything about a stranger's blood and pain. While it's not your job to fix difficult or dangerous situations all on your own, look for ways to band together with other believers in order to show your neighbors genuine care.

Jesus didn't aim these words at others. His story is for any of us who consider ourselves all-out committed to God.

PRAY IT

God, train me to show real love to people who are different from me. Help me see and act beyond my comfortable world.

day96

april 6

READ IT

Deuteronomy 30:11 – 31:29, Luke 11:5 – 32, Proverbs 8:32 – 36

"Now then, my children, listen to me; blessed are those who keep my ways."

PROVERBS 8:32

LIVE IT

Wisdom is like the recipe for a perfect chocolate chip cookie. You can rave about it all you want, but the formula doesn't do any good sitting on the counter. You need to mix up a batch of dough and bake it. Just like that, you need to get wisdom off the pages of the Bible and make it real.

Remember where this passage starts earlier in Proverbs 8. The voice of the Lord's wisdom calls out, explaining his vast knowledge and the happiness God felt when he made human beings. Now wisdom speaks again. She instructs you to listen and grow wise. You should watch her comings and goings, because when you find wisdom you find life. When you fail to locate God's practical wisdom, you might as well hand yourself over to disaster.

And there's a little instruction here you don't want to miss: "Blessed are those who keep my ways" (Proverbs 8:32). Wisdom can't bring you the Lord's deep happiness if you don't put it into action. It doesn't matter how much you know if it doesn't affect your life.

Like James 1:22 says, "Do not merely listen to the word, and so deceive yourselves. Do what it says." If you only learn God's wisdom and do nothing about it, you're just kidding yourself. You're not really living wisely.

PRAY IT

God, don't let me slide by learning more and more about how you want me to live but never doing anything about it. I promise to put your word into action.

READ IT

Deuteronomy 31:30–32:52, Luke 11:33–54, Psalm 42:1–6a

"As the deer pants for streams of water, so my soul pants for you, my God."

PSALM 42:1

LIVE IT

No one had to teach you to feel thirsty. That craving for fluids results from a complex bodily system that measures water volume along with the presence of minerals like salt. When your fluid levels drop out of balance, your brain forces you to quench your thirst.

So picture yourself as the deer in Psalm 42. You bounce through the forest, expecting to happen upon a stream. When you don't find the refreshment you're looking for, you sniff the air for moisture. Then your pace slows to a deliberate hunt. Soon every instinct tells you the only thing that matters is finding water. That's what real longing for God feels like.

When you truly thirst for God, the deepest part of you wonders where and how you can connect with him. Like in Psalm 42, maybe you feel beat up by an awful sadness, as if you have consumed nothing for days except tears. Or maybe everyone around sees your pain and mockingly wonders why God hasn't helped you.

This song hints at a couple of ways to quench your thirst. You can keep hoping in God, trusting that soon you won't feel so far from him. And you can purposely go on the hunt for God's people, finding ways to both hang out with people and worship God. Whatever you do, don't give up on finding God. You must obey your thirst.

PRAY IT

Lord, I thirst for you. Help me find you when I feel beat up and isolated. Show me how and where to meet with friends who follow you.

day98 april 8

READ IT

Deuteronomy 33:1 – 34:12, Luke 12:1 – 34, Psalm 42:6b – 11

> *"And everyone who speaks a word against the Son of Man will be forgiven, but anyone who blasphemes against the Holy Spirit will not be forgiven."*
>
> Luke 12:10

LIVE IT

Jesus didn't have an amplifier and giant speaker when he addressed the crowd in Luke 12, a group so intense they trampled each other. Yet the warnings Jesus spoke that day must have sounded alarmingly loud.

The Lord started by announcing that hypocrites have nowhere to hide. He particularly picked on the Pharisees, religious fakes who pretended to be perfect. Jesus also reminded his listeners that God deserves utter respect. He has authority over hell, yet he also knows how to tenderly care for his own.

Most startling are Jesus's words about an unforgiveable sin. Keep in mind that the Lord also said that "every kind of sin and slander can be forgiven" (Matthew 12:31). So of all the possible kinds of wrongdoing in the world, only one type of sin is beyond pardon, "blaspheming" or "speaking against" the Holy Spirit. It's the specific sin of calling Jesus's powerful acts evil and accusing him of partnering with the devil (v. 24).

You might worry your sins are too big to forgive. But God promises that "if we confess our sins, he is faithful and just and will forgive us our sins and purify us from all unrighteousness" (1 John 1:9). If you admit your failings to God and ask for forgiveness, you can be certain you aren't beyond hope. Get the Lord's mercy and press on.

PRAY IT

Lord, sometimes I'm not sure I deserve forgiveness. I worry I have made you mad forever. But I will admit my sins and count on your forgiveness.

READ IT

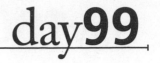

Joshua 1:1–2:24, Luke 12:35–59, Psalm 43:1–5

> *"Have I not commanded you? Be strong and courageous. Do not be afraid; do not be discouraged, for the LORD your God will be with you wherever you go."*
>
> JOSHUA 1:9

LIVE IT

God's stunning plans were coming together. After forty years of wandering in the desert, his people were finally once again poised to enter the land promised to their ancestor Abraham (Genesis 12:6–7). The Lord mapped out property stretching from the southern desert to Lebanon in the north, from the Euphrates in the east to the Mediterranean Sea in the west.

Besides the passing of the old generation of escaped slaves that had refused to enter the land, there was another major shift for the new nation. Moses was gone, and Joshua now stood as the head of the people.

Joshua was one of only two men unafraid to storm the land forty years earlier, convinced the Lord was on their side. Along with his friend Caleb, he stood up to the entire Israelite nation (Numbers 14:1–9). Joshua obviously wasn't a coward, but as the people readied their military invasion, God gave him an extra boost of courage. The Lord had commanded this next step, and would go with Joshua wherever he went. Joshua had no reason to feel discouraged or give in to fear.

That's the secret to obtaining God's boldness. When you follow the Lord's command, you don't have to worry what lies ahead. When you do his will, you don't have to feel anxious. Be courageous and press on. You can be sure the Lord is with you.

PRAY IT

God, I need your courage every day of my life. I intend to obey your commands. I'm convinced you're with me wherever I go.

day100 april 10

READ IT

Joshua 3:1 – 5:12, Luke 13:1 – 30, Proverbs 9:1 – 12

> *"Jesus answered, 'Do you think that these Galileans were worse sinners than all the other Galileans because they suffered this way? I tell you, no!'"*
>
> Luke 13:2 – 3

LIVE IT

A mom gets cancer and dies. A terrorist guns down a camp full of teenagers. An airplane crashes and hundreds lose their lives. Some say such episodes of evil have a quick and easy explanation: Bad things happen to bad people.

That's the assumption between the lines at the start of this scene. Unidentified sources tell Jesus about victims "whose blood Pilate had mixed with their sacrifices" (Luke 13:1). Though the Bible doesn't offer more details, it sounds like people from northern Israel had died at the hand of the Roman governor while offering their usual animal sacrifices at the Jerusalem temple.

The person who brought this news must have worn a face that said, "They got what they deserved," because Jesus immediately declares that tragedy doesn't work that way. The Galileans were no worse sinners than those who escaped dying that day. Nor were people crushed by a falling tower any more evil than their neighbors.

Jesus doesn't want us pointing fingers when bad things happen. For that matter, you don't need to be buried with guilt when tragedy hits you. Bad things happen to everyone, and in God's sight, all human beings are sinners (Romans 3:23). We all have the same need, whether life seems smooth or sad. The Lord wants all of us to repent — to quit sinning and turn to him.

PRAY IT

Lord, it's not my job to measure how guilty other people may or may not be. I want to come clean about my own sin and recommit myself to following you.

READ IT

Joshua 5:13–7:26, Luke 13:31–14:14, Psalm 44:1–12

> *"At the sound of the trumpet, when the men gave a loud shout, the wall collapsed; so everyone charged straight in, and they took the city."*
>
> JOSHUA 6:20

LIVE IT

God told Joshua he had already handed over the fortified city of Jericho to his people. So rather than launch the usual attack, the Israelite army was to march around the city and shout—once a day for six days, then seven times on the seventh day. Just as God promised, the city wall collapsed at the sound of a trumpet blast, and the army rushed in.

That sounds absurd, except that excavations in Jericho in the 1930s showed that the city walls had collapsed so completely that attackers could easily have climbed over the rubble to capture the city. Even more astonishing, the walls didn't fall inward, as in a normal attack. Archaeologist John Garstang discovered Jericho's walls had collapsed outward, a sign that another force was at work. The rubble supports the Bible's claim that God leveled the city. Archaeology backs up other details recorded in the Bible. The city was well defended (Joshua 2:5). The battle didn't last long (6:15). The city was burned completely (v. 24).

Your faith is grounded not only in the claims of Scripture, but in evidence found in the rocks and rubble of Israel. And there's a spiritual lesson here too. The Lord's miraculous power is mightier than any obstacle you can ever face. So when God makes a promise to act on your behalf, you can believe him. He keeps his word.

PRAY IT

God, you're more powerful than I can understand. I will trust your promises no matter how outrageous they seem.

day102 april 12

READ IT

Joshua 8:1–9:15, Luke 14:15–35, Psalm 44:13–26

"Awake, LORD! Why do you sleep? Rouse yourself! Do not reject us forever. Why do you hide your face and forget our misery and oppression?"

PSALM 44:23–24

LIVE IT

It can be frustrating when you can't get someone's attention. Now imagine if that someone is your god, to whom you've dedicated your life. When priests of the false god Baal couldn't persuade their master to answer their prayers, the prophet Elijah unleashed a great taunt. He told them, "Shout louder! ... Perhaps he is deep in thought, or busy, or traveling. Maybe he is sleeping and must be awakened" (1 Kings 18:27).

"Busy" is actually a polite way to say, "Perhaps your God is visiting the bathroom." Yet worshipers of ancient gods had even bigger worries. Their deities often dozed off, and they had to be awakened by loud cultic rituals. So the worshipers of Baal not only screamed but slashed themselves "until their blood flowed" (v. 28).

A god can't do you much good if he can't keep his eyes open or if you have to torture yourself to get his attention. But Scripture tells us that the God who watches over us "will neither slumber nor sleep" (Psalm 121:4). That's a vivid way to remember that the Lord's care never ends.

Knowing that the Lord doesn't sleep might not quiet the worries expressed in Psalm 44—that God needs to be prodded, or that he's rejected you. Yet the last lines of this song answer that concern. God will rise up. He will help you. He will rescue you. Why? Not because of anything special you do. You can count on his care because of his unfailing love.

PRAY IT

God, you never sleep or take a vacation. You never stop caring for me. While I wait for your help, I will trust in your nonstop love.

READ IT

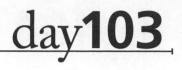

Joshua 9:16–10:43, Luke 15:1–32, Psalm 45:1–9

> *"So he got up and went to his father. But while he was still a long way off, his father saw him and was filled with compassion for him; he ran to his son, threw his arms around him and kissed him."*
>
> LUKE 15:20

LIVE IT

The guy best known as "the prodigal son" couldn't wait to break out of his father's house. He was likely in his teens and single, and by asking for his share of the family wealth, he was telling his dad, "I wish you were dead."

Lots of people read "The Parable of the Lost Son" as a warning against wandering into wildness. The son had barely received his money before he runs away and wastes everything. He ends up feeding pigs, an insulting job that made him ritually unclean. The son doesn't come to his senses until he almost starved.

Yet you could also call this "The Parable of the Waiting Father." The dad must have been actively watching for his son, because he spots his boy a long way in the distance. The father has every reason to lash out, but he welcomes his son home.

Or you could also call this "The Parable of the Lost Sons," because there's another brother at home. He always works hard, but he only serves his father out of duty. He never stops to enjoy his father's love. He's just as lost as his younger brother, only in a different way.

Maybe you're the younger brother who needs to come home to the Lord. Or perhaps you're the older brother who needs to serve God from the heart. Either way, you have a Father whose love never stops.

PRAY IT

Lord, sometimes I feel lost, even when I haven't left home. I want to live your way and enjoy your love.

day104 april 14

READ IT

Joshua 11:1 – 12:24, Luke 16:1 – 18, Proverbs 9:13 – 18

"Folly is an unruly woman; she is simple and knows nothing."

PROVERBS 9:13

LIVE IT

You already met the wise woman of Proverbs 8. She's the personification of the Lord's practical intelligence, the knowledge you need to thrive in real life. Call that lady "Wisdom." Now you get to meet a rowdy woman. She's named "Folly," and she embodies everything unwise.

These two women couldn't be more different, but their profiles in Proverbs 9:1 – 6 and 9:13 – 18 fit together almost line-by-line. Make sure to read them both, comparing where they match or differ.

Folly is unruly, meaning she's loud and undisciplined. She's also simple, unsure about her path in life. She knows absolutely nothing, so she can't tell the difference between right and wrong. Like Wisdom, she calls out from her house high atop the city. Also like Wisdom, she beckons naive people to come close, inviting everyone who lacks sense. But unlike Wisdom, she serves stolen water (5:15 – 16) and secret food (30:20). Little do visitors know that her house is jammed with dead bodies. By entering her home, her guests have already expired.

If you live against God, you're hanging out in Folly's house. You're also missing out on the grand banquet Wisdom serves. She has fine food and fresh drinks. Everyone who enters her home learns how to escape their simple ways, and she points them down a sophisticated path. And none of Wisdom's guests ever drop dead.

PRAY IT

God, teach me to choose wisdom over folly. I want to experience real life, and I know that only happens when I listen to you.

READ IT

Joshua 13:1 – 14:15, Luke 16:19 – 17:10, Psalm 45:10 – 17

> *"When Joshua had grown old, the LORD said to him, 'You are now very old, and there are still very large areas of land to be taken over.'"*
>
> JOSHUA 13:1

LIVE IT

Unless you're a crazed fan of ancient maps, your eyes will glaze over when you read the geographic features marking the land boundaries between Israel's twelve tribes. But there's a story behind these lists.

Joshua 10 – 11 sounds as if every last corner of the land God promised has been conquered. Cities fell from north to south, and a total of thirty-one petty kings lost their thrones. But then the Lord speaks up in Joshua 13. He breaks the news to Joshua that he has grown too old to finish conquering the land. Yet there's an extended list of places the people haven't occupied.

While the Lord promises to continue driving out the inhabitants of the land, the people's commitment to his purposes begin to fade. They fail to destroy the worship sites dedicated to pagan gods, letting those unpleasant altars stand. And so the Lord lets their enemies live. By the start of the Bible's next book, he says, "I will not drive them out before you; they will become traps for you, and their gods will become snares to you" (Judges 2:3).

Once again you spot the big lesson of this section of the Bible. While today it's not your job to drive out worshipers of other religions, it's still your task to rid your life of anything that tempts you away from God. If you don't, you will end up snared.

PRAY IT

God, teach me to be faithful to you and obey you in every way I know how. I don't want anything to pull me away from you.

day106 april 16

READ IT

Joshua 15:1 – 16:10, Luke 17:11 – 37, Psalm 46:1 – 11

> *"Jesus asked, 'Were not all ten cleansed? Where are the other nine? Has no one returned to give praise to God except this foreigner?' "*
>
> Luke 17:17 – 18

LIVE IT

Nowadays a skin disease won't get you kicked out of church. But Old Testament believers were just beginning to grasp God's perfect holiness. To safeguard their health and to teach them about purity and obedience, the Lord laid down laws not only about right and wrong but also about ritual cleanliness.

Leprosy was a condition that made its victims spiritually unclean, banning them not only from worship but from all contact with family and friends. The law forced them to live on the fringes of towns and villages in heartwrenching poverty and isolation (Leviticus 13:45 – 46).

In this scene Jesus meets ten men suffering from this untreatable condition. Their uncleanliness means they can't approach him, but they beg for his pity. The Lord sends them to the priests, the only people who can verify their healing. As they obey, all ten men are cleansed. Nine men run off, no doubt to celebrate with family and friends. Only one detours back to thank Jesus.

Saying thanks is always the right thing to do. But the guy who came back got even more, not just a physical cure but a spiritual healing that made him truly "well" (Luke 17:19). When God drops good things in your life, say thanks. When you do, you get more than the gift. You get a sweet connection with the one who gives you everything good.

PRAY IT

God, forgive me when I receive your gifts and simply take off to enjoy them. Thanks for everything good you give me.

day107

READ IT

Joshua 17:1–18:28, Luke 18:1–30, Psalm 47:1–9

> *"For the LORD Most High is awesome, the great King over all the earth."*
>
> PSALM 47:2

LIVE IT

Your family almost certainly has unspoken rules about who controls various parts of your home. There might be a kitchen boss, a garage master, and a yard chief. A pet might dominate a corner or couch, you might be in charge of a bedroom, and everyone understands who commands the remote control.

That's what gods were like in the ancient world. The deities of Israel's neighbors were masters of a particular city, region, or kingdom. Those areas often overlapped, and followers argued over which god was most powerful.

The God of the Bible isn't tied to a particular place. Even in the Old Testament, where he chose Israel as his special people and the temple in Jerusalem as the place of his intense presence, he nevertheless ruled an infinite domain. Scripture says "God reigns over the nations" (Psalm 47:8) and proclaims "God is the King of all the earth" (v. 7). He rules over every notable person and every monarch on earth. And he deserves praise from all people. This song instructs people of every nation to clap to God and shout with joy.

God is bigger than any so-called god in your world. He's more powerful than anyone who tries to rule your school or act like the boss of you. He's the all-powerful Lord, the ultimate King over every place you can ever go.

PRAY IT

God, you're the boss of me and of my whole world. I won't make anything an idol. I won't let anyone rule me but you.

day108 april 18

READ IT

Joshua 19:1 – 21:19, Luke 18:31 – 19:10, Proverbs 10:1 – 10

"The proverbs of Solomon: A wise son brings joy to his father, but a foolish son brings grief to his mother."

Proverbs 10:1

LIVE IT

If the Lord comes to you in a dream and promises to give you whatever you ask, your fellow human beings would like you to request an end to war and hunger. But no one would be shocked if you asked for a fast car or a beachfront estate.

Soon after Solomon became ruler of Israel, the Lord appeared to the new king in a dream. He said, "Ask for whatever you want me to give you" (1 Kings 3:5). Rather than wishing for long life or wealth, Solomon asked for a wise heart to govern the nation and to discern right from wrong. The Lord was so pleased with Solomon's request that he promised to give the king not only unmatched wisdom but also riches and fame (vv. 3:10 – 15). Solomon soon became known as the wisest man that ever lived (4:29 – 34).

Parts of the book of Proverbs came from Agur (Proverbs 30:1) and King Lemuel (31:1), yet Solomon is regarded as the author of much of the book's contents (1:1). As you launch into Proverbs 10:1 – 22:16, you reach the core of his pithy words. These short but highly useful proverbs give you wisdom for real life.

It's tempting to rush through these short sayings. But ponder them one by one. God wants to teach you through the wisdom of the most sensible human ever.

PRAY IT

Lord, you have wisdom far beyond what I possess. Use the proverbs in this book to teach me your best way to live.

READ IT

Joshua 21:20–22:34, Luke 19:11–44, Psalm 48:1–8

> *"Now that the LORD your God has given them rest as he promised, return to your homes in the land that Moses the servant of the LORD gave you on the other side of the Jordan."*
>
> JOSHUA 22:4

LIVE IT

It's like getting a B when you could have earned an A. Or jogging a twelve-minute mile when you know you can run an eight. Or giving five dollars to a good cause when you know you can afford ten dollars or more. There's something not quite right in this passage about two-and-a-half tribes wanting to live east of the Jordan River.

Back when the Israelites were getting ready to enter the Promised Land, the tribes of Reuben, Gad, and half of Manasseh said they didn't want to cross the Jordan. They liked the land on the east of the river, and they persuaded Moses to let them live there (Numbers 32:1–5).

That area is called the "Transjordan," and Bible scholars argue whether it was right for tribes to settle there. Moses had commanded the tribes to help conquer the land west of the Jordan (vv. 20–23). When Joshua lets them go home after the battles have ended, he calls the Transjordan the land given them by "Moses the servant of the Lord," as if it didn't come from God.

That territory might have been good, but it wasn't the best. It was almost the Promised Land, but not quite. That's a choice you face every day. You can try, or you can go all-out. You can be good, or you can be great. You can settle, or you can pursue God's very best. What will you choose?

PRAY IT

God, forgive me when I don't follow you all-out. I don't want to settle. I want your very best plans for me.

day110 april 20

READ IT

Joshua 23:1–24:33, Luke 19:45–20:26, Psalm 48:9—14

"Choose for yourselves this day whom you will serve.... But as for me and my household, we will serve the LORD."

JOSHUA 24:15

LIVE IT

By the time Joshua was a very old man, God had defeated all of Israel's enemies. Life was going well, and the people had seen with their own eyes everything the Lord had accomplished. Like Joshua told Israel's leaders, "You know with all your heart and soul that not one of all the good promises the LORD your God gave you has failed. Every promise has been fulfilled" (Joshua 23:14).

At that moment, the Israelites had everything going for them. They had every reason to trust God and obey his commands. But Joshua sensed something evil brewing. After reminding the people of everything the Lord had done to rescue them, he challenged the people to "fear the LORD and serve him with all faithfulness" (24:14). They needed to throw away every false god and serve the Lord only.

Joshua called for a decision. He told the people to choose then and there whom they would follow, the Lord or other gods. As for him, he was sticking with God.

Joshua reminded everyone that God is holy and that following him can be hard. While a whole crowd of Israelites swore they would obey the Lord, it wouldn't be long before the nation would rebel and wander into wild sin. It's easy to say you intend to follow the Lord. But nice words don't matter if you walk away.

PRAY IT

Lord, I don't want to say one thing and do another. I don't want to promise to obey you and then walk away. Teach me to serve you only.

april 21

day111

READ IT

Judges 1:1–2:5, Luke 20:27–21:4, Psalm 49:1–20

> *"Even Moses showed that the dead rise, for he calls the* LORD *'the God of Abraham, and the God of Isaac, and the God of Jacob.' He is not the God of the dead, but of the living, for to him all are alive."*
>
> LUKE 20:37–38

LIVE IT

Have you ever watched a devious classmate ask a complicated but irrelevant question to throw a teacher off track? That's the scene you witness in Luke 20. A group of religious experts hits Jesus with a question so complex that it makes mathematical word problems sound easy.

The Lord's interrogators describe an impossible string of events, a woman widowed by one brother after another. The issue isn't seven marriages, which were in line with ancient laws about keeping a family name alive. The problem is the question that comes at the end: "At the resurrection whose wife will she be?" (Luke 20:33).

Jesus brushes off the question and takes the conversation in another direction. Why? Because the religious experts are Sadducees. They don't even believe the dead will rise. They think their riddle proves the foolishness of this basic belief.

The Lord answers by explaining the real nature of heaven. The life you will enjoy post-death doesn't have to do with getting married. It's a completely new experience. And the bigger point is that the Lord wants you to be assured he has an eternal home planned for you. He goes way back to the account of Moses at the burning bush (Exodus 3:6) to prove that God brings the dead back to life. Heaven is hard for our limited minds to grasp. But you can be sure heaven exists.

PRAY IT

Lord, I believe you that heaven is a real place and my real destination after I die. I trust you to bring me home to you.

day112 april 22

READ IT

Judges 2:6–3:31, Luke 21:5–38, Proverbs 10:11–20

> *"After that whole generation had been gathered to their ancestors, another generation grew up who knew neither the LORD nor what he had done for Israel. Then the Israelites did evil in the eyes of the LORD."*
>
> JUDGES 2:10–11

LIVE IT

Maybe you're growing up in a Christian family, a group of people that trusts Jesus as the one-and-only Savior and that aims to follow him wholeheartedly. That's an unbeatable advantage as you build your own relationship with the Lord. But don't assume you get your family's faith automatically.

Judges reports that the generation that conquered the Promised Land served the Lord "throughout the lifetime of Joshua and of the elders who outlived him and who had seen all the great things the LORD had done for Israel" (Judges 2:7).

After those folks died, the next generation slid into evil. They worshiped Baal, the god of the Canaanites, and the Ashtoreths, pagan goddesses of the Philistines. These false gods were allegedly in charge of the fertility of people, herds, and crops. Instead of counting on the Lord for those good things, the Israelites looked to pagan gods to ensure them success.

It's no secret why the Israelites stopped trusting God. That next generation "knew neither the LORD nor what he had done for Israel" (Joshua 2:10). Either their parents didn't tell them the stories of God's mighty power, or they weren't paying attention.

If you want to walk closely with the Lord, you have to meet him firsthand. You need to apply his promises and commands to your life. You have to make your own choice to live as his child, because God doesn't have grandchildren.

PRAY IT

God, thanks for putting believers among my family and friends. I won't take my relationship with you for granted. I will make faith my own.

READ IT

Judges 4:1–5:31, Luke 22:1–38, Psalm 50:1–15

> *"Now Deborah, a prophet, the wife of Lappidoth, was leading Israel at that time. She held court under the Palm of Deborah."*
>
> JUDGES 4:4–5

LIVE IT

Once Israel turned away from God, the people entered a vicious cycle that continued for hundreds of years. They developed bad habits of sin ... they suffered attacks by fierce enemies ... they cried to God ... the Lord raised up a leader called a "judge" to save them ... and the people went back to their sin as soon as that leader died (Judges 2:10–19).

A judge wasn't a court official but a spiritual, political, and military ruler all rolled into one. The book of Judges gives us accounts of leaders like Ehud, Gideon, Samson, and one of the greatest judges ever, Deborah.

Deborah led the nation from the shade of a palm tree named after her. When she ordered one of Israel's commanders to attack an enemy army, he refused to enter the battle without her. Deborah pointed out that credit for the victory would go to a woman, and glory went not only to Deborah but also to a second woman, Jael, who killed the enemy commander by pounding a stake through his head. (As women were considered secondary citizens back then, Deborah and Jael's actions were worth calling special attention to.) The days of the judges often weren't happy, but Deborah sang to praise God and celebrate the people who volunteered to fight.

God isn't telling you today to take up arms against your enemies. But no matter what he asks, you can be like Deborah. You can step up, do your duty, and teach others to do theirs.

PRAY IT

God, help me to obey you even when others don't. I'm going to be brave and believe you will help me do your work.

day114 april 24

READ IT

Judges 6:1 – 7:8, Luke 22:39 – 62, Psalm 50:16 – 23

> *"Peter sat down with them. A servant girl saw him seated there in the firelight. She looked closely at him and said, 'This man was with him.' But he denied it."*
>
> LUKE 22:55 – 57

LIVE IT

Everyone tells you, "Don't be afraid to tell people about Jesus." But that expectation can feel unrealistic when you watch what happened to one of Jesus's closest friends and followers.

Don't be quick to slam Peter. Soon he would preach a spontaneous message that persuaded three thousand people to believe in Jesus (Acts 2:14 – 41). Tradition says he was crucified upside-down after insisting he was unworthy to die like his Lord. Yet here this bold guy crumples when a little servant girl confronts him.

Jesus had predicted Peter would disown him (Luke 22:34), and hindsight shows several reasons he failed. Peter was under intense pressure from Satan (v. 31). He was overconfident, presuming he was ready to go to prison and die for Jesus (v. 33). Peter often acted without thinking, like when he drew a sword and cut off a man's ear trying to protect Jesus (John 18:10). Then Peter lost contact with Jesus, lurking in the shadows when he could have stayed near (Luke 22:54).

Yet the biggest reason Peter didn't stand up for his Lord is that he lacked the boldness that would come from the Holy Spirit alone (Acts 2:1 – 17). If you want to face your world unafraid, don't expect to do it on your own. God stands ready to give you the right words (Luke 21:15). Ask him to make you bold, and count on him to help.

PRAY IT

Lord, I need you to make me bold through the power of your Holy Spirit. I want to stand up for you, but I need your help.

READ IT

Judges 7:8b – 8:35, Luke 22:63 – 23:25, Psalm 51:1 – 9

"Have mercy on me, O God, according to your unfailing love; according to your great compassion blot out my transgressions."

Psalm 51:1

LIVE IT

From the time you were little your parents taught you to say, "I'm sorry." After a while they prodded you to "Say it like you mean it." If you're truly fortunate, they told you, "Tell God you're sorry too."

There's a specific story behind Psalm 51, the Bible's famed song of confession. The heading says King David penned these words after the prophet Nathan called out his sin with Bathsheba.

David should have been leading his troops in battle, but he was lounging around the palace when he spied a beautiful woman bathing. David sent for her, slept with her, and got her pregnant. If that weren't enough, he conspired to kill her husband, sending a loyal soldier into the heat of battle (2 Samuel 11:1 – 27). When God sent Nathan to confront David, the prophet compared the king to a wealthy rancher who stole a poor man's only lamb (12:1 – 14). That's when David poured out his heart to God. He admitted all the evil he had done against the Lord.

Everyone sins, but the big choice is always what you do about your failures. Admitting you're wrong to God and others might be the toughest thing you ever do, but you get a head start when you make David's words your own. Pray them and invite God to wash you clean.

PRAY IT

God, I admit I'm not perfect. I can't begin to count my sins. But I want to admit them one by one to you. Thanks for your forgiveness.

day116 april 26

READ IT

Judges 9:1–57, Luke 23:26–56, Proverbs 10:21–30

> *"One of the criminals who hung there hurled insults at him: 'Aren't you the Messiah? Save yourself and us!'"*
>
> Luke 23:39

LIVE IT

As the hours ticked down to Jesus's crucifixion, he was surrounded by mockers. The soldiers who captured him ridiculed and beat him, wrapping his eyes in a blindfold and demanding he say who had hit him. They uttered "many other insulting things" (Luke 22:65), and that was just the start.

Jesus was taken to the Roman governor, Pilate, then to the king of Judea, Herod. When Jesus refused to answer Herod's questions, he and his soldiers decked him out in a royal robe (23:11).

As Jesus hung on the cross, rulers and everyday people continued to sneer. Then the two criminals being executed on either side of Jesus got mixed up in the fight. One of the criminals taunted Jesus, daring him to prove his identity as the Messiah by saving himself and them. But the other recognized an essential fact about Jesus. The other two guys were getting what they deserved, but Jesus had done nothing wrong.

The Bible says that Jesus was like his human brothers and sisters in every way (Hebrews 2:17). That implies he had quirky habits or less-than-perfect physical traits just like the rest of us—points others would find easy to tease. But this mocking at the cross questioned his character, his truthfulness, even his sanity. When Jesus went to the cross for human sin, his pain wasn't just physical. He was ridiculed and rejected, all for your sake.

PRAY IT

Lord, you suffered for me in ways I can barely begin to imagine. Thank you for the price you paid on the cross.

READ IT

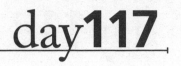

Judges 10:1 – 11:40, Luke 24:1 – 35, Psalm 51:10 – 19

> *"Whatever comes out of the door of my house to meet me when I return in triumph from the Ammonites will be the LORD's, and I will sacrifice it as a burnt offering."*
>
> JUDGES 11:31

LIVE IT

Parents aren't perfect. Their children get the brunt of their issues, and the scene of Jephthah and his daughter shows a family at its worst.

The Israelites had fallen into another cycle of sin, doing evil by serving the false gods of all their neighbors. When the Israelites abandon the Lord, he hands them over to be crushed by their enemies. The people cry to God, but he tells them to beg their new gods for help.

After the Israelites get rid of their false gods, the Lord can't stand to watch their misery any longer and raises up Jephthah to save them. But the judge makes a reckless vow, promising to sacrifice to God the first thing that welcomes him home after his victory. Unfortunately, the first one out the door is not an animal, as he expected, but his daughter. It's not clear if Jephthah kills his daughter or if he sacrifices her by not letting her marry. Either way, the girl suffers horribly for her father's stupidity.

If you or a friend is caught in an intense home situation, get help from an adult you trust. If you suffer the brunt of your parents' bad choices, remember the Lord loves you even when parents seem like they don't (Isaiah 49:15). And if you see yourself falling into bad patterns you might see at home, ask God to show you how to break the cycle of sin.

PRAY IT

God, help my family grow in its commitment to you. Thanks for good times at home. Work with us to solve our problems.

day118 april 28

READ IT

Judges 12:1 – 13:25, Luke 24:36 – 53, Psalm 52:1 – 9

> *"He said to them, 'Why are you troubled, and why do doubts rise in your minds? Look at my hands and my feet. It is I myself! Touch me and see.'"*
>
> Luke 24:38 – 39

LIVE IT

The fact that Jesus would die and come back to life was no secret. The Lord had explained it all along, but his disciples never really got it (Luke 9:22, 9:44 – 45, 18:31 – 33). So when Jesus suddenly appears among them and wishes them peace, they're confused. These closest followers of Jesus stand in the presence of their risen Lord yet feel shaken and scared, wondering if they're chatting with a ghost. Their joy and amazement leaves their minds and emotions in a jumble.

Jesus could have turned harsh at their lack of understanding. Instead he points to clear evidence he's back from the dead. He lets his friends examine where his hands and feet were nailed to the cross. He invites them to reach out and touch. He eats a chunk of fish. And then he uses Scripture to prove that his resurrection went exactly according to plan. It's the same way he unfolded the facts for a couple of confused followers on the road to Emmaus (24:13 – 35).

If Jesus didn't rise from the dead, the rest of your faith falls apart (1 Corinthians 15:12 – 14). The Lord wants you to know that he was seen by people just like you who could verify he was truly alive. The resurrection is not a hopeful wish or a hallucination. If you wonder if Jesus really rose from the dead, read the Bible accounts (Matthew 28:1 – 20, Mark 16:1 – 8, Luke 24:1 – 53, John 20:1 – 21:25). The eyewitness evidence is all there.

PRAY IT

Lord, you rose from the dead and made it clear you were really alive. I serve a risen Savior.

READ IT

Judges 14:1–15:20, John 1:1–28, Psalm 53:1–6

> *"In the beginning was the Word, and the Word was with God, and the Word was God."*
>
> JOHN 1:1

LIVE IT

You might not realize you're reading the Christmas story when you flip through the first words of the gospel of John. While Matthew and Luke detail the Lord's birth in Bethlehem, John launches into the meaning of his arrival for you and your world.

John starts by giving the Lord an usual name, "the Word." To both Jews and Greeks the name stood for the powerful intelligence that created and rules the universe. Its use in John 1:1 tells you three crucial facts. "In the beginning was the Word" means Jesus is eternal, existing forever before creation. "The Word was with God" says Jesus relates with God as a face-to-face equal. "The Word was God" reveals that Jesus is distinct from God yet also truly God.

That might be tough to grasp, but it helps explain what comes next. Even though Jesus is God, he left heaven and was born as a human being. As John says, he "became flesh and made his dwelling among us" (v. 14). When you look at Jesus, you see everything you need to know about God.

By coming to earth, Jesus gives every human a chance to decide for or against God. Not everyone recognizes him. Some outright reject him. Yet "to all who did receive him, to those who believed in his name, he gave the right to become children of God" (v. 12). That isn't the usual Christmas story, but it still comes with a gift.

PRAY IT

Lord, you were born on earth as a baby and you grew up to show me God. I recognize you as my Lord and Savior now and forever.

day120 april 30

READ IT

Judges 16:1 – 17:31, John 1:29 – 51, Proverbs 10:31 – 11:8

> *"'No razor has ever been used on my head,' he said, 'because I have been a Nazirite dedicated to God from my mother's womb. If my head were shaved, my strength would leave me.'"*
>
> Judges 16:17

LIVE IT

Your parents can drag you to church, but they can't make you love God. The Lord can map out a spectacular purpose for your life, but you might run away from his plan. That's how it was with Samson. He was drafted by God even before he was born, but he always had a tough time getting in line with the Lord's program.

Samson was the world's original superhero, except his strength wasn't a product of computer-generated imagery. His power came from the Lord, who chose him to rescue Israel from the Philistines, brutal neighbors who lived on the Mediterranean plains. Samson was to commit himself to God as a Nazirite, a vow that included no alcohol and no haircuts (Judges 13:1 – 8). As long as his locks grew uncut, he would have phenomenal strength.

Samson's parents were on board from the start, but their son constantly fought against God. His rebellion grew worse until he shared the secret of his strength with a Philistine woman, Delilah. After he lost his strength, his enemies made him a slave in a pagan god's temple. Only at the end of his life did Samson fully submit to God (16:28 – 31).

This guy was a powerful defender of God's people. But he never became as great as the Lord must have intended. Although he was a person with unlimited potential, much of what he did in life isn't worth imitating.

PRAY IT

God, you have an amazing design for my life. I want to stay close to you and live out your plan. Show me when I'm getting off track.

READ IT

Judges 18:1 – 19:30, John 2:1 – 25, Psalm 54:1 – 7

> *"He made a whip out of cords, and drove all from the temple courts, both sheep and cattle; he scattered the coins of the money changers and overturned their tables."*
>
> JOHN 2:15

LIVE IT

You wouldn't smile if enemies crept into your room and turned it into a shrine to an archrival team. You would tear down every bit of memorabilia and carry it to the curb. Now picture Jesus back in the ancient temple, seeing people who care nothing about God making his holy house into a mall. He's more than a little upset.

The merchants that deeply offended Jesus thought they were providing necessary services to worshipers who often traveled long distances. Some sold animals required for sacrifices, like cattle, sheep, and doves. Others swapped money, exchanging normal Roman coins for special temple currency. Still others collected mandatory temple taxes. But all these activities happened in the wrong place, the courtyard of God's temple. They also came at a steep price, cheating ordinary worshipers.

Jesus made a whip and chased out animals and owners. He tossed tables, making money fly. He drove away everything that didn't honor his Father. He defended his divine right to cleanse the temple. Then he predicted he would be killed and raised back to life three days later.

People who tag Jesus as a meek and mild guy don't understand his zeal for doing the right thing . . . correcting injustice . . . rescuing the hurting . . . worshiping authentically. You don't become like Jesus by flipping tables. But you start to resemble him when you can identify what's truly important and when his holy passion drives everything you do.

PRAY IT

Lord, you're my example in doing things that matter. Fill me with passion for everything you care about.

day122 may 2

READ IT

Judges 20:1–21:25, John 3:1–21, Psalm 55:1–11

> *"For God so loved the world that he gave his one and only Son, that whoever believes in him shall not perish but have eternal life."*
>
> John 3:16

LIVE IT

Don't say John 3:16 is your favorite verse in the Bible and move on. Hit pause and look around at what's going on.

A Pharisee named Nicodemus came to visit Jesus at an hour when no one else would spot him. This spiritual leader was far ahead of his hypocritical peers, recognizing Jesus as a teacher from God authenticated by powerful miracles. But the Lord didn't congratulate Nicodemus on his insight. Instead he challenged him to think harder. Jesus insisted Nicodemus needed to be "born again," a phrase that means "born anew" or "born from above."

Being a decent person like Nicodemus doesn't make you friends with God. Belonging to a Christian family or keeping religious rules doesn't do it either. If you want an actual relationship with the Lord, the Holy Spirit has to work a miracle in you, one that starts when you believe in Jesus. When you understand that Jesus is the world's Savior and personally begin to count on him, you're born again in a brand new way.

Jesus could have ridiculed Nicodemus for not having everything figured out. Instead, the Lord explained how we can all truly meet God. Jesus didn't show up on earth to condemn the human race, but to lead us home to heaven. God loves us so much that he sent his Son into the world so we can live forever with him.

PRAY IT

Lord, you show us how to be born into a new relationship with you. I believe in you. I look forward to my forever home in heaven.

READ IT

Ruth 1:1–2:23, John 3:22–36, Psalm 55:12–23

> *"But Ruth replied, 'Don't urge me to leave you or to turn back from you. Where you go I will go, and where you stay I will stay. Your people will be my people and your God my God.'"*
>
> RUTH 1:16

LIVE IT

The happy book of Ruth starts with miserable sadness. Back in the time of the judges, famine struck Israel, and a man fled with his family east into Moab. Soon Elimilech died, leaving a widow, Naomi, and two sons. The young men married local women, but then they also died, leaving two more widows, Orpah and Ruth. In an era when a woman had no resources to survive without a husband or sons, life was lonely and desperate. Naomi was convinced God was against her.

When Naomi heard there was again food in Israel, she made up her mind to return home. As she told the wives of her dead sons to return to their families, everyone wept. But then one daughter-in-law showed astonishing loyalty. Ruth vowed to stay with Naomi until death. She promised to go to Naomi's homeland, become part of her people, and worship her God. If you want a role model of loyalty to people and God, Ruth is your unbeatable example. Whether you're a girl or guy, she shows what commitment looks like in real life.

The book of Ruth details the rest of what becomes a very happy story. Not only does the Lord provide for two widows, but he also gives Ruth a husband in one of the Bible's best-known love stories. In the end Ruth, a foreigner, becomes a great-grandmother of King David (Ruth 4:13–17) and gains an honored place in the family line of Jesus.

PRAY IT

God, teach me true commitment to family and friends. Give me stamina to stay loyal and keep loving others no matter what we face.

day124 may 4

READ IT

Ruth 3:1–4:22, John 4:1–26, Proverbs 11:9–18

> *"Yet a time is coming and has now come when the true worshipers will worship the Father in the Spirit and in truth, for they are the kind of worshipers the Father seeks."*
>
> John 4:23

LIVE IT

Christians dig at each other over which church is best. They split over the style of music or how dressed up worshipers should be. They might even act like God never shows up at a church building down the block. That's a bit like the skirmish happening in the background when Jesus meets a woman at a well.

Old Testament law limited real worship to one place, the temple in Jerusalem. It was the only location on earth where people could give offerings and sacrifices (1 Kings 8:22–53). The woman in this scene was a Samaritan, a despised racially-mixed cousin of the Jews. Her people thought it was acceptable to worship at a rival temple on Mount Gerizim. The religious disgust between Jews and Samaritans was so extreme that Jesus, as a Jew, should have had nothing to do with that woman. Yet he asks her for water and engages her in a meaningful conversation—one that could lead to her salvation.

This discussion between Jesus and the woman also signals greater things are about to change in God's relationship with his people. When Jesus died and came back to life, he did away with the Old Testament system of worship (Hebrews 10:1–10). Because of the Holy Spirit, people can connect with God anywhere.

To worship "in the Spirit and in truth" (John 4:24) means you give God praise in the way he commands, empowered by the Holy Spirit working inside you and recognizing the real facts about God. And you don't have to go to a special place in Israel to do that. You can worship right now.

PRAY IT

Lord, I want to worship you in the way you desire. I want my words and life to center on you.

READ IT

1 Samuel 1:1 – 2:26, John 4:27 – 42, Psalm 56:1 – 13

> *"LORD Almighty, if you will only look on your servant's misery and remember me, and not forget your servant but give her a son, then I will give him to the LORD for all the days of his life."*
>
> 1 SAMUEL 1:11

LIVE IT

Maybe you strike bargains with God — or try to. If the Lord scores you an A on an exam, you promise to become a doctor and cure cancer. Or if God gets you a car, you say you're willing to give rides to church for the rest of your life.

Although you might not always follow through with these promises, Hannah meant the vow she made to God. Driven by the anguish of a woman unable to have children, she promises to fully dedicate her child to God if she's ever able to conceive. When she gives birth to a son, she calls him Samuel, a name that sounds like the Hebrew words "Asked from God." When the boy is two or three years old, Hannah presented him in the Lord's house. She kept her promise of dedication, then broke out in praise.

Samuel grew up in the temple, serving under a high priest, Eli, whose sons committed atrocious sins. Unlike those evil offspring, Samuel learned to listen to the Lord from a young age (1 Samuel 3:1 – 18). He became a great prophet. At the end of his life, Samuel challenged the Israelites to recall if he had ever cheated any of them. No one could think of a time he failed in his commitment to God (12:1 – 5).

Samuel shows you how to dedicate your life to God from start to finish. As you read the history of Israel in 1 Samuel, watch him grow. Then imitate his all-out devotion.

PRAY IT

God, I won't try to bargain with you. I commit myself to you and won't hold back. Train me to serve you well.

day126 may 6

READ IT

1 Samuel 2:27–4:22, John 4:43–5:15, Psalm 57:1–6

> *"My heart, O God, is steadfast, my heart is steadfast; I will sing and make music."*
>
> Psalm 57:7

LIVE IT

Enemies send you running for cover, but probably not into a cave. The Bible lists two times David fled to a hole. The first was in a place called Adullam (1 Samuel 22:1–5), an experience that inspired David to write Psalm 142. The second was in En Gedi (1 Samuel 24:1–7), the story behind this song.

King Saul had been on the hunt, chasing David to slay him. The king happened to choose a cave as a bathroom, the very cavern where David was hiding. Instead of slaughtering Saul, David crawled up unobserved and sliced a corner off the royal robe, a garment that's symbolic of Saul's kingly authority. David quickly regretted even this small disrespect for the person God had chosen as king and forbade his soldiers to harm Saul.

Like three other psalms (Psalms 58, 59, 75), these lyrics were set to the tune "Do Not Destroy." We don't have the music for this song, yet it isn't hard to catch the mood. David flips rapidly from describing the terrors of his situation to frantic prayers to praising the God who rules the whole world.

When you're in an awful situation, it's natural to tell God about your troubles. Explaining how badly you need him to rescue you might feel easy. But as you struggle to survive, don't forget to worship. Your God deserves praises higher than the sky. His glory fills the entire earth, even the place you hide.

PRAY IT

God, I depend on you for protection. Keep me safe when I face difficulties. Encourage me and help me remember to praise you.

READ IT

1 Samuel 5:1–7:17, John 5:16–30, Psalm 57:7–11

> *"But the following morning when they rose, there was Dagon, fallen on his face on the ground before the ark of the LORD!"*
>
> 1 SAMUEL 5:4

LIVE IT

The "ark of God" or "ark of the covenant" was the most sacred object in ancient Israel, because God's presence dwelt within it. Built according to a pattern God gave Moses (Exodus 25:10–22), this gold-covered wood chest measured four feet long and two feet deep and high. It contained two stone tablets listing the Ten Commandments (v. 16). Each year on the Day of Atonement, Israel's high priest sprinkled blood on the ark's gold cover to gain forgiveness of sin (vv. 17–22, Leviticus 16:15).

The ark was normally housed inside the tabernacle in the Most Holy Place, but when the Israelite's moved, the portable box was carried on poles. The ark made the Jordan River split so the Israelites could cross on dry ground (Joshua 3:6–4:18). It also went before the people during the march around Jericho (6:1–14).

The Israelites ran into trouble when they began to think the ark had magic power of its own, like the ability to win battles (1 Samuel 4:1–11). But like the Philistines found out, the ark's true power came from God. When they put the ark in a temple to their pagan god, it knocked the Philistine's false god Dagon flat.

The Lord doesn't let you play with his power like magic. If you need his strength, just ask. You won't get hold of God's power without going directly to him.

PRAY IT

Lord, you have unbeatable power, but I can't manipulate you to do what I want. I trust you to use your strength to help me.

day128 may 8

READ IT

1 Samuel 8:1 – 10:8, John 5:31 – 47, Proverbs 11:19 – 28

"A generous person will prosper; whoever refreshes others will be refreshed."

PROVERBS 11:25

LIVE IT

You can watch a professional golfer to learn how to swing, or you can study a hack to learn what not to do. Proverbs 11 gives you that same option. You can see how righteous people act and the good results that follow, or you can witness the disasters that befall people who live against God.

Proverbs goes out of its way to give you good and bad examples of handling money. Like this one: "One person gives freely, yet gains even more; another withholds unduly, but comes to poverty" (Proverbs 11:24). Logic says making a habit of giving will leave you impoverished. But that's not how the Lord works. When you give away your time, money, or energy, he gives you more. When you hang on to what you have, you finish with even less.

When you refresh others, God makes sure you receive what you need. When you give, you often get even more. Jesus once said, "Give, and it will be given to you. A good measure, pressed down, shaken together and running over, will be poured into your lap. For with the measure you use, it will be measured to you" (Luke 6:38).

There's one catch. If you give just to get more, the Lord sniffs that out. You spoil the joy of real generosity, and that's not the kind of giving the Lord rewards.

PRAY IT

God, teach me to be generous with everything you give me. Show me how to give wisely. I trust you to keep supplying what I need.

READ IT

1 Samuel 10:9 – 12:25, John 6:1 – 24, Psalm 58:1 – 11

> *"Jesus then took the loaves, gave thanks, and distributed to those who were seated as much as they wanted. He did the same with the fish."*
>
> John 6:11

LIVE IT

Jesus did a miracle no one could miss. He took a boy's small lunch of loaves and fishes and fed a crowd of five thousand men plus women and children. Everyone ate as much as they wanted, and there were leftovers galore. That's a scene so significant it's included in each of the Gospels (Matthew 14:13 – 21, Mark 6:32 – 44, Luke 9:10 – 17).

The people witness this miraculous event and want more. They call Jesus "the Prophet who is to come into the world" (John 6:14), a holy spokesperson foretold by Moses more than a millennium before (Deuteronomy 18:15). When Jesus perceives that they want to force him to lead a rebellion against the Romans, he goes away to pray. Even after he walks across the Sea of Galilee to the far side of the lake, the crowd finds him.

Keep reading to see how the next scene plays out. It might seem like Jesus now has an enormous fan base eager for his spiritual teaching. Yet Jesus realizes that the crowd follows him simply because they hunger for another free meal (John 6:25 – 27). They don't want him; they just wanted to get filled up.

And that begs a big question. Do you chase after Jesus because you want to know him more — or do you just want more of the good things he can give you?

PRAY IT

Lord, I like all the blessings you send my way. But that isn't why I follow you. Purify my motives. Keep me close to you.

day130 may 10

READ IT

1 Samuel 13:1 – 14:23, John 6:25 – 59, Psalm 59:1 – 8

> *"The LORD has sought out a man after his own heart and appointed him ruler of his people, because you have not kept the LORD's command."*
>
> 1 SAMUEL 13:14

LIVE IT

When the Israelites assembled a yearbook for the class of 1026 BC, Saul definitely got voted "Most Likely to Succeed." In the year the son of Kish ascended to the throne of Israel, he looked as if he was headed for outrageous success. "Headed" is the appropriate word, because Saul stood a head taller than anyone else in the nation, a detail Scripture notes twice (1 Samuel 9:2, 10:23).

This good-looking guy (9:2) was famed as a gifted military leader, but his dubious character was visible right from the start. On the day the Lord decided to appoint him king, the entire nation gathered before the prophet Samuel, but Saul was nowhere to be found. God had to speak up from heaven and reveal that the future king was hiding among the luggage (10:22).

Then Saul led an attack on a Philistine outpost. When the enemy fought back, the Israelites fled. Because Samuel was slow to show up and give advice from the Lord, Saul lit up a burnt offering. This grave offense against God's rules for worship cost him his throne.

God isn't looking for followers who necessarily stand out because of their looks, talents, or intelligence. The first quality he looks for is a heart that belongs to him. If you don't keep the Lord's commands, none of your other good qualities matter.

PRAY IT

God, give me a heart that beats with yours. I choose to care about the things that matter to you and to obey your commands.

READ IT

1 Samuel 14:24–15:35, John 6:60–7:13, Psalm 59:9–17

> *"Simon Peter answered him, 'Lord, to whom shall we go? You have the words of eternal life. We have come to believe and to know that you are the Holy One of God.'"*
>
> John 6:68–69

LIVE IT

Put yourself in the scene in John 6:60–71 and replay in your mind the events of the last hours. Everything starts when the Lord turned a little boy's snack into a feast for thousands. Just when a mob is ready to sweep Jesus into power, he vanishes. Many hours and miles later, you catch up with Jesus and he begins one of his famous talks. But this time he dubs himself "the bread of life" (v. 35) and instructs you to eat his flesh and drink his blood (v. 53). What could that possibly mean? What should you do now?

Many hear those words and call them too hard to accept. They sound creepy to Jews forbidden to ever taste blood. Many turn around and go home.

When Jesus calls himself the bread of life, he means he's the spiritual nourishment you require to meet your deepest needs. When he tells you to eat his flesh and drink his blood, he looks ahead to the cross and instructs you to feed on him to get life, counting on his death to make you right with God.

You won't follow Jesus for long if you go home every time his teaching puzzles or challenges you. Peter expressed perfectly why this isn't the time to walk away. Jesus is the Son of God. He tells you how to get eternal life. There's nowhere else to go.

PRAY IT

Lord, I plan to keep following you even when it's confusing or challenging. You're the only one who gives me real life that lasts forever.

day132 may 12

READ IT

1 Samuel 16:1 – 17:37, John 7:14–44, Proverbs 11:29 – 12:7

> *"The LORD does not look at the things people look at. People look at the outward appearance, but the LORD looks at the heart."*
>
> 1 Samuel 16:7

LIVE IT

Recall that King Saul was exceptionally tall and good looking (1 Samuel 9:2). God wanted to replace him back when he broke the law by offering a burnt sacrifice (13:14). Then Saul gave the Lord another reason to find a new king when he kept herds of bleating sheep and lowing cattle instead of destroying them as commanded (15:1 – 35).

After those episodes, the Lord sent his man Samuel looking for a new king. The prophet arrived in Bethlehem knowing the Lord had picked one of Jesse's sons to take the throne. As Samuel studied Jesse's oldest son, it seemed like Israel might end up with another Saul. The prophet was awed by Eliab's impressive exterior — his appearance and height. But God had already rejected Jesse's seven oldest boys. The Lord reminded Samuel what matters: People judge based on outward appearances. God looks at the heart.

Jesse and his sons seemed to overlook the youngest brother, David, yet no one would call him homely. He was tanned and healthy from his tough jobs outside. Most importantly, he had the inner qualities God desired.

Every day, you're measured by people who have forgotten what matters most. They judge your externals instead of looking deeper. You can't change the way your entire culture thinks, but you can always be sure the Lord notices the real you. And he likes what he sees.

PRAY IT

God, I'm tired of being judged for things that don't matter. Thanks for looking deeper and caring about who I really am.

READ IT

1 Samuel 17:38–18:30, John 7:45–8:11, Psalm 60:1–4

"'Then neither do I condemn you,' Jesus declared. 'Go now and leave your life of sin.'"

John 8:11

LIVE IT

Many Bibles add a note to John 7:53–8:11 explaining that the passage isn't found in the earliest manuscripts of the Bible, hand-copied documents that date back nearly two thousand years. That doesn't mean these words aren't factual or they don't accurately reflect everything else we know about Jesus. Take that "textual note" as a reminder of how seriously scholars treat the Bible. They aim to tell you everything they can about the trustworthiness of God's holy book.

This passage is where you find famous words everyone roughly repeats as "Let the one who has never sinned cast the first stone" (John 8:7). But there's far more here than that snippet.

That group of religious hypocrites was looking for a way to trap Jesus, so they brought him a woman they thought deserved stoning, the law's full consequence for sexual sin. Even though she was caught "in the act," they didn't bring her male partner. While the Bible doesn't say what Jesus doodled on the ground, when he stood to speak, his wisdom forced the woman's accusers to walk away.

Then Jesus spoke some words worth pondering. No matter what you do wrong, the Lord doesn't condemn you. But his good news doesn't stop there. He gives you not just forgiveness but freedom. He tells you to go and sin no more.

PRAY IT

Lord, I need your forgiveness for my sins. I also need you to help me break free from the bad things I do. Thanks for never giving up on me.

day134 may 14

READ IT

1 Samuel 19:1–20:42, John 8:12–30, Psalm 60:5–12

> *"David got up from the south side of the stone and bowed down before Jonathan three times, with his face to the ground. Then they kissed each other and wept together—but David wept the most."*
>
> 1 Samuel 20:41

LIVE IT

Peter, James, and John were close friends with Jesus, but they dozed while he prayed in such awful agony that he sweat blood (Mark 14:37, Luke 22:39–46). The apostle Paul went on the road with Barnabas to spread the good news about Jesus, but they split after a sharp fight (Acts 15:36–41). So as you study this scene with David and Jonathan, know that it likely ranks as the Bible's ultimate example of male bonding.

Jonathan should have hated David. Any political advisor would have told him to exterminate David long before this scene. As the oldest son of King Saul, Jonathan might have assumed he would someday ascend to the throne. As David grew more and more popular, all the people and even Saul recognized that David threatened Jonathan's future role as king (1 Samuel 18:7).

As Saul tried harder to kill David, Jonathan went against his father and sided with the guy who had become his best friend. When David finally had to flee Saul, he and Jonathan wept together and swore that their godly friendship would never end. (That kissing, by the way, shows up almost three dozen times in the Bible as an ancient cultural greeting.)

You can't survive life on your own, and you can't get along without friends who have your back. So when you tick through the long list of qualities you look for in a friend, make sure loyalty comes somewhere near the top.

PRAY IT

Lord, give me friendships that last even through the worst circumstances of life. Be the bond between us that won't break.

may 15 **day135**

READ IT

1 Samuel 21:1–23:29, John 8:31–59, Psalm 61:1–8

> *"From the ends of the earth I call to you, I call as my heart grows faint; lead me to the rock that is higher than I."*
>
> Psalm 61:2

LIVE IT

Many psalms sound pretty, but they're far more than lush words. David and others wrote their songs to express their thoughts and emotions. They divulged real-life struggles and celebrated hard-fought triumphs. By creating these songs for ancient public worship, they let you in on their experience of God.

Instead of rushing through these words, look for what they say line by line. David says "hear my cry" (Psalm 61:1) because he wants the Lord to pay attention to everything that follows. "From the ends of the earth" (v. 2) says he feels as far away from God as he can get. "As my heart grows faint" (v. 2) means his emotions, thoughts, and will are about to collapse. "The rock that is higher than I" (v. 2) isn't just a picturesque safe place, but a name for God himself. "Refuge" and "strong tower" are fortresses that give protection from a "foe" (v. 3) in war. David wants nothing more than to "dwell in your tent forever" (v. 4), to live close to God in the tabernacle. He longs to take refuge under the Lord's "wings" (v. 4), the only place young birds find complete safety.

You can pray these powerful words as your own. Or you can write your own songs to God. What thoughts and emotions do you need to tell him? What struggles or triumphs do you want him to know about? Or what images describe how you picture the Lord?

PRAY IT

Lord, I want to pray these songs to you. Help me also to find my own fresh words to talk to you.

day136 may 16

READ IT

1 Samuel 24:1–25:44, John 9:1–34, Proverbs 12:8–17

> *"From the fruit of their lips people are filled with good things, and the work of their hands brings them reward."*
>
> Proverbs 12:14

LIVE IT

Decent people work hard because it's the right thing to do. But it doesn't hurt your motivation to know that doing good brings a reward.

Proverbs 12 is full of unnamed role models who persistently choose to do good, and their assorted good acts bring results worth getting. When people are righteous, meaning "holy" and "upright," their houses can't be knocked down (v. 7). Someone who is prudent earns applause by planning for the future and making careful decisions (v. 8). Those who work their land harvest ample food (v. 11). The innocent escape trouble (v. 13).

The Bible doesn't always tell you exactly what to expect when you do right. This passage doesn't detail the results of living honestly (v. 9), caring for animals (v. 10), taking advice (v. 15), overlooking insults (v. 16), or telling the truth (v. 17). But the Lord still makes you a bold promise to bless your good choices in his time and his way. Like the apostle Paul wrote, "Let us not become weary in doing good, for at the proper time we will reap a harvest if we do not give up" (Galatians 6:9).

You might not be sure what kind of crop to expect from God, but making choices is like putting seeds in the ground. Seeds always sprout something. Whenever you do right, you glorify God, benefit others, and put yourself in a place where you're guaranteed to grow.

PRAY IT

God, help me choose to do good in all the choices I face today. It's the right thing to do, and I trust you to bring real rewards.

READ IT

1 Samuel 26:1–28:25, John 9:35–10:21, Psalm 62:1–12

> *"The thief comes only to steal and kill and destroy; I have come that they may have life, and have it to the full. I am the good shepherd."*
>
> John 10:10–11

LIVE IT

God has forever been tagged with a reputation for being out to wreck everyone's pleasure. But you don't have to buy that untruth. Just listen to what Jesus has to say for himself.

The Lord was once again taking on the religious rule keepers when he described a scene familiar to everyone within earshot, the common sheep pen. Everyone could picture the walled or fenced enclosure — or cave — with a single opening. The world is full of thieves, says Jesus, people who climb over the wall or break through the fence to harm the sheep.

But there's another person in this scene. The good shepherd names each animal. By day he leads his flock to safe pasture. Each evening he protects them in the pen, tending their wounds and sleeping across the doorway to keep out deadly threats. The sheep know his voice so well they won't follow anyone else, including imposters who try to imitate his unique call.

Jesus aimed his story at the Pharisees, a crowd that truly did take the fun out of life by piling on unnecessary rules and picking at everyone's faults. It's like they're thieves, out to kill sheep. But Jesus? He came to give abundant life — the nourishment, protection, and help you need. Once you understand that Jesus is a shepherd always on guard for your good, letting him lead you seems like the obvious choice.

PRAY IT

Lord, you're the good shepherd who watches over me. You lead me to real life and protect me from deadly harm. I will follow you wherever you take me.

day138 may 18

READ IT

1 Samuel 29:1–31:13, John 10:22–42, Psalm 63:1–11

> *"I have seen you in the sanctuary and beheld your power and your glory. Because your love is better than life, my lips will glorify you."*
>
> Psalm 63:2–3

LIVE IT

When you feel thirst for God, you eagerly seek him. When you glimpse him, you naturally respond with worship. But you don't want to chase and praise a made-up God. You don't want to settle for anything less than the real thing.

David saw the Lord "in the sanctuary" (Psalm 63:2). That sounds like he somehow looked into heaven and spotted God, but he's actually talking about meeting the Lord in the tabernacle. David made a habit of going to worship at that Old Testament tent, which was located first in a place called Nob (1 Samuel 21:1), then in Jerusalem (Psalm 76:2).

David didn't think God lived at Nob or Jerusalem, but he sought the Lord in the place where God promised to be especially present. David approached in the manner the Lord himself commanded.

David also observed God's "power and glory." He noticed power that can silence liars. He perceived that the Lord's strength hunts down enemies and sends them to the grave. He counted on God for help and hid in his protection. He took time to appreciate the Lord's glory, his bright shining essence, a beauty that shows off his greatness, authority, and perfection.

You can meet God wherever you want. You can trust him to be the closest friend you will ever find. But he's far more than a human buddy. Relate to him with respect. Worship him with appropriate awe.

PRAY IT

Lord, thank you for being close to me and letting me see you. Show me how to give you the respect you deserve.

READ IT

2 Samuel 1:1–2:7, John 11:1–44, Psalm 64:1–10

> *"I am the resurrection and the life. The one who believes in me will live, even though they die; and whoever lives by believing in me will never die."*
>
> John 11:25–26

LIVE IT

Jesus wasn't the only person who came back to life in the Gospels. The Lord raised the dead daughter of a synagogue leader (Matthew 9:18–26). He brought back a poor widow's only son (Luke 7:11–17). And there's this scene where he raised a good friend.

Jesus didn't rush to help Lazarus the moment he heard he was sick. For two days after he received the news, Jesus stayed many miles away on the far side of the Jordan. He didn't delay because he was scared of murderous enemies. He waited because he saw an opportunity to display God's glory.

Lazarus's sisters weren't happy Jesus showed up too late to heal their brother. Martha confronted him even before he reached their home, and Mary soon fell at his feet sobbing. Jesus wept with them, then ordered Lazarus to walk out of the grave. His shocked family unwrapped their stinking brother and welcomed him back.

Jesus raised the dead to demonstrate he had authority over life and death. And he proved his most astonishing promise, that if you believe in him, you will live forever. Jesus is "the resurrection" for believers who die. And he is "the life" for those still living when he returns. He will change them instantly and make them ready for their new life in heaven (1 Thessalonians 4:16–17).

PRAY IT

Lord, I know that you have power unlike anyone else. I trust you to be the resurrection and the life. You will bring me home to live with you forever.

day140 may 20

READ IT

2 Samuel 2:8–3:21, John 11:45–12:11, Proverbs 12:18–27

> *"The war between the house of Saul and the house of David lasted a long time. David grew stronger and stronger, while the house of Saul grew weaker and weaker."*
>
> 2 Samuel 3:1

LIVE IT

Long before this scene, Saul's disobedience made him unfit to be king (1 Samuel 13:14). The Lord picked David as the new ruler (16:13), and from that time forward, God's spirit left Saul (v. 14). Saul took his own life rather than be tormented by warring Philistines (31:4).

Saul's death seemed like it should end Israel's infighting, bringing God's pick to the throne. But the tragedy 'didn't settle anything. It ignited a struggle for the kingdom between David's army and Saul's remaining family and allies. Since David's beloved friend Jonathan had died in battle, Saul's next-eldest son Ish-Bosheth was crowned king of Israel, while David rules only his own tribe, Judah. But when Ish-Bosheth angered Abner, the head general went over to David's side.

You might not track all of those details. But words from Abner make sense of what's going on: "Must the sword devour forever? Don't you realize that this will end in bitterness?" (2 Samuel 2:26). When nations, tribes, and individuals turn against God, violence spreads and life turns bitter.

You can't control what happens in your larger world. But you can do everything in your power to get along with the people around you. Like the apostle Paul wrote, "If it is possible, as far as it depends on you, live at peace with everyone" (Romans 12:18).

PRAY IT

God, train me to obey you at home, school, work, and everywhere I relate to people. Teach me to treat others the way you treat me.

READ IT

2 Samuel 3:22–5:5, John 12:12–36, Psalm 65:1–13

> *"The streams of God are filled with water to provide the people with grain, for so you have ordained it."*
>
> Psalm 65:9

LIVE IT

People can forget that milk comes from cows, eggs pop out of chickens, and that peanuts, potatoes, and onions grow in dirt. Rarely do people take stock of all the good things they enjoy in life and recognize they came from God.

David starts Psalm 65 by alerting the Lord to get ready for his people's praises. He called everyone to come and worship the God who answered their prayers. As in several other psalms, he shouted thanks for the Lord's spiritual blessings, like forgiveness and letting people live close to him. There are typical phrases that applauded God's awesome power in creating mountains and calming roaring seas.

Then at verse 9 this song takes an unusual turn, when David starts listing details about the Lord's natural provisions for humankind. People assume their own hard work feeds hungry mouths, yet God is ultimately the one who cares for the land. He waters the ground and enriches the soil (v. 10). He produces so much grain it spills out of harvesters' carts (v. 11). He clothes the hillsides with grass and covers them with flocks (vv. 12–13).

God's care for you isn't limited to "spiritual" stuff. He enthusiastically supplies you with food, clothes, and everything else you need (Matthew 6:30–32). He's the source of every perfect gift (James 1:17). So whenever anything good drops into your life, give God the credit and say thanks.

PRAY IT

God, forgive me when I take you and your gifts for granted. You give me everything I need. You fill my life with good things.

day142 may 22

READ IT

2 Samuel 5:6–6:23, John 12:37–13:17, Psalm 66:1–12

> *"Now that I, your Lord and Teacher, have washed your feet, you also should wash one another's feet. I have set you an example that you should do as I have done for you."*
>
> John 13:14–15

LIVE IT

You probably bare your feet in flip-flops all the time, or at least any day it's even a little bit warm. But the challenge of scrubbing between someone else's grimy toes probably sends you running. Yet the Lord did that and more.

Nobody among Jesus's disciples sported a pedicure. They were a dozen burly guys who traveled extensively with their master, trudging down dusty dirt roads wearing open sandals made of leather or woven grass. Whenever they arrived at a destination, it was the job of the lowest household servant to unlace their sandals and wash their feet (1 Samuel 25:41).

That's the humble role Jesus took when he stood up from his meal, shed his outer robe, wrapped himself in a towel, and proceeded to wash his disciples' feet. Until the Lord reached Peter, apparently no one protested the culturally shocking deed of a teacher washing his followers' stinking feet. Yet to reject this footwashing, Jesus said, was to reject him. This act was an example the Lord meant them to follow.

Most days don't present you with opportunities to literally wash other people's feet. But that memorable Bible scene shows you what kind of humility Jesus wants you to put into action every chance you get. You can do acts so out of the ordinary that you catch people off guard. Your Master served you. Now it's time for you to serve others.

PRAY IT

Lord, you put servanthood on display when you scrubbed your disciples' feet. Help me find ways today to follow your example.

READ IT

2 Samuel 7:1–8:18, John 13:18–38, Psalm 66:13–20

> *"Your house and your kingdom will endure forever before me; your throne will be established forever."*
>
> 2 SAMUEL 7:16

LIVE IT

Suppose God chose you as the recipient of an astounding promise: Not only will you rule as king or queen as long as you breathe, but your descendants will sit on your throne forever … and ever … without end. But guess what? There's a bigger surprise still to come.

David rose to the throne amid intrigue and bloodshed. His rival Ish-Bosheth was murdered and David became king of all Israel. David attacked Jerusalem, made it his royal home, and brought God's ark to the city. And "after the king was settled in his palace and the LORD had given him rest from all his enemies around him" (2 Samuel 7:1), the Lord revealed what lay ahead. God reminded David how he swept him from tending sheep to the throne. He vowed to make the king as famous as anyone on earth, granting a lasting dynasty and more. David's throne would be "established forever" (v. 16).

That promise was fulfilled hundreds of years later when Jesus the eternal King was born to David's line (Matthew 1:1–17). And that ancient history matters. Right from the start, God had a plan that one day would involve you. He knew ahead of time he would send Jesus as a royal successor to David, all to show you himself and save you. If the Lord cares that much about showing you his love, make sure you let him into your life today.

PRAY IT

God, thank you for having an ancient plan to reach me. I won't shut you out of my life.

day144 may 24

READ IT

2 Samuel 9:1 – 10:19, John 14:1 – 31, Proverbs 12:28 – 13:9

> *"Jesus answered, 'I am the way and the truth and the life. No one comes to the Father except through me.'"*
>
> John 14:6

LIVE IT

As John 14 starts, you catch the disciples with their stomachs knotting up and tears halfway down their cheeks. Right after Jesus washed their feet (13:1 – 17), he predicted that one of his closest followers would sell him out (vv. 18 – 30). Then they learned Peter would deny knowing Jesus (vv. 31 – 38).

'You can see why the disciples are troubled in this scene. But Jesus dropped an even more dismaying detail: He was leaving. Sure, there was an upside. Jesus said he was departing to prepare a home for his disciples. Thomas spoke up and said they had no idea what he's talking about. How could they know the way if they didn't know where he was headed?

The Lord said they already knew the way because they knew him. Then Jesus made one of the most monumental statements ever. Jesus said, "I am the way," the path to the Father and to their home in heaven. He said, "I am the truth," the one who showed them everything they needed to know about God. He said, "I am the life," the guy who gave them an abundant existence both then and forever (14:6).

Jesus spoke those words when his anxious disciples needed them most. Not long before he would go to the cross, he told them exactly what they needed to know. They're the same facts you can count on. Jesus himself is your path. He never lies. He leads you to true life.

PRAY IT

Lord, you're the way, the truth, and the life. I can't get to God without you. I won't let go of you.

may 25

day145

READ IT

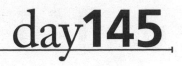

2 Samuel 11:1 – 12:31, John 15:1 – 16:4, Psalm 67:1 – 7

> *"Why did you despise the word of the LORD by doing what is evil in his eyes? You struck down Uriah the Hittite with the sword and took his wife to be your own."*
>
> 2 SAMUEL 12:9

LIVE IT

You already caught a glimpse of this scene back in Psalm 51 (april 25). That's the song where David pours out a confession after the prophet Nathan calls out his sins against Bathsheba and Uriah. This passage gives you the whole story.

After using his royal power to summon Bathsheba to the palace and sleep with her, David multiplied his wrongs by plotting to cover up Bathsheba's pregnancy. He ordered her husband back from battle and told him to go home on furlough, but Uriah was too loyal to enjoy his wife while other warriors were still at risk. So David sent this good man into a battle and made sure Uriah was on the front lines where he was sure to be killed.

David saw the evil in what he had done when Nathan told him a story about a rich man who stole a poor man's beloved lamb. Even though the king confessed his sin, the Lord promised to send disaster on David. Another man would sleep with his wives, a scene that played out years later (2 Samuel 15:1 – 18, 16:20–22). And the innocent son born to David and Bathsheba would die.

The king's confession and sorrow show real repentance—quitting sin and turning back to God—yet sin still had a deadly price. When you admit your failings, you can always count on God to cleanse you from sin and call you back close to him. But forgiveness doesn't necessarily do away with consequences. God's mercy doesn't always fix your bad choices.

PRAY IT

God, I can't expect you to always undo the damage my sin causes. When I do wrong, help me to make things right.

day146 may 26

READ IT

2 Samuel 13:1–39, John 16:5–17:5, Psalm 68:1–6

"A father to the fatherless, a defender of widows, is God in his holy dwelling."

Psalm 68:5

LIVE IT

You would weep if an earthquake flattened your home or a fire sent all your possessions up in smoke. But imagine losing your family, or being left alone in this world for any reason at all. It wouldn't be a surprise if you weren't sure where you could turn for help.

Psalm 68 starts by contrasting people who are good and bad. The wicked melt like wax near a flame, but the righteous celebrate in the Lord's presence. They find solid reasons to praise him. One is that God "rides on the clouds" (v. 4), an obvious dig at the Canaanite god Baal, famous in the ancient world as "the rider of the clouds." But Baal doesn't control the weather; God does. He's the one who sends rain on parched desert ground.

There's another reason to honor God. The Lord looks out for those who have lost everything and everyone. He's "a father to the fatherless" and "a defender of widows." He "sets the lonely in families" and "leads out the prisoners with singing" (vv. 5–6).

In the worst imaginable crisis, you can look to your powerful Lord for help. Whenever you feel isolated, he comes close. No matter why you're lonely or who left you all alone, God makes a promise he won't break. "Never will I leave you," he says. "Never will I forsake you" (Hebrews 13:5).

PRAY IT

God, you feel my agony when I'm lonely. I know you stay close, but help me sense your presence too. Put me with people who can help me trust you.

may 27 **day147**

READ IT

2 Samuel 14:1–15:12, John 17:6–26, Psalm 68:7–14

> *"My prayer is not for them alone. I pray also for those who will believe in me through their message, that all of them may be one."*
>
> John 17:20–21

LIVE IT

You're in the Bible, even if your name isn't on the page. As the few short hours counted down to the Lord's crucifixion, he prayed for his future followers, including you.

Jesus had just told his closest friends that as long as they live in this world they can't escape "trouble," literally "pressure," but they can have confidence and courage, because he's already defeated "the world"—anything that fights against him (John 16:33).

Then Jesus looked up and prayed. He reminded the Father that he's headed to the cross so his followers can gain eternal life, not just a never-ending supply of years, but a close relationship with him (17:1–5). He prayed first for the people following him at that moment. Then, he thought of everyone else who will ever believe in him.

The Lord's request was straightforward. He wanted all of us to be one, just as he and the Father are one. When believers reach complete unity, everyone else will know Jesus really came from heaven. And they will understand his authentic love.

If our unity filled Jesus's mind right before he went to the cross, it must be extremely important to him. If getting together and growing with other believers isn't an essential part of your life, you're missing one of Jesus's ultimate priorities for you. How well you connect with other believers tops his list of concerns.

PRAY IT

Lord, connect me with other believers so completely that everyone can see we're one. Then everyone will know you're for real.

day148 may 28

READ IT

2 Samuel 15:13–16:14, John 18:1–24, Proverbs 13:10–19

> *"Where there is strife, there is pride, but wisdom is found in those who take advice."*
>
> Proverbs 13:10

LIVE IT

There's a reason people don't get along. Battles happen when we don't back down from what we want. Maybe you have never thought of that as "pride," but that's what it is. Proverbs points out that whenever you encounter strife, there's an evil pride behind it.

There's a good kind of pride that gives you healthy self-respect. It helps you stand up for yourself when others try to slam you down, and it doesn't hesitate to celebrate accomplishments (Galatians 6:4). But there's also a dark pride that's one of the sins God hates most (Proverbs 6:16–17). It caused Satan to rebel against the Lord and get ejected from heaven (Ezekiel 28:15–17). It makes human beings think they deserve more honor than God (Isaiah 2:11). And it causes conflict between you and the people around you.

The pride Proverbs is talking about makes people push themselves ahead of others and demand their own way. The apostle James details the outcome. He writes, "For where you have envy and selfish ambition, there you find disorder and every evil practice" (James 3:16). Self-centeredness causes turmoil and all kinds of bickering.

When you find yourself at odds with someone, you're rarely the whole cause of the problem. But you can study yourself to see how your pride might have started or intensified the conflict. Realizing your own faults is the first step to ending whatever battle you face.

PRAY IT

God, forgive me when I let the wrong kind of pride control me. Help me see when I'm putting myself first—and help me stop it.

READ IT

2 Samuel 16:15–18:18, John 18:25–40, Psalm 68:15–20

> *"The reason I was born and came into the world is to testify to the truth. Everyone on the side of truth listens to me."*
>
> John 18:37–38

LIVE IT

The religious leaders who opposed Jesus wanted to get rid of him, but they couldn't execute anyone without permission from authorities of the Roman Empire, which had ruled Israel for decades. So those leaders dragged Jesus to the palace of the Roman governor, Pilate, demanding a death sentence.

Pilate cared nothing about Jewish law. Historians outside the Bible report his constant hostility toward the people he governed, including killing Jews who were angry that he had seized money from their temple to construct an aqueduct to carry water to Jerusalem.

The Lord knew his enemies had gotten to Pilate when the governor asked if Jesus considered himself the king of the Jews. Jesus replied that a political kingdom wasn't his goal. He was born to speak truth. That's when Pilate retorted, "What is truth?" (John 18:38). We can't tell if that was an honest question or a sarcastic statement that truth can't be known. We do know that Pilate refused to defend a fact he knew to be true: Jesus wasn't guilty of anything.

Jesus once told a group who believed in him that "If you hold to my teaching, you are really my disciples. Then you will know the truth, and the truth will set you free" (8:31–32). If you're really on God's side, you love truth. You speak truth. You live truth. You stand up for truth.

PRAY IT

Lord, you always speak truth. Teach me to recognize truth when I hear it. Help me stand up for truth wherever people fight against it.

READ IT

2 Samuel 18:19 – 19:43, John 19:1 – 27, Psalm 68:21 – 27

> *"The king was shaken. He went up to the room over the gateway and wept. As he went, he said: 'O my son Absalom! My son, my son Absalom! If only I had died instead of you.'"*
>
> 2 Samuel 18:33

LIVE IT

Even the best believers sometimes make bad choices that bring disastrous consequences. The sad scenes playing out in 2 Samuel go all the way back to David's sin against Bathsheba and Uriah.

The Lord had picked David to take Saul's place as king because he was a guy with God's heart (1 Samuel 13:14). But that extreme passion for God didn't make David a perfect man. After David's own sexual offense with Bathsheba, his son Amnon raped Tamar, who was David's daughter and Amnon's half-sister. Although that act of violence enraged David, he did nothing to bring his son to justice (2 Samuel 13:21).

Two years later, another of David's sons, Absalom, killed Amnon to avenge the rape. Absalom fled, and for three years David wouldn't speak to his son. During that time, Absalom gained a crowd of followers. He eventually staged a coup and drove his father from the throne, then slept with his father's concubines as the prophet Nathan had predicted (12:11). The rebellion ended with Absalom dead and David brokenhearted. "My son, my son Absalom!" he wailed. "If only I had died instead of you" (18:33).

David's ongoing bad choices only made these problems worse. And the scenes you observe in 2 Samuel show what happens when you let evil get out of hand. Don't miss the point that sin is best stopped when it's small. Problems are best fixed before they get completely twisted.

PRAY IT

Lord, I hate when evil wins. Discipline me to do right. Teach me how to help others make your right choices.

may 31 **day151**

READ IT

2 Samuel 20:1–21:22, John 19:28–20:9, Psalm 68:28–35

> *"Summon your power, God; show us your strength, our God, as you have done before."*
>
> Psalm 68:28

LIVE IT

Help me. Then help me again. That's the cry of many psalms. But Psalm 68 comes right out and says it. "Summon your power," David pleads. "Show us your strength ... as you have done before" (Psalm 68:28).

Maybe you worry God gets worn out by your prayers. How many times can the Lord stand to hear about your cruel friends? Does he really need another prayer session about your homework? Or would he like to shut you out when you tell him once again about problems that drag on for years, like parents who battle through a divorce and still don't stop fighting?

If the prayers of the Bible are any guide, you can pour out your heart to God without limit. The Lord never tires of the same old requests. Jesus even told his disciples to keep praying boldly, driving home his point with a story about a guy who wouldn't stop pounding on his neighbor's door in the dead of night until he got what he needed (Luke 11:5–10).

When you feel like your prayers have become nonstop requests, there's another point you can learn from Psalm 68. No matter how desperate David felt or how many times he asked for help, he never stopped proclaiming God's power. Even more often than he made a request, he repeated how awesome God is.

PRAY IT

God, summon your power once again. I need your help like I have needed it so many times before. Thanks for never getting tired of my prayers.

day152 june 1

READ IT

2 Samuel 22:1–23:7, John 20:10–31, Proverbs 13:20–14:4

> *"Then he said to Thomas, 'Put your finger here; see my hands. Reach out your hand and put it into my side. Stop doubting and believe.'"*
>
> John 20:27

LIVE IT

Thomas often gets knocked for not instantly believing that Jesus had risen from the dead, and he's been tagged as "Doubting Thomas" for two thousand years. But there's another way to look at this disciple. He's a tough-thinking follower.

The risen Jesus had already appeared to others. Mary Magdalene met him at the empty tomb. Then all of the disciples except Thomas were hiding in a locked room when Jesus appeared among them, wished them well, and showed them his wounded hands and side.

When the other disciples told Thomas what they had seen, he wasn't impressed. For Thomas, secondhand testimony wasn't enough. He not only wanted a chance to see Jesus up close like the others, but he wouldn't be convinced without the hard proof of touching the Lord's wounds.

The disciples didn't kick Thomas out of their group when he demanded firsthand evidence. Nor did Jesus scold Thomas for holding out. When the Lord once again appeared through locked doors, he simply offered Thomas his hands and side. And that's all the disciple really needed.

You can give people who struggle with faith piles of information about Jesus. What they often need in addition to facts is a personal encounter with the risen Lord. So don't just try to argue someone into being a Christian; do your best to introduce them to Jesus.

PRAY IT

Lord, I haven't seen you, but I believe. But some of my friends struggle. Use me to share truth and show them you're real.

june 2 **day153**

READ IT

2 Samuel 23:8–24:25, John 21:1–25, Psalm 69:1–12

> *"David was conscience-stricken after he had counted the fighting men, and he said to the LORD, 'I have sinned greatly in what I have done.' "*
>
> 2 SAMUEL 24:10

LIVE IT

Counting soldiers sounds smart. If you're a king about to go to war, it seems wise to know how many people stand on your side of the battle line. But God had a different view of the census David undertook.

Fighters gathered around David as soon as he fled Saul, soon numbering in the hundreds (1 Samuel 22:1–2). Starting as a band of misfits, these men became known for daring exploits. During his reign as king, David had his three mighty warriors and the thirty mighty men, along with a trio of additional well-known warriors.

Yet something goes awry when David counts the troops under his command. The plan is opposed by his commanders, but the king's word wins out. When David discovers he has more than a million soldiers at hand, he knows he has sinned.

David needed an army to defend the nation. But his census was evidence he had unwisely turned to human might instead of to the Lord. As David himself once wrote, "Some trust in chariots and some in horses, but we trust in the name of the LORD our God. They are brought to their knees and fall, but we rise up and stand firm" (Psalm 20:7–8).

God gives you abilities, resources, and everything else you need to thrive. But as soon as you count on those gifts more than God, you're acting like David. And that doesn't end well.

PRAY IT

God, I'm glad you make me strong. But you're the real source of my power. Help me remember to keep relying on you.

day154 june 3

READ IT

1 Kings 1:1–2:12, Acts 1:1–22, Psalm 69:13–28

> *"But you will receive power when the Holy Spirit comes on you; and you will be my witnesses in Jerusalem, and in all Judea and Samaria, and to the ends of the earth."*
>
> Acts 1:8

LIVE IT

After dying on the cross, Jesus rose from the grave. For forty days he showed himself to hundreds of people, offering persuasive proof he was truly alive (1 Corinthians 15:3–8).

But what's next? You know the story, but the disciples were clueless about what was to come. Ecstatic to have Jesus back from the dead, they were terrified of their religious opponents. As they puzzled over their next steps, the Lord gave them a crucial hint. They were to wait for power from the Holy Spirit, then tell the world about him.

Immediately, before Jesus ascended to heaven, he mapped out a strategy. His followers were to start telling his story in Jerusalem, God's holy city and the site of the crucifixion and resurrection. They were next to go to their own neighborhood of Judea, then to their foreign cousins in Samaria. Finally they would take the news about Jesus to the world's far reaches.

You're still part of that plan. Jesus commanded all of his followers to "go and make disciples of all nations, baptizing them in the name of the Father and of the Son and of the Holy Spirit, and teaching them to obey everything I have commanded you" (Matthew 28:19–20). God gives each person a different part of that plan—praying, giving, sending, going. As you puzzle over your own next steps, ask him exactly what he wants you to do.

PRAY IT

Lord, I want the whole world to meet you. Show me how, when, and where you want me involved in your plan to tell everyone about you.

READ IT

1 Kings 2:13–3:15, Acts 1:23–2:21, Psalm 69:29–36

"The LORD hears the needy and does not despise his captive people."

PSALM 69:33

LIVE IT

It's easy to look the other way when you walk by someone begging money. Or to forget about the hundreds of homeless people in any sizeable city. Or to shut out images and sounds of a billion hungry people around the globe. But God never closes his eyes or plugs his ears to the needy.

At first glance Psalm 69 isn't all about the poor. David starts by asking the Lord to save him from waters that have risen to his neck. He can't find a foothold. Waters keep washing over him. He's almost out of energy to call for help (vv. 1–3).

Then David goes on to tell God that people hate him for no reason. He feels like an alien among his own family. His heart breaks with weeping. When he hungers, his enemies feed him "gall," a bitter, poisonous herb. When he thirsts, they give him "vinegar," a drink made from sour wine (vv. 4–21).

Those details all add up to a solid description of the experience of people who struggle with poverty, and at the end of this song David offers hope to the poor. They will be glad when he praises the Lord. Their hearts will live when they seek God. Why? Because "The LORD hears the needy" (v. 33).

When you connect with God's heart, you can't help but care about people who don't have much in this world.

PRAY IT

God, help me see this world the way you see it. It's not all about rich, famous, popular people. You care about people who have nothing.

day156 june 5

READ IT

1 Kings 3:16–5:18, Acts 2:22–47, Proverbs 14:5–14

> *"They devoted themselves to the apostles' teaching and to fellowship, to the breaking of bread and to prayer."*
>
> Acts 2:42

LIVE IT

Not long before this scene, Peter had completely denied knowing Jesus (Luke 22:54–62). Now you catch him mid-sermon telling an enormous crowd about his Lord. And Peter had some explaining to do.

Right after the resurrection, he and the other close followers of Jesus hid from their religious opponents (John 20:19). Not much later, as they waited together as Jesus commanded, they experienced a blast of power that sounded like wind and looked like tongues of fire. When the disciples opened their mouths, natives from across the Mediterranean world heard them speak their home languages. Peter had to clarify that the Lord's followers weren't drunk. Their ability to speak languages they had never learned came from the Holy Spirit (Acts 2:1–21).

That's when Peter told the story of Jesus. In response, three thousand people became believers that day. And look what they started to do. They heard the apostles teach ... stuck close to each other ... ate meals and celebrated the Lord's Supper together ... prayed ... watched God do miracles ... shared their possessions ... and praised God.

Getting together with other Christians can turn into a lot of things that have little to do with God. But those early believers show you solid experiences to make part of your everyday life. They're exactly what you need to grow close to God and each other. So be like those first believers. Devote yourself to these things.

PRAY IT

God, I want you to be in charge of the times I get together with other Christians. Call us out when we're not doing things to help us grow.

READ IT

1 Kings 6:1 – 7:22, Acts 3:1 – 26, Psalm 70:1 – 5

> *"In the eleventh year in the month of Bul, the eighth month, the temple was finished in all its details according to its specifications. He had spent seven years building it."*
>
> 1 Kings 6:38

LIVE IT

Seven years is roughly the span you will spend in middle school and high school. It's not forever, but it's hardly the blink of an eye. That's how long Solomon dedicated to building a temple to worship God.

For an Old Testament believer, there was only one correct place to worship. At first, that was the tabernacle, a tent-like worship structure (Exodus 25:1 – 8). As David settled into his reign as king, he felt embarrassed luxuriating in a palace while the Lord dwelled in a tent. God, however, didn't think it was right for David, a man of war, to build his new home. That job would fall to his son, Solomon (2 Samuel 7:1 – 17).

Solomon constructed an exquisite building to honor God, filling it with silver and gold and all the furnishings necessary for worship. The temple became the only place on earth where Old Testament believers could legally offer the all-important sacrifices the Lord prescribed. Sacrificing anywhere else was as sinful as worshiping a foreign god.

When Jesus died and rose, he did away not only with having to follow the Old Testament rituals for salvation, but needing to worship in the temple where those rituals took place (Hebrews 10:10 – 18). Nowadays you might prefer to praise God on a mountain peak, in a stained-glass cathedral or modern auditorium, at school or out in the street. Where you worship isn't important. What matters is that you give God all the honor he deserves.

PRAY IT

Lord, you deserve all the worship I can give you. I will praise you wherever I go.

day158 june 7

READ IT

1 Kings 7:23–8:21, Acts 4:1–22, Psalm 71:1–8

> *"Salvation is found in no one else, for there is no other name under heaven given to mankind by which we must be saved."*
>
> Acts 4:12

LIVE IT

People say you're safe to follow whatever religion you want, because they all say the same things and all point to the same God. Dedicated followers of almost every belief system disagree with that thought, and a couple thousand years ago the apostle Peter stood up and declared it isn't true.

Peter and John had been seized and put before the religious experts. They had heard reports of a man lame since birth leaping and jumping and praising God, and they wanted to know by what power the disciples had healed him (Acts 3:1–10). Peter had already told a crowd of astonished witnesses that the power wasn't their own. The real healer was Jesus (vv. 11–26).

When Peter continued his sermon in front of the religious leaders, he uttered a statement even more bold: Not only is Jesus the powerful healer, but he's the only one who can save us. Faith in him is the only way home to heaven. Those leaders were astonished by the disciples' courage, and the healing spoke for itself. But they forbade Peter and John to say anything more.

People might call you intolerant for claiming Jesus is the one real God and the only one who rescues humankind from sin. But you be the judge. Should you listen to people—or to God? He's the one who tells you to spread what you have seen and heard.

PRAY IT

Lord, you're the one Savior of me and my world. Make me unafraid to speak up about you to people who don't believe.

READ IT

1 Kings 8:22–9:9, Acts 4:23–5:11, Psalm 71:9–18

> *"But will God really dwell on earth? The heavens, even the highest heaven, cannot contain you. How much less this temple I have built!"*
>
> 1 Kings 8:27

LIVE IT

Solomon didn't think he was building a temple to contain God any more than you would expect the Lord to fit in a backyard playhouse. But the Lord had promised to make his house the place of his special presence, so Solomon invited him home with a lofty prayer of dedication.

Solomon began by telling God no other god was like him, "you who keep your covenant of love with your servants who continue wholeheartedly in your way" (1 Kings 8:23). This one-of-a-kind being couldn't be contained. But Solomon asked God to always be present with his people, then offered massive sacrifices of celebration.

The Lord answered Solomon's sincere prayer. Another Old Testament account says that when Solomon finished praying, fire came down from heaven and consumed the sacrifices, and God's presence filled the temple. The Israelites saw the Lord's glory, knelt facedown, and worshiped with the chorus, "He is good; his love endures forever" (2 Chronicles 7:3).

That scene might seem long ago and far away. Yet the Lord does the same thing now when he comes to live in you. Like the apostle Paul wrote, "Don't you know that you yourselves are God's temple and that God's Spirit dwells in your midst?" (1 Corinthians 3:16). When God lives in you, expect to see his glory.

PRAY IT

Lord, you're a God unlike any other, and you never break your promise to love me. Live in me now through your Holy Spirit. I want you present in my life.

day160 june 9

READ IT

1 Kings 9:10–11:13, Acts 5:12–42, Proverbs 14:15–24

> *"As Solomon grew old, his wives turned his heart after other gods, and his heart was not fully devoted to the LORD his God, as the heart of David his father had been."*
>
> 1 KINGS 11:4

LIVE IT

One glance at the Ten Commandments tells you instantly what matters most to God. Rule number one: "You shall have no other gods before me" (Exodus 20:3). If you aim to put God first, then you guard against anything that can knock him out of that top spot, like falling for guys or girls not totally devoted to him.

In the Old Testament the Lord laid down clear rules against marrying worshipers of other gods. He said, "Do not intermarry with them. Do not give your daughters to their sons or take their daughters for your sons, for they will turn your children away from following me to serve other gods" (Deuteronomy 7:3–4). And the Lord didn't drop that rule in the New Testament. The apostle Paul writes, "Do not be yoked together with unbelievers. For what do righteousness and wickedness have in common? Or what fellowship can light have with darkness?" (2 Corinthians 6:14).

Solomon brought catastrophe on himself by disobeying that core command. Having hundreds of wives wasn't against the law in his day. But when his foreign wives pulled him into sin, the Lord ripped away most of his kingdom.

You're not likely looking for a spouse right now, but the principle still applies. If you bind yourself to nonbelievers—like you do in dating, marriage, and some other partnerships and friendships—you risk everything that matters most.

PRAY IT

Lord, I need help obeying this command. Show me where my relationships get in the way of following you, and show me what to do about it.

READ IT

1 Kings 11:14–12:24, Acts 6:1–7:19, Psalm 71:19–24

> *"In those days when the number of disciples was increasing, the Hellenistic Jews among them complained against the Hebraic Jews because their widows were being overlooked in the daily distribution of food."*
>
> Acts 6:1

LIVE IT

You can't claim you love people if you don't do anything to help their practical needs. It makes you look like a hypocrite if your spiritual talk isn't matched by real-life action.

In the commotion of rapid growth in the early church, some of the neediest believers were being neglected. Hellenistic widows were getting overlooked as food was handed out to the needy each day. These "Hellenistic Jews" had grown up far from Israel and felt at home in Greek culture. "Hebraic Jews" grew up in Israel and spoke Aramaic. And the cultural clash between these groups harmed elderly widows with no means of support. Moreover, the dispute weighed on the apostles, who felt their focus should be on prayer and teaching rather than handing out food.

The solution was appointing leaders dedicated to caring for daily needs. At the head of that team came Stephen, a man highly respected for his faith and spiritual power. His miraculous acts brought him violent hostility from the religious authorities, a story that plays out in Acts 7 and 8.

The point here is that a beloved spiritual leader took charge of meeting practical needs. He didn't feel torn between feeding people and preaching. He did both, providing living proof that it's not okay to tell people about Jesus but neglect urgent physical needs, or to meet those needs but forget to speak up about the Lord. Real love looks after every kind of need.

PRAY IT

Lord, teach me to love in a way that cares for people's needs, whatever they are.

day162 june 11

READ IT

1 Kings 12:25–14:20, Acts 7:20–43, Psalm 72:1–20

> *"After forty years had passed, an angel appeared to Moses in the flames of a burning bush in the desert near Mount Sinai. When he saw this, he was amazed at the sight."*
>
> ACTS 7:30–31

LIVE IT

Back in the earliest days of the church, Stephen oversaw distribution of food to needy widows. Through God's power he also did astounding miracles. And when Jews tried to argue with him about Jesus, his wisdom silenced his opponents. The losers of those debates concocted charges against him and brought him before the Jewish ruling council (Acts 6:8–15).

As Stephen defended himself, he told the story of Israel from Abraham to Moses to Jesus. Along the way he highlighted episodes where the Israelites rebelled against God, then charged his listeners with being just as stubborn as their ancestors. Not only had they resisted the Holy Spirit and killed the prophets, they had murdered the Savior of the world.

At that point his opponents were cut to the heart, furious that their sin had been exposed. That teeth-gnashing indicates they're like animals ready to tear their victim apart. All it took was Stephen's vision of Jesus in heaven that caused them to stone him.

When Stephen was killed, he became the first Christian ever to die for his faith in Jesus. That's a fate believers around the world still face. Even if you never endure that ultimate violence, how do you respond to everyday hostility—or just being ignored? Stephen died for something he knew was real. Why are you willing to suffer for Jesus?

PRAY IT

Lord, be with believers around the world who suffer for their faith more than I do. Help me to speak up about you even when I might pay a price.

june 12

day163

READ IT

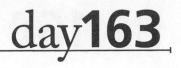

1 Kings 14:21 – 16:7, Acts 7:44 – 8:3, Psalm 73:1 – 14

> *"My feet had almost slipped; I had nearly lost my foothold. For I envied the arrogant when I saw the prosperity of the wicked."*
>
> Psalm 73:2 – 3

LIVE IT

You might want to make Psalm 73 your new favorite song. If it rocked with a solid tune, it would echo through your heart and mind more than anything you have loaded on a playlist.

This song is credited to Asaph, a guy who clanged cymbals when the ark of God moved to Jerusalem (1 Chronicles 15:16 – 19). Asaph might be the actual lyricist, or the song might have been written by someone in his family (25:1 – 9).

Asaph was surrounded by evil people enjoying wild success. He was so envious of their prosperity that he almost quit trusting God. He observed that evil people didn't struggle. Their bodies didn't break. Because they didn't have problems like normal people, they wore pride as a necklace and violence like the latest fashion. They had plenty of time to dream up ways to sin, and they thought God wouldn't notice. In Psalm 73, Asaph wonders if it's been a waste to stay pure.

Keep reading the rest of this song to find out what happens to these evildoers. It isn't pretty. In the end, Asaph discovers the Lord has grabbed him by the hand and will never let go.

Whenever you feel like Asaph, remind yourself that you serve a just God. If your life falls apart, recall that you still have everything you need. You have God. And if you're near him, that's enough.

PRAY IT

Lord, help me make sense of life when I see evil people succeed. When I get frustrated, I know that you're everything I need.

day**164** june 13

READ IT

1 Kings 16:8–18:15, Acts 8:4–40, Proverbs 14:25–35

> *"The fear of the Lord is a fountain of life, turning a person from the snares of death."*
>
> Proverbs 14:27

LIVE IT

You can easily flip a faucet to access an endless stream of water for drinking, cooking, and getting clean, but the Israelites never took water for granted.

After escaping slavery in Egypt, God's people spent forty years wandering in a desert. When they couldn't locate an adequate supply of water, they experienced desperate and deadly thirst (Exodus 17:1–7). When the people arrived in the Promised Land, they found more than milk and honey: The land's springs gave them reliable fresh water for people, animals, and crops. Yet in that dry and scorching hot region, water was always a precious commodity (2 Chronicles 32:2–4).

When the Bible declares that "the fear of the Lord is a fountain of life" (Proverbs 14:27), it's saying that living for God with awe-filled respect is as good as stumbling across water in the desert. Relating to him with reverence is the difference between living and dying. And awe for the Lord is like a "fountain," a free-flowing supply of fresh water. That's a source far better than rain collected in cisterns that quickly turns warm and stale.

The book of Jeremiah calls it a sin to turn away from the Lord, "the spring of living water," to rely on a cistern you dig for yourself (Jeremiah 2:13). But when you choose to respect God, you experience his thirst-quenching, life-saving waters.

PRAY IT

Lord, you fill me with awe. Teach me to live for you with total respect. You will quench my thirst and save me.

june 14 **day165**

READ IT

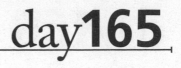

1 Kings 18:16–19:21, Acts 9:1–31, Psalm 73:15–28

> *"I have been very zealous for the LORD God Almighty. . . . I am the only one left, and now they are trying to kill me too."*
>
> 1 KINGS 19:10

LIVE IT

Nothing makes you want to give up on following God like feeling as if you're all alone. That's how the prophet Elijah felt after his spectacular clash with the prophets of the false god Baal.

Elijah appeared on the scene in 1 Kings 17 to confront the evil king Ahab, who gave Baal equal status with the Lord. Because of this terrible sin, Elijah vowed that no rain would fall in Israel until he called for it (v. 1).

Three years later, the land was parched and the nation starving. Then Elijah threw down a challenge to hundreds of prophets of Baal and Asherah. He assembled a large sacrifice and invited his opponents to do the same. When their gods didn't answer loud prayers to set their offering ablaze, the Lord sent fire that consumed not only Elijah's sacrifice but a water-drenched wood and rock altar.

After that confrontation, Elijah fled for his life. He soon found himself alone and despairing, convinced he was the only one who followed God. But the Lord didn't leave Elijah to suffer alone. He gave the prophet food and rest. He made a stunning appearance and promised to give Elijah an assistant and thousands of others to support him.

When you commit your life to God, you're never as alone as you might fear. God himself is with you, and he will surround you with others who follow him too.

PRAY IT

God, help me know that you're close when I feel all alone. Give me friends who want to know and obey you.

day166 june 15

READ IT

1 Kings 20:1–21:29, Acts 9:32–10:23a, Psalm 74:1–9

> *"At Caesarea there was a man named Cornelius, a centurion in what was known as the Italian Regiment. He and all his family were devout and God-fearing."*
>
> Acts 10:1–2

LIVE IT

It's easy to miss the enormous spiritual shift that occurs in the middle of the book of Acts. For nearly two thousand years of Bible history, God's plan for the world centered on the nation of Israel. But suddenly, God connected the apostle Peter with a centurion named Cornelius, a commander of about a hundred men in the Roman military.

Cornelius was a "God-fearer," someone who followed Old Testament practices but who wasn't born an ethnic Jew. This military man was a Gentile, with family roots in Italy. As a God-fearer, he believed in one God and rejected the countless Roman gods and goddesses and the immorality that went along with their worship. He cared for the poor and needy, and he made a frequent habit of prayer.

Long before Cornelius, God had promised to bless the entire world through Abraham (Genesis 12:3). Jesus had sent his followers to tell every nation about him (Matthew 28:18–20). But up to this moment, the new Christians you read about in Acts were all born to the people of Israel. When Cornelius heard about Jesus and believed, he became the first recorded non-Jewish disciple.

That's significant. It proves that God's plan to save people extends to everyone, including non-Jews. That's probably you. So when Cornelius believed, he became a sign of God's care for you. You can look to him as an example of true devotion. He's part of your own spiritual story.

PRAY IT

God, thanks for loving every nation, people, and race. You reach out to everyone on earth, including me.

june 16

day167

READ IT

1 Kings 22:1–53, Acts 10:23b–11:18, Psalm 74:10–17

> *"But God is my King from long ago; he brings salvation on the earth."*
>
> Psalm 74:12

LIVE IT

Some people give God no respect. They expect the Lord to prove himself by sending an instant answer to prayer or doing an on-demand miraculous act. When God ignores their tests, they "mock", attacking the Lord and defying his commands. They "revile," abusing him with harsh words (Psalm 74:10).

When the Lord seems to let these insults go on forever, Psalm 74 asks him to powerfully halt them. But then the song offers a longer and bigger view of God. It lists the Lord's powerful actions in making and governing the world, wrapping his accomplishments in poetic language. His power split the sea from land, a picture drawn from creation (Genesis 1:6–8). He took on "Leviathan," a sea monster in pagan literature, crushing that serpent's head and proving his dominance over evil. He opened springs in the desert to quench his people's thirst (Numbers 20:8–13), and he dried up waters to let them march onward (Exodus 14:21–31). He rules the day, night, and seasons.

When people challenge your faith, you don't need on-the-spot proof of God's power. You can look back to everything he's already done, all the ways he has shown he's your King "from long ago" (Psalm 74:12). And you can point people to Jesus, the one who "brings salvation on the earth" (v. 12). He's the best sign of God's existence, power, and love.

PRAY IT

God, your actions in every time and place prove that you reign. You sent Jesus so I can know that you're real.

day168 june 17

READ IT

2 Kings 1:1 – 2:25, Acts 11:19 – 12:19a, Proverbs 15:1 – 10

> *"Suddenly an angel of the Lord appeared and a light shone in the cell. He struck Peter on the side and woke him up. 'Quick, get up!' he said, and the chains fell off Peter's wrists."*
>
> Acts 12:7

LIVE IT

Christians felt the heat of persecution almost immediately after Jesus rose from the dead. His closest followers hid from their religious opponents (John 20:19). Peter and John were put on trial for teaching about the Lord (Acts 4:1 – 5:42). Stephen was killed for his faith (7:54 – 60). After his death, "a great persecution broke out against the church in Jerusalem," scattering believers everywhere (8:1 – 3).

As time passed, there was little relief from the new believers' suffering. Soon one of the Lord's best friends, James, was beheaded, and another, Peter, was tossed in prison, sure to face the same doom.

Peter was shackled between two guards when an intense light filled his cell. He woke when an angel hit him, and as he got up his chains fell off. Until the reality of his escape sunk in, he thought it was all too good to be true. Peter's freedom was so shocking that when he arrived at a house where others were praying for him, a servant girl ran away happy and left him at the door.

Suffering for your faith should never surprise you, because the Bible shows it's an inescapable fact of following Jesus. Sometimes God pulls off surprising rescues that leave you and others gleefully bewildered. But even in the worst of circumstances, you can be sure the Lord watches over you.

PRAY IT

God, make me bold and unafraid to speak up about my faith, even if it causes me pain. I trust you to look after me no matter what comes.

READ IT

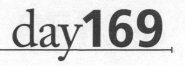

2 Kings 3:1–4:37, Acts 12:19b–13:12, Psalm 74:18–23

"While they were worshiping the Lord and fasting, the Holy Spirit said, 'Set apart for me Barnabas and Saul for the work to which I have called them.'"

Acts 13:2

LIVE IT

The New Testament Saul is a guy best known by his Roman name, Paul. Maybe you caught his first Bible appearance as a young man who guarded the coats of religious leaders who stoned Stephen, then went on the road to kill Christians (Acts 8:1–3). It was hard to miss his dramatic meeting with Jesus, who knocked him down with a blinding light on his way to Damascus, capital of modern Syria (9:1–19).

After that meeting, Paul immediately began to preach Jesus as God's Son (v. 20). Early Christians were scared to accept him as a true disciple (v. 26). They became convinced when they heard his story and he kept talking about Jesus despite threats of death (vv. 27–30).

Paul became one of several teachers in the church at Antioch, a city not far from Damascus, but what happened next changed the world forever. The believers sent Paul to take the good news about Jesus to cities in what is now Turkey. He soon became a missionary across the Mediterranean, and from that time on, he was the world's leading evangelist and teacher of Christianity.

Paul obediently went wherever the Holy Spirit led him, doing the tasks the Lord called him to do (13:2). If you want to serve God like Paul, your goal isn't to relive his story or retrace his steps. Start by asking God what he wants you to accomplish, then act.

PRAY IT

Lord, show me the next steps I can take to serve you. Help me to see the gifts and opportunities you put in my life.

day170 june 19

READ IT

2 Kings 4:38–6:23, Acts 13:13–41, Psalm 75:1–10

> *"Elisha sent a messenger to say to him, 'Go, wash yourself seven times in the Jordan, and your flesh will be restored and you will be cleansed.'"*
>
> 2 Kings 5:10

LIVE IT

Suppose you have a huge prayer you want God to answer. You try to entice him to say yes by making him an equally huge promise. Whatever you dream up as a bribe to the Lord can't compare to what Naaman offered for his healing — an outrageous haul including 750 pounds of silver and 150 pounds of gold.

Naaman was the general of the army of Aram, an area roughly equivalent to modern Syria. He was afflicted with leprosy, the same dreaded skin disease seen in Luke 17:11–19 (april 16). Naaman's master, the king of Aram, sent him to Israel with a rich gift for God's prophet, hoping for a cure. But Elisha wanted none of the wealth. He sent the general to do a ridiculously simple task, dipping seven times in an ordinary nearby river.

Naaman almost left without getting the healing God had in store for him, but by the time he went home he gained a couple of crucial lessons. First, God doesn't need a bribe to do us good. His gifts come free, no strings attached. Second, the Lord is the one and only God. Naaman vowed to never worship any other god, and took home a film of river dirt as a reminder.

When you need something from God, don't show up with a bribe. Just always put God first. Tell the Lord what you need, and watch for his answer.

PRAY IT

God, I can't do anything to get favors from you. Thanks for all your kind gifts to me. I trust you to answer my prayers as you see best.

READ IT

2 Kings 6:24–8:15, Acts 13:42–14:7, Psalm 76:1–12

> *"We had to speak the word of God to you first. Since you reject it and do not consider yourselves worthy of eternal life, we now turn to the Gentiles."*
>
> Acts 13:46

LIVE IT

"Since you don't want anything to do with God's news of eternal life through Jesus, we're going to give it to others." The apostle Paul's stinging words are tough to hear, but you need to understand what they mean.

Those words catch Paul in the middle of a speech that started in Acts 13:13. One Sabbath he went to a local place of Jewish worship, where the synagogue leader invited him to speak, a common custom for guests.

Everyone probably liked Paul's talk until he brought up the message of salvation through Jesus (v. 23), who was executed on the cross but raised from the dead by God (vv. 29–30). Paul then told the crowd that only through Jesus could their sins be forgiven. Faith in him was the only way to be "justified" with God, or made right with him (vv. 38–39).

Some of the Jews who heard this message accepted it. Others fought it, and they are the people Paul warned so sternly. If that group of Jews thought they were too good to need God's forgiveness through Jesus, then Paul would take the message to non-Jews.

Plenty of people nowadays think they deserve to go to heaven and don't need to take God up on his offer of forgiveness. But Jesus is the only way the Lord gives guilty people eternal life. It's never smart to put him off or reject him.

PRAY IT

God, you offer me forgiveness of sins through Jesus. I need that. I accept it. Help others understand the need for your free gift.

day172 june 21

READ IT

2 Kings 8:16–9:37, Acts 14:8–28, Proverbs 15:11–20

> *"Then Jehu went to Jezreel. When Jezebel heard about it, she put on eye makeup, arranged her hair and looked out of a window."*
>
> 2 Kings 9:30

LIVE IT

Jezebel's story reads more like a reality TV script than the usual Bible account. But here you see an evil queen meet an ugly death.

Jezebel first appears as the wife of Israel's King Ahab (1 Kings 16:31). Her systematic attempt to kill off God's prophets forced Elijah to flee for his life after his victory against the prophets of the false god Baal (19:1–9).

Ahab and Jezebel made a frightening pair. Like the Bible says, "There was never anyone like Ahab, who sold himself to do evil in the eyes of the Lord, urged on by Jezebel his wife" (21:25). Even after Ahab was killed in battle, Jezebel continued to exert terrible control through her sons Joram and Ahaziah.

When a man named Jehu was anointed the next king of Israel, the Lord commanded him to destroy Ahab's household. Jehu drove his chariot "like a maniac" (2 Kings 9:20) to hunt down Joram and Ahaziah. When Jezebel heard Jehu closing in on the palace, she did herself up like a queen. She put on makeup, fixed her hair, and posed in a window. A push from her servants sent her to a bloody death on the street below, where dogs devoured her body.

There's nothing happy in Jezebel's story, but it signals that God is just. He doesn't let evil people live forever. He puts a stop to blatant sin.

PRAY IT

Lord, I want to be loyal to you and give you the respect you deserve. You deal with people who refuse to quit sinning and turn to you.

june 22 **day173**

READ IT

2 Kings 10:1 – 11:21, Acts 15:1 – 21, Psalm 77:1 – 9

> *"It is my judgment, therefore, that we should not make it difficult for the Gentiles who are turning to God."*
>
> Acts 15:19

LIVE IT

Some Christians pretend they never argue. But they do. Even the best believers have to figure out how to survive conflict, and the early Christians show how it's done.

Early on in the history of the church, Peter and Paul didn't always see eye to eye, especially when it came to bringing the gospel to the Gentiles. But not long after Peter and Paul came into agreement and began to take the good news about Jesus to non-Jews, others began to say new Gentile believers couldn't be saved without keeping all the laws God laid down in the Old Testament, especially circumcision. So the most experienced church leaders gathered in Jerusalem to sort out the truth. In the end, the apostles and others said old laws weren't binding on new followers of Jesus. They commanded Gentile believers to keep a few simple rules to avoid sin and prevent needless conflict between believers with Jewish or Gentile roots.

That model of getting together in "councils" to settle major differences has been followed numerous times since the birth of the church. But you can watch and learn from this scene to handle conflict in your own life, especially with other Christians.

You start by bringing the problem out in the open. Then you listen to everyone involved. But you don't settle for everyone's opinions—you look for answers in Scripture. And as you work toward a decision, you remember that Jesus gives you an unbreakable connection with your adversary. As Peter said, "We believe it is through the grace of our Lord Jesus that we are saved, just as they are" (Acts 15:11).

PRAY IT

Lord, sometimes I want to run from conflict. Other times I want to fight. Teach me your way to work through disagreements.

day174 june 23

READ IT

2 Kings 12:1–14:22, Acts 15:22–41, Psalm 77:10–20

"Your ways, God, are holy. What god is as great as our God?"

Psalm 77:13

LIVE IT

You're in trouble, so you cry to God for help, hoping he hears all your moaning. The more you think about your situation, the more you ache. You can't sleep, and you don't have words big enough to describe your pain. You wonder if God will always feel so distant. Maybe he's forgotten to be sympathetic and forgiving, or he's so angry he's out of compassion for you.

That's the gist of Psalm 77:1–9. The first part of this song from Asaph acts like a giant question, asking what many believers feel when they hit life's tough spots. What's going on? Where is God? Why bother to trust him?

The rest of Psalm 77 serves up the answer. Asaph decides to purposely remember all the good things God has already done. He remembers the years when the Lord's power in his life was obvious. He recalls God's amazing miracles.He won't stop rolling these thoughts around in his mind.

Asaph thinks back to creation and the Lord's choice of Israel, but you can make your own list of reasons you look to God, trusting his love and power. Whether you keep your list in your head or write it down, it gives you facts to think about whenever you get discouraged. And you can put verse 13 at the top of your list. Your God is always perfectly pure and right. There's no one who compares to him.

PRAY IT

God, you give me all kinds of reasons to trust you. Help me make a plan to remember them when I need them most.

june 24 **day175**

READ IT

2 Kings 14:23–15:38, Acts 16:1–15, Psalm 78:1–8

> *"Jeroboam son of Jehoash king of Israel became king in Samaria, and he reigned forty-one years. He did evil in the eyes of the LORD."*
>
> 2 KINGS 14:23–24

LIVE IT

You're not alone if all the Bible kings confuse you. Nearly four dozen ruled in the hundreds of years after King Saul came to Israel's throne (1 Samuel 10:1–27). The list of kings is extra long because after King Solomon, the nation split into a northern kingdom (Israel) and a southern kingdom (Judah), creating two royal lines.

The staggered sequence of these rulers show up in the introduction of each king. For example, Jeroboam became king of Israel fifteen years into the rule of King Amaziah of Judah (2 Kings 14:23). Far more important than the chronology, however, is the description of each king. A few do right, yet many completely reject God.

You probably know families where everyone takes the wrong path in life until someone finally chooses a better way. While all of Israel's kings consistently did evil, some of Judah's kings broke loose from past sinful patterns to live for God. A few even built on the godly habits of the previous king, like Azariah, also known as Uzziah (15:1–7), and Jotham, his son (vv. 33–38).

You might be surrounded by people who don't follow God. Your own family might not be fully committed to him. But these old royal stories prove it's possible for you to do something completely new. You can choose God now.

PRAY IT

God, help me choose to love you even when no one else does. Help me break bad patterns around me and live for you.

day176 june 25

READ IT

2 Kings 16:1 – 17:41, Acts 16:16 – 16:40, Proverbs 15:21 – 30

"They replied, 'Believe in the Lord Jesus, and you will be saved—you and your household.'"

Acts 16:31

LIVE IT

What would you say if someone asked you straight-up what it takes to know God and go to heaven? While you might never hear anyone utter those exact words, people all around you have spiritual questions that need understandable answers. That's exactly what the apostle Paul knew how to give.

As Paul and his partners spread the good news about Jesus in the city of Philippi, they were stalked by a slave woman who was able to tell the future. When she shouted that Paul preached the truth about how to be saved, Paul grew annoyed and commanded an evil spirit to leave her. This angered the woman's owners, who used her abilities to make money for themselves. As a result, Paul and Silas were stripped, beaten, and jailed.

Other prisoners listened as the two men prayed and worshiped God in the middle of the night. A massive earthquake popped open the prison doors and shook off everyone's chains. The jailer feared he would be killed for allowing his prisoners to escape, so he prepared to end his own life. When Paul spoke up that the prisoners were all there, the jailer asked a famous question: "What must I do to be saved?" (Acts 16:30).

Some people watch your every move. Others listen to you relate to God. Still others have deep needs that trigger big questions. You can give them all a simple message: People are saved by believing in Jesus Christ. It's a promise everyone can count on.

PRAY IT

Lord, help me notice the people around me who watch me and wait for me to speak. Help me hear their spiritual questions and speak truth about you.

june 26 **day177**

READ IT

2 Kings 18:1 – 19:13, Acts 17:1 – 21, Psalm 78:9 – 16

> *"Now the Berean Jews ... received the message with great eagerness and examined the Scriptures every day to see if what Paul said was true."*
>
> Acts 17:11

LIVE IT

If you're looking for Bible people to imitate, the Bereans are tough to beat. Scripture applauds their "noble character" (Acts 17:11), all because of a habit you can start building right now.

The apostle Paul was on the second of his four missionary trips, a three-year trek westward to spread the news about Jesus (15:36 – 18:22). Whenever he arrived in a city, he headed first for the Jewish synagogue. He used Scripture to reason with people, explaining that Jesus was the Messiah predicted in the Old Testament, the Savior who had to suffer and rise from the dead (17:1 – 4).

In Thessalonica, some of the Jews and Gentiles—both women and men—became convinced that Jesus was everything Paul said he was. Others violently objected, starting a riot aimed at Paul and Silas. But the people of Berea gave the truth about Jesus a friendly welcome. These Bereans "received the message with great eagerness." Their enthusiasm was good, and their next move was even better: they "examined the Scriptures every day to see if what Paul said was true" (v. 11).

You have a chance today and every day to search the Old and New Testament to understand the Bible's own reliability. And you can use the Bible to test the truthfulness of everything you hear and read. That's a solid habit you need right now and for the rest of your life.

PRAY IT

Lord, teach me to value truth. I will study your word to understand its teachings and make sure my faith is real.

day178 june 27

READ IT

2 Kings 19:14–20:21, Acts 17:22–18:8, Psalm 78:17–31

> *"Hezekiah received the letter from the messengers and read it. Then he went up to the temple of the LORD and spread it out before the LORD. And Hezekiah prayed to the LORD."*
>
> 2 KINGS 19:14–15

LIVE IT

Hezekiah was unlike any king of Judah before or after him. Check how the Bible sums him up: "He held fast to the LORD and did not stop following him; he kept the commands the LORD had given Moses. And the LORD was with him; he was successful in whatever he undertook" (2 Kings 18:6–7).

Living close to God didn't mean Hezekiah escaped difficult times. Six years into his reign, forces of the Assyrian Empire obliterated the northern kingdom of Israel forever (v. 10). Eight years later, all of the walled cities of his own southern kingdom of Judah had fallen (v. 13).

Hezekiah had reason to be terrified, because his royal city of Jerusalem was the last thing left for the Assyrians to attack. Their commander mocked God and hurled insults at the king, even threatening that common people would grow so hungry they would eat their own waste (vv. 17–37). When the king received a final threatening letter predicting his defeat, he knew exactly what to do. He went to the temple and laid the letter before the Lord. Then he prayed. He praised the Lord's greatness and pleaded for help.

Hezekiah didn't escape deadly trouble, and neither will you. But you too can run to God and lay all your problems before him. Don't hesitate for a moment to tell him what you need.

PRAY IT

God, I will turn to you when I'm in trouble. I won't wait to pray to you. I will come running when I need help.

june 28 **day179**

READ IT

2 Kings 21:1–22:20, Acts 18:9–19:13, Psalm 78:32–39

> *"They remembered that God was their Rock, that God Most High was their Redeemer."*
>
> PSALM 78:35

LIVE IT

Here they go again. Psalm 78 tells the highs and lows of Israel throughout its long history, detailing not only the mightiness of the Lord's powerful acts on behalf of his people but also their nonstop stubbornness. You can't read these words and not feel astonished that people keep fighting against God. What does it take for people to learn that trusting the Lord and obeying his commands (v. 7) is the best choice they could ever make?

Psalm 78 describes miracles anyone would be eager to see. The Lord split the sea to free his people from slavery. He led them with a pillar of fire. He made water gush from rocks, then showered bread and meat from heaven. Yet "in spite of all this, they kept on sinning; in spite of his wonders, they did not believe" (v. 32).

Because of his people's rebellion, God lets them experience futility and terror (v. 33). It isn't until the Lord lets his people suffer that they remember he's their rock.

So what does it take for you to trust God and obey him? You're not wise if you wait for the hard knocks of life to push you back to him. It's far better to let his goodness pull you close. Like Romans 2:4 says, you're making a rude mistake if you ignore the Lord's compassion. His kindness is meant to convince you to quit sin and turn to him.

PRAY IT

God, I don't want to brush off your kindness. Teach me to live close to you before life gets hard.

day180 june 29

READ IT

2 Kings 23:1–24:7, Acts 19:14–41, Proverbs 15:31–16:7

"Those who disregard discipline despise themselves, but the one who heeds correction gains understanding."

Proverbs 15:32

LIVE IT

You know how it goes. You act up and do something wrong, and your parents come back at you with some variety of discipline. Back when you were little, you might have gotten a time out. Now you're more likely to lose a privilege or end up doing extra chores. But do you learn from that experience?

The Bible tries hard to convince you that discipline—no matter where it comes from—is one of the best gifts you can ever receive. Correction gives life (Proverbs 15:31). Learning from discipline gives you wise friends (v. 31). Paying attention to tough lessons makes you smart (v. 32). Discipline assures you of God's love (3:12). Hating correction means you're stupid (12:1).

You're wise if you accept those statements as facts so true you can't wait to put them into action. And here's another intriguing piece of information you don't want to ignore: "Those who disregard discipline despise themselves" (15:31).

To "despise" yourself means you consider yourself worthless or even hate the core of who you are. When you refuse to learn from correction—whether it's doled out by parents, teachers, coaches, pastors, or God himself—you're doomed to go on doing wrong. You continue to injure others. You no doubt offend God again and again. And along with all that, you tell everyone how much you disrespect yourself.

PRAY IT

God, thanks for discipline, even when it's painful. Help me to learn whatever you're trying to teach me whenever I face correction.

june 30 **day181**

READ IT

2 Kings 24:8–25:30, Acts 20:1–38, Psalm 78:40–55

"Nebuzaradan the commander of the guard carried into exile the people who remained in the city, along with the rest of the populace."

2 Kings 25:11

LIVE IT

You know about God's discipline. The Bible asserts that his correction is a sign of his love (Proverbs 3:12). Keep that fact in mind as you watch the final events of 2 Kings unfold.

Decades before the drama of 2 Kings 24–25, Josiah had led the nation of Judah back to God by teaching the people all the laws the Lord had spoken to Moses. The king's passion for God ushered in some of the best years in the nation's history (22:1–23:30). But the Lord was still fed up with the sins committed by rulers before Josiah, and rulers after him quickly returned to doing evil (2:31–37).

Remember that many hundreds of years earlier, the Lord had threatened to drive his people from the land he had promised them if they disobeyed his commands. "I will scatter you among the nations," he said. "Your land will be laid waste, and your cities will lie in ruins" (Leviticus 26:33). As a consequence of sin, God had allowed Israel to be conquered by the Assyrians (2 Kings 18:10). 2 Kings records how Judah fell to the Babylonians, and its people were led as slaves to a distant land.

Exile was the Lord's ultimate discipline. As strange as it might seem, this toughness was an act of love. Whenever the Lord disciplines you, his aim is to bring you back to himself and teach you to follow him.

PRAY IT

God, teach me to obey when you discipline me. I don't need tough correction for you to get my attention.

day182 july 1

READ IT

1 Chronicles 1:1–2:17, Acts 21:1–26, Psalm 78:56–72

> *"Then Paul answered, 'Why are you weeping and breaking my heart? I am ready not only to be bound, but also to die in Jerusalem for the name of the Lord Jesus.'"*
>
> Acts 21:13

LIVE IT

After spending years zigzagging the world with the message of Jesus, the apostle Paul knew firsthand that violent opposition lurked wherever he went. Despite this constant danger, Paul always pressed on. He declared, "My only aim is to finish the race and complete the task the Lord Jesus has given me—the task of testifying to the good news of God's grace" (Acts 20:24).

The next hazards Paul faced would be more perilous than ever. The Holy Spirit alerted him that prison and hardship lay ahead (v. 23), but after tearing himself away from his close friends in Ephesus (vv. 36–38), he set sail for Jerusalem. Believers along the way urged him not to continue, and a prophet named Agabus warned him that religious authorities in Jerusalem would tie him up and hand him over to the Romans for trial. Paul replied that he was ready not only to be bound but also to die for Jesus.

Maybe you wonder how you would react if someone threatened to hurt you for your faith. You might not want to know if you were about to encounter that kind of danger. But Paul made up his mind ahead of time that he was willing to pay any price to tell everyone about Jesus. God doesn't intend for you to go looking for ways to get hurt for him. But he does want you to decide to keep doing the tasks he gives you.

PRAY IT

Lord, I want to always act on your plan for my life. Help me keep following you whether the path is easy or hard.

july 2 **day183**

READ IT

1 Chronicles 2:18–4:8, Acts 21:27–22:21, Psalm 79:1–13

> *"When the seven days were nearly over, some Jews from the province of Asia saw Paul at the temple. They stirred up the whole crowd and seized him."*
>
> Acts 21:27

LIVE IT

Countless friends had warned the apostle Paul not to go to Jerusalem, and their worst fears come true shortly after he reaches the city. Religious opponents whip up a crowd against Paul. They seize him and drag him from the temple. A Roman commander intervenes moments before the mob kills Paul, but the apostle still goes to prison. The last chapters of Acts tell the rest of his story.

Life doesn't always turn out the way you hope, and God doesn't always make bad situations instantly better. Parents fight, and some divorce. Someone close feels a strange pain, then receives a deadly diagnosis. Your schoolwork overwhelms you, and you fail a class. What are you supposed to do when awful things happen that you can't change?

As the crowd kept shouting "Get rid of him!" (Acts 21:36), Paul must have felt relieved to be bound and led to safety. He lets his captors know he isn't a terrorist, and he stands up for his rights as a Roman citizen (22:25–29). Then he presses on to accomplish what he came to do. He tells his enemies about Jesus.

When life beats you up, God still has a plan and a purpose for every minute of your day. He hasn't left you. He lifts you up if you let him. He helps you press on through life's hardest circumstances.

PRAY IT

God, help me to trust you when my fears come true. You still have a plan for me, and you won't ever stop caring for me.

day184 july 3

READ IT

1 Chronicles 4:9–5:26, Acts 22:22–23:11, Proverbs 16:8–17

"In their hearts humans plan their course, but the LORD establishes their steps."

PROVERBS 16:9

LIVE IT

Most days you wake to must-do tasks—school, chores, practice, work. You might get rare breaks when no one is on you about things you have to get done. You maybe even look forward to turning sixteen or eighteen or twenty-one and running your own life. Some people think that's when everything comes under an individual's total control. They should think again.

The Lord designed you with a mind capable of plotting a path through life. It's a phenomenal sign of maturity when you start to dream up goals and take steps to meet them. But don't ever forget that God rules you.

Proverbs 16:9 hints at how the Lord guides you. He's the one who ultimately chooses your path, so don't be shocked if he nudges you one way or another to keep you going his way. He doesn't alter your course to ruin your life. His plans for you are good (Jeremiah 29:11), better than you can imagine (Ephesians 3:20). And when God "establishes" your steps, he makes your footing sure. Like Proverbs 3:6 says, "In all your ways submit to him, and he will make your paths straight."

The Lord's major goal for your life isn't for you to clock a few more years and then do your own thing. He wants you to grow up and choose to follow him every day.

PRAY IT

Lord, I dream of doing all kinds of things, and I like to plan for my future. But I want you to lead where I go and what I do.

july 4

day185

READ IT

1 Chronicles 6:1–81, Acts 23:12–35, Psalm 80:1–7

> *"These are the men David put in charge of the music in the house of the LORD after the ark came to rest there."*
>
> 1 CHRONICLES 6:31

LIVE IT

Don't let your eyes glaze over when you read the lists of temple workers in 1 Chronicles. Each of those people had a place in the Lord's plans. So do you.

The musicians, priests, and temple assistants remembered here are long gone. Yet they were actual people. They were born and they died, and for all the days they had breath they served God. Aaron and his sons (1 Chronicles 6:3) served as priests. Asaph and his boys (1 Chronicles 6:39) come in a long succession of musicians. Thousands of years later, his family is still famous for writing at least twelve Old Testament psalms (Psalms 50, 73–83).

This passage describes the parcels of land given to these servants of God. As they took responsibility for the spiritual leadership of Israel, the Lord made sure their practical needs were met.

These lists aren't all that different from names and faces that appear on a modern church website: people paid to work as pastors, youth directors, or other staff members. There are also real-life principles here. You can be part of supporting your spiritual leaders, because the Lord cares about their needs (1 Timothy 5:17–18). And whenever and however you serve God, you can be certain he watches out for you.

PRAY IT

God, I worry that if I serve you I won't have any time or money or energy left for me. Help me to trust you to care for my needs whenever I pour myself out for others.

day186 july 5

READ IT

1 Chronicles 7:1–9:1a, Acts 24:1–27, Psalm 80:8–19

> *"As Paul talked about righteousness, self-control and the judgment to come, Felix was afraid and said, 'That's enough for now! You may leave.'"*
>
> Acts 24:25

LIVE IT

As the apostle Paul stands before Felix, governor of Judah, he faces three charges. He's accused of igniting riots across the Roman Empire, teaching people to disobey the law of Moses, and polluting the temple by bringing a Gentile into an area reserved for Jews (Acts 21:27–29).

Paul's opponents argue that these crimes deserve death, but Felix seems unconvinced and unconcerned. By the end of Acts 24, two years have passed. When Felix exits his post, he leaves Paul in prison.

In the meantime, Paul and Felix have intriguing conversations, at least one of which is attended by Felix's wife Drusilla, who is Jewish. Felix is already well acquainted with "the Way" (24:22), a common name for the early Christian faith, and he's eager to hear Paul talk about Jesus. But when Paul brings up purity, self-control, and a future judgment of sin, the governor sends the apostle back to his cell. Maybe Felix's Jewish wife starts feeling guilty for marrying a man who didn't worship God, because she doesn't come back for more conversations. The governor just hopes Paul's friends will pay a bribe to gain his release.

Jesus wants you to tell people about him. When you do, you can't control how they react. Some run away. Others keep talking for all kinds of reasons. And a few truly want to meet your Lord. Whatever happens, your task is to keep speaking truth.

PRAY IT

Lord, give me the right words to tell people about you. I don't want to make people mad, but I do want them to know the truth.

july 6 **day187**

READ IT

1 Chronicles 9:1b–10:14, Acts 25:1–22, Psalm 81:1–7

> *"I removed the burden from their shoulders; their hands were set free from the basket. In your distress you called and I rescued you."*
>
> Psalm 81:6–7

LIVE IT

In Psalm 81 God isn't talking about lifting weights. Or moving furniture. Or trying to hoist a car barehanded. But he does remind his people that he's freed them from an unbearable burden.

You have to dig back into the Old Testament story to get the full point of this song from Asaph or his descendants. The lyrics instruct the Lord's people to sing to the God "of Jacob," the father of Israel's twelve tribes (Genesis 49). The people should blow a ram's horn "at the New Moon" (Numbers 28:11–15). This was all part of the religious law God gave his people when he freed them from slavery in Egypt.

That experience of bondage was the scene of real-life heavy lifting for God's people. As the slaves labored for centuries on various pharaohs' vast building projects, they carried baskets loaded with weighty bricks and other materials. Their shoulders were crushed by heavy burdens. But the Lord heard their cries (Exodus 2:23–25) and rescued them. He released them from the control of cruel taskmasters and put them on a road to new life.

When you feel flattened by things too heavy to bear, the Lord hears your prayers. While you can't predict when and how he will relieve the pressure, you can still shout for joy to God. Today and always he's your strength.

PRAY IT

God, you're my strength when I'm weak. Lift the burdens I feel right now. Send me relief however you can.

day188 july 7

READ IT

1 Chronicles 11:1–12:22, Acts 25:23–26:23, Proverbs 16:18–27

"These were the chiefs of David's mighty warriors—they, together with all Israel, gave his kingship strong support to extend it over the whole land, as the LORD had promised."

1 CHRONICLES 11:10

LIVE IT

Immense accomplishments sound all the more amazing when they're done solo—like shattering a home run record, scaling Mount Everest, or circling the globe in a sailboat. Yet no great feat happens without help.

The Lord had a plan for David that started with his appointment as king over Israel, an act of blessing initiated through Samuel (1 Samuel 16:13). God later made an astonishing promise that one of David's descendants would always rule on the throne (2 Samuel 7:16), a vow fulfilled when Jesus the eternal King was born to David's line (Matthew 1:1–17).

David's forty-year reign was marked by significant deeds. He attacked the supposedly unbeatable city and made it his capital, Jerusalem. He brought the ark of God to the city, giving worship its rightful place at the heart of the nation. He calmed tensions between northern and southern tribes, and he extended peace in every direction. But it took the strong support of his mighty warriors for David to make his kingship strong throughout the land.

There's nothing truly great you can accomplish on your own. You need parents, pastors, teachers, coaches, friends, and countless others behind you no matter what you want to accomplish. And if there's something you think you can do well on your own, remind yourself that you will do even better if you partner with others.

PRAY IT

Lord, thanks for surrounding me with people to give me support and insight in everything I do. Train me to give others the kind of help you give me.

READ IT

1 Chronicles 12:23–14:17, Acts 26:24–27:12, Psalm 81:8–16

> *"What I am saying is true and reasonable. The king is familiar with these things, and I can speak freely to him. I am convinced that none of this has escaped his notice, because it was not done in a corner."*
>
> ACTS 26:25–26

LIVE IT

Most prisoners would do anything to break out of jail. But the apostle Paul saw interrogation and imprisonment as opportunities to declare the facts about Jesus.

When Felix ends his term as governor, he leaves Paul in prison (Acts 24:27). Paul's religious opponents still want him dead, and they convince the next governor, Festus, to put him on trial. When these enemies can't prove any of their charges against Paul, the governor concludes the quarrel is "about their own religion and about a dead man named Jesus who Paul claimed was alive" (25:19). Rather than let the charges be dismissed and go free, Paul appeals his case to Caesar. He wants to preach Christ to the highest officials of the empire.

Before shipping off to Caesar, Paul appears before King Agrippa, who is visiting. When Festus interrupts and laughs that Paul's great learning is making him insane, Paul offers a brilliant defense. He declares that his faith is reasonable. Then he points out that the facts about Jesus are open for examination. All the events of the Lord's life, death, and resurrection happened in plain sight.

For two thousand years the Christian faith has made sense to countless people. Why? Because anyone can test the facts about Jesus. When you tell people about the Lord, you're not asking them to accept crazy beliefs. You can invite them to check the facts for themselves.

PRAY IT

Lord, help me understand all the reasons there are to believe in you. And give me opportunities to share my faith with others.

day190 july 9

READ IT

1 Chronicles 15:1–16:36, Acts 27:13–44, Psalm 82:1–8

> *"As the ark of the covenant of the* LORD *was entering the City of David, Michal daughter of Saul watched from a window. And when she saw King David dancing and celebrating, she despised him in her heart."*
>
> 1 CHRONICLES 15:29

LIVE IT

It might not fit your style to dance with enthusiasm for the Lord. But David couldn't help celebrating when he brought the ark of God into Jerusalem. He wasn't about to let anyone halt his extreme joy.

The ark had been a physical sign of the Lord's spiritual presence with Israel since the days of wandering in the desert (Deuteronomy 31:9). After God's people entered the Promised Land, they parked the ark for centuries at Shiloh (Joshua 18:1). David moved it to Jerusalem, where later it would find its home in the new temple Solomon built (1 Kings 8:6).

Ushering the ark into the holy city was an epic event, and David is so overflowing with happiness that he strips to a loincloth and dances wildly before God. His wife Michal accuses the king of prancing half-naked in front of the slave girls, but David says he would rather become even more undignified and humiliated than refrain from celebrating God (2 Samuel 6:20–22). David doesn't care what anyone thinks about his deep love for God. He would rather look like an idiot than fail to give the Lord the honor he deserves.

The world is jam-packed with people who look down at your faith. They especially don't understand your enthusiasm for following Jesus. But don't be afraid to let them know what you think and feel. Your God is real. So is your passion for him.

PRAY IT

God, I want to be unashamed about my relationship with you. Alert me when I let what others think control me.

july 10 **day191**

READ IT

1 Chronicles 16:37–18:17, Acts 28:1–16, Psalm 83:1–18

> *"O God, do not remain silent; do not turn a deaf ear, do not stand aloof, O God."*
>
> Psalm 83:1

LIVE IT

There's no worse sensation than feeling like God is standing in some far-off corner of the universe with his back turned to you and his hands plugging his ears, ignoring your desperate prayers.

In Psalm 83 Asaph writes of growling enemies who form cunning conspiracies to destroy God's people. He names all the surrounding nations as allies in a plot against the Lord. He pleads for God to blow them away like tumbleweed, and he wants everyone to know the Most High rules the entire earth. And as Asaph waits for an answer, he worries that God isn't listening.

You can be sure that the Lord hears your prayers. Psalm 116:1 shouts, "I love the Lord, for he heard my voice." Not only does he hear your prayers, but his answers are superior to anything you can ask. They're more immense than your biggest dreams. Ephesians 3:20 praises God as the one "who is able to do immeasurably more than all we ask or imagine."

That same verse adds an intriguing twist. The Lord does bigger and better things "according to his power that is at work within us." You might be waiting for God to alter your situation. Yet he might be working to change something about *you*. As you glance around for the Lord's answers to your prayers, don't just look outside. Check what he's doing inside too.

PRAY IT

Lord, I trust you to answer my prayers in the right way at the right time. Don't just fix my world. Work inside my heart.

day192 july 11

READ IT

1 Chronicles 19:1 – 22:1, Acts 28:17 – 31, Proverbs 16:28 – 17:4

> *"For two whole years Paul stayed there in his own rented house and welcomed all who came to see him. He proclaimed the kingdom of God and taught about the Lord Jesus Christ — with all boldness and without hindrance!"*
>
> Acts 28:30–31

LIVE IT

The book of Acts has a relatively happy ending. After multiple missionary journeys the apostle Paul travels back to Jerusalem, where he is promptly arrested (Acts 21:27 – 36). His imprisonment drags on, and he nearly dies in transit to Rome (27:1 – 28:10). But the last words of Acts show him freely preaching about Jesus while he awaits his trial before Caesar.

That's not the end of Paul's story. While in Rome he likely wrote his letters to the Colossians, Ephesians, Philippians, and Philemon, which all detail his ongoing work. Each Roman official who heard Paul up to this point had found him innocent, so there's good reason to think Caesar heard his case and set him free.

Ancient tradition reports that Paul went to Spain to preach Jesus in a place where the Lord was unknown, a wish he expressed in Romans 15:24. Tradition says that Paul was again arrested under a new, more hostile emperor, Nero, then condemned and beheaded for his faith in Jesus.

Paul's friend Luke likely finished the book of Acts where he did simply to avoid delay in sending this account to Theophilus (Acts 1:1). But the abrupt conclusion implies a bold truth. The spread of the good news about Jesus didn't end with Paul. Along with every Christian who ever lived, you too are part of the story of telling the world about him (v. 8).

PRAY IT

Lord, you've given me the job of spreading the good news about you. Train me to tell your story well.

READ IT

1 Chronicles 22:2–23:32, Romans 1:1–17, Psalm 84:1–7

> *"For I am not ashamed of the gospel, because it is the power of God that brings salvation to everyone who believes."*
>
> Romans 1:16

LIVE IT

Most of what you read in the first five books of the New Testament—from Matthew to Acts—are fast-paced stories. The accounts of Jesus and of the early church explain what happened from when Jesus was born on earth to the first years of a new movement made up of believers just like you.

When you flip to Paul's letter to the Romans, you find a detailed explanation of your faith that reads more like a textbook. But don't let that bog you down. This amazing letter from the apostle Paul tells you how and why your faith works. It explains how sinful people can become friends with a holy God.

You can spend the rest of your life studying this book, but the facts here all come down to one point: the gospel or "good news" about Jesus "is the power of God that brings salvation to everyone who believes" (Romans 1:16). "Salvation" captures everything God does for you. It means you're saved from the *penalty* of sin, eternal separation from God in hell. You're rescued from the *power* of sin, its ability to enslave you to doing wrong. And you will live forever apart from even the *presence* of sin when the Lord brings you home to heaven.

You receive all those good gifts when you believe the truth that Jesus is God's Son who died on the cross for your sins. That powerful message is nothing to be embarrassed about.

PRAY IT

God, you save me from sin through Jesus. I'm glad that by believing in him I can be friends with you and live forever in heaven.

day194 july 13

READ IT

1 Chronicles 24:1–26:19, Romans 1:18–32, Psalm 84:8–12

> *"Better is one day in your courts than a thousand elsewhere; I would rather be a doorkeeper in the house of my God than dwell in the tents of the wicked."*
>
> Psalm 84:10

LIVE IT

Do you have a special place where you expect to feel close to God? Maybe it's at church. Or youth group. Or it might be a Christian camp, a retreat site, or a mission project locale. That sensation of connecting with God in a special place gives a tiny taste of how Old Testament saints thought about the temple.

Back in the days when the Israelites wandered in the desert, the Lord promised to be with his people at the tent-like tabernacle. Later the permanent temple built by Solomon became the location of the Lord's focused presence. The tabernacle and temple were the only places where the Lord accepted sacrifices for sin. They were the only locations for true worship.

Getting close to God meant going to the temple, and believers ached to be in his courts (Psalm 84:10). The temple felt like home (v. 3). It was the place to praise God (v. 4). People trekking to worship in Jerusalem could count on God turning their hot desert journey into a hop between spring-fed pools (v. 6). And they knew it was better to have a minor role serving in the temple than to live in an evil person's posh tent (v. 10).

You don't have to go to a temple to get near God, yet you can still passionately pursue his presence. You're not limited to a specific place. Any time you reach out to him he's right there.

PRAY IT

God, my relationship with you isn't all about feelings. But thanks for always being close—and for times I sense you're with me.

july 14

day195

READ IT

1 Chronicles 26:20–27:34, Romans 2:1–16, Psalm 85:1–7

> *"But because of your stubbornness and your unrepentant heart, you are storing up wrath against yourself for the day of God's wrath, when his righteous judgment will be revealed."*
>
> Romans 2:5

LIVE IT

Think of the first few chapters of Romans as the worst mid-term report card you could ever get. You're not just struggling to survive a tough class. You're completely failing. Unless you find the right remedy, you're doomed.

You're not the only one with issues. Romans 1:18 kicks off the Lord's negative evaluation of the whole human race when it says, "The wrath of God is being revealed from heaven against all the godlessness and wickedness of people, who suppress the truth by their wickedness." The Lord is furious because people know the facts about his power and love, but they push him out of their minds. The result is all kinds of ugly sin.

Romans 2 asserts that stubborn human hearts pile up reasons for the Lord to unleash on evildoers the wrath they deserve. Both Jews (people who know God's law) and Gentiles (people who don't) reject him. While Romans 2:7–11 might sound like people can earn their way to heaven, it teaches that authentic faith proves itself through good deeds. Once you accept Christ into your life, you can't help but want to show that love to others through your actions. And the bad news keeps coming. Paul goes on to write, "There is no one righteous, not even one" (3:10).

These harsh chapters aren't meant to make you abandon hope. They simply point out your dire need for Jesus. Unless you get a true picture of your own failings, you won't take seriously the remedy he offers through the cross.

PRAY IT

God, it's tough to hear what you think of my sin. Help me look honestly at my sins. Get me ready to admit I need Jesus to make me friends with you.

day196 july 15

READ IT

1 Chronicles 28:1–29:30, Romans 2:17–3:8, Proverbs 17:5–14

> *"Starting a quarrel is like breaching a dam; so drop the matter before a dispute breaks out."*
>
> Proverbs 17:14

LIVE IT

People usually deal with conflict in one of two ways. You either avoid the situation—or dig in and fight. Put another way, you either pretend everything's okay—or you lash out until others crumble.

Jesus said, "Blessed are the peacemakers" (Matthew 5:9), but don't take that to mean Christians are pushovers. God doesn't want you to "fake peace," pretending that everything's okay when it's not. He also doesn't want you to "break peace," winning a battle at any cost. The Lord filled the Bible with wise ways of handling conflict, no matter who you butt heads with or why you fight.

The apostle Paul wrote, for example, "If it is possible, as far as it depends on you, live at peace with everyone" (Romans 12:18). Those words recognize that peace should be your goal, but solving a problem isn't completely in your control. Paul also said, "Do not let the sun go down while you are still angry" (Ephesians 4:26). That's not a command to solve every problem before bedtime, but not to let an issue linger. Jesus himself provided a series of courageous practical steps to take when someone wrongs you (Matthew 18:15–17).

Most fights aren't worth the air it takes to argue. So the next time you see a conflict coming, check if you can put Proverbs 17:14 into action. Try to stop the fight before it starts.

PRAY IT

God, teach me not to flee conflict or always fight until I win. Train me in your smart ways to make peace.

july 16

day197

READ IT

2 Chronicles 1:1 – 17, Romans 3:9 – 31, Psalm 85:8 – 13

> *"For all have sinned and fall short of the glory of God, and all are justified freely by his grace through the redemption that came by Christ Jesus."*
>
> Romans 3:23 – 24

LIVE IT

The first part of Romans contains almost non-stop bad news, detailing the dire situation of the rebellious human race. When you come face-to-face with the Lord's honest evaluation of the people he created, it's astonishing he didn't dump us like the hopeless enemies we are. Instead he hatched a plan to rescue us from evil and make us new people.

The apostle Paul declares "there is no one righteous, not even one" (Romans 3:10), passing along God's message that all of us are sinful in what we think, say, and do. Some people sin in ways everyone can see. Some kinds of wrongdoing cause more devastation than others. But all people miss God's perfection. Not only that, but it's simply not possible to do good to make up for the bad we have done. None of us will ever be good enough to be friends with God on our own. Like Paul says, "no one will be declared righteous in God's sight by the works of the law" (v. 20).

Yet God creates a totally different way for you to get right with him. He "justifies" everyone who has faith in Jesus. That means he declares us not guilty, so it's "just-as-if-I-never-sinned." Because Jesus offered himself as a sacrifice for sins, God can forgive everything you have ever done wrong. It's all an amazing gift that comes from God's grace, his favor you don't deserve.

PRAY IT

God, I admit I have done wrong. I need your forgiveness. I trust that Jesus paid for my sins when he died on the cross.

day198 july 17

READ IT

2 Chronicles 2:1–5:1, Romans 4:1–15, Psalm 86:1–10

"Hiram king of Tyre replied by letter to Solomon: 'Because the LORD loves his people, he has made you their king.'"

2 CHRONICLES 2:11

LIVE IT

Back in the times of David and Solomon, the area surrounding the city of Tyre was famed for its thick cedar forests, much like northern California is known for giant redwoods. A stand of surviving trees is protected in a preserve in modern Lebanon called the "Cedars of God."

It's no surprise that King Solomon turned to Hiram, king of Tyre, for beautiful wood and skilled help to build the temple. Hiram had long been friends with Solomon's father, David, and he provided timber and labor for David's royal palace (1 Chronicles 14:1). So Solomon asked for cedar logs and an artisan skilled in working precious metals and rich yarns.

When Hiram replied, he declared that God must love his people to have given them a king like Solomon. He recognized that the Lord had given David's son intelligence and solid judgment. He promised to send the materials and the worker Solomon needed. And Hiram praised the Lord, whom he called "the God of Israel, who made heaven and earth!" (2 Chronicles 2:12).

Hiram knew Solomon. He even knew something about Solomon's God. The king of Tyre no doubt worships the gods of his own land, so it is strange that he would say Solomon's God is the ultimate ruler of the universe. Perhaps he accepted God as one among many. These two men likely disagreed about God, yet they made the most of their friendship. They let you glimpse how you can get along with people who don't follow Jesus.

PRAY IT

Lord, you're the one-and-only God. Teach me how to connect with people who don't yet worship you.

READ IT

2 Chronicles 5:2–7:10, Romans 4:16–5:11, Psalm 86:11–17

> *"Therefore, the promise comes by faith, so that it may be by grace and may be guaranteed to all Abraham's offspring."*
>
> Romans 4:16

LIVE IT

Unlike plenty of people you meet, the Lord doesn't think promises are meant to be broken. Numbers 23:19 assures you that "God is not human, that he should lie." So when the Lord says he makes you his friend because of what Jesus accomplished on the cross, it's a relief to know you can count on his words.

The apostle Paul wrote his letter to the Christians in Rome to tell them how to get right with God. He starts by detailing humankind's problem with sin. He explains that God "justifies" or "declares innocent" everyone who believes in Jesus. Then he keeps hammering the point that this "justification" happens through faith, not through doing good works. It's a gift that flows from the Lord's grace, the favor he gives you even when you don't deserve it. It's a sign God loves you even at your worst (Romans 5:8).

Some of God's words might seem too good to be true, but God guarantees his promises, giving you even more reason to trust. You can dare to be like Abraham, who "did not waver through unbelief regarding the promise of God, but was strengthened in his faith and gave glory to God," because he was "fully persuaded that God had power to do what he had promised" (4:20–21).

When God makes a promise to you, he keeps it. He has all the love and power he needs to make it come true.

PRAY IT

God, I trust your promises to me, especially your words that I can be your friend by believing in Jesus.

day200 july 19

READ IT

2 Chronicles 7:11–9:31, Romans 5:12–21, Proverbs 17:15–24

"A friend loves at all times, and a brother is born for a time of adversity."

PROVERBS 17:17

LIVE IT

Some adult in your life has probably said you need to be the kind of friend you want to have. God agrees.

The Bible highlights good friends at their best—and worst. Ruth vowed to stay with her mother-in-law Naomi wherever she went, pledging to stick close until death (Ruth 1:16–18). Jonathan saw through his father Saul's evil rage and swore friendship with David, the young guy God had picked to be Israel's next king (1 Samuel 20:1–42). When Jesus set out for an agonizing prayer session hours before he went to the cross, he took along Peter, James, and John for support. But his friends dozed off when he needed them most (Matthew 26:36–46).

Life is good when you're surrounded by people who pass the Proverbs 17:17 test of real friendship. Real friends never stop loving, and they don't quit your relationship when circumstances get rough. But steady companions can be few and far between.

God tells you to seek the best friends possible in your quest to follow him (2 Timothy 2:22). Yet you start by becoming the friend you hope to find. It's tough to demand loyalty from others if you're not willing to give it yourself. You can't expect people to stick with you if you don't stick with them.

PRAY IT

Lord, train me to be a friend worth having. I need your help to live up to the high expectations I have of others. I want to be the kind of friend I need others to be.

READ IT

2 Chronicles 10:1 – 12:16, Romans 6:1 – 14, Psalm 87:1 – 7

> *"But Rehoboam rejected the advice the elders gave him and consulted the young men who had grown up with him and were serving him."*
>
> 2 Chronicles 10:8

LIVE IT

The Israelites should have spotted this ugly scene coming. Years earlier, God grew angry at King Solomon for worshiping the pagan gods of his many foreign wives. The Lord vowed to rip away much of Solomon's kingdom as a consequence of sin, though not until after the king's death (1 Kings 11:9 – 13).

After Solomon dies his son Rehoboam ascended to the throne. An old enemy named Jeroboam (vv. 26 – 40) returned from Egypt to plead with Rehoboam for relief from the heavy burdens of taxation and forced labor Solomon had put on the people to undertake his lavish building projects (v. 28). Jeroboam spoke not just for himself but for the entire nation.

Older advisors told Rehoboam that showing kindness to his new subjects would earn their undying affection. Yet younger counselors urged Rehoboam to pile even more severe loads on the people and to beat them not merely with whips embedded with razor-sharp metal but with poisonous scorpions. When Rehoboam thundered his verdict, the kingdom split just as God had predicted.

Proverbs 19:20 says, "Listen to advice and accept discipline, and at the end you will be counted among the wise." But foolish advice doesn't do you any good. When you turn to others for wisdom, not just any voice will do. Choose carefully whom you listen to. Bad advice is worse than no advice at all.

PRAY IT

God, I want to listen to people who can give me advice worth taking. Teach me to rely on voices that speak your wisdom.

day202 july 21

READ IT

2 Chronicles 13:1–15:19, Romans 6:15–7:6, Psalm 88:1–9a

"For the wages of sin is death, but the gift of God is eternal life in Christ Jesus our Lord."

Romans 6:23

LIVE IT

It's bad news and good news all in one breath. That's the two-part message of Romans 6:23.

Scripture doesn't shy away from the terrible news of people's sin and its outcomes. The Bible's first pages describe Adam and Eve's failure in the garden of Eden, which started humankind's rebellion against the Lord. Old Testament books spell out God's laws, and prophets speak out when God's people fall short. The apostle Paul's letter to the Romans builds a case outlining the sinfulness of all people.

Romans 6:23 explains that death is the result of human rebellion. That consequence is more than a physical body ceasing to function. Spiritual death is a total and permanent separation from God and everything good.

That's unbearably bad news. Yet the Bible also declares the supremely good news that the Lord gives eternal life to everyone who believes in Jesus. It's a free gift that means more than your body lasting forever. It's not just a span of time but a quality of existence. The Bible says that eternal life is all about you knowing the only true God (John 17:3).

Eternal life isn't something that happens when you die. It starts when you first believe, and it lasts forever. If you trust in Jesus, you have already crossed over from death to life (5:24). That's good news. Believe it.

PRAY IT

God, thank you for your free gift of eternal life. I'm glad I get to live forever with you. I'm happy I can live close to you now and forever.

READ IT

2 Chronicles 16:1 – 18:27, Romans 7:7 – 25, Psalm 88:9b – 18

> *"What a wretched man I am! Who will rescue me from this body that is subject to death? Thanks be to God, who delivers me through Jesus Christ our Lord!"*
>
> Romans 7:24–25

LIVE IT

Sin is like quicksand. The more you struggle against it, the more stuck you realize you are. Yet there's a solution to your problem. You need outside help to scramble free.

In Romans 7 the apostle Paul describes the awful predicament of being trapped in a sin you can't escape. He starts by admitting that the Lord's commands are perfectly good, helping him spot evil he should avoid and making sin appear "utterly sinful" (v. 13). Yet something happens whenever Paul hears God's laws. Something inside deceives him and entices him to sin.

Has someone ever forbidden you to do something wrong, yet their command made sin even more tempting? It's like when your parents tell you not to talk back, and you instantly think of more mouthy comments. Paul says that's your sinful nature battling inside you. You want to do right, yet a tug inside makes doing wrong more appealing. As Paul says, "For I do not do the good I want to do, but the evil I do not want to do — this I keep on doing" (v. 19).

Paul feels so stuck that he screams he's a wretched man. Yet he hints at a solution. Through Jesus Christ, God rescues you from sin.

PRAY IT

God, I feel trapped by sin. I fail to do the good things I want to do, and I do bad things I wish I wouldn't. Rescue me!

day204 july 23

READ IT

2 Chronicles 18:28 – 21:3, Romans 8:1 – 17, Proverbs 17:25 – 18:6

> *"Should you help the wicked and love those who hate the LORD? Because of this, the wrath of the LORD is on you."*
>
> 2 Chronicles 19:2

LIVE IT

When Jehu the prophet challenges King Jehoshaphat about helping the wicked and loving people who hate God, it might sound like he's going against Jesus's command to "love your enemies and pray for those who persecute you" (Matthew 5:44). But Jehu was out to make a different point.

Jehoshaphat ruled the southern kingdom of Judah at the same time Ahab reigned in the northern kingdom of Israel. Ahab and his wife Jezebel had a reputation as the most evil leaders in the history of God's people. When Jehoshaphat allied himself with Ahab by letting his son marry Ahab's daughter (2 Chronicles 18:1), God wasn't happy with the cozy relationship between the royal families.

When Jehoshaphat goes into battle with Ahab against a common enemy, the king of Aram, the Lord grows even more upset. That's when Jehu the prophet speaks up. Jehoshaphat sinned by teaming up with a king bent on evil. The king wasn't merely befriending notorious Ahab; he had become a partner in crime.

All day long you meet people who don't know God. They need your love and help, and the Bible is jammed with ideas for reaching out to them. But you have to be honest with yourself and not cross an important line. If you let nonbelievers lead you into sin, you're not exactly demonstrating God's kindness.

PRAY IT

Lord, I want to show your love to everyone around me, whether they know you or not. Help me be on guard against getting pulled away from you.

READ IT

2 Chronicles 21:4–23:21, Romans 8:18–39, Psalm 89:1–8

> *"Neither height nor depth, nor anything else in all creation, will be able to separate us from the love of God that is in Christ Jesus our Lord."*
>
> Romans 8:39

LIVE IT

Romans 8 is like a dense note from a friend that you need to read and reread from beginning to end to understand everything it says. Just when you think you grasp everything, you spot more life-altering truth.

The apostle Paul starts this chapter by solving the problem that made him cry out in Romans 7. You and every human being are mired in sin, battling evil from the inside out. But God fixes what all the rules in the world can't. He sends his Holy Spirit to transform your mind and heart so you can obey God. With the same power residing in you that raised Jesus from the dead, you're sure to live a new life (Romans 8:11).

Then Paul hits more unforgettable truths. He says the pain you suffer for following Jesus is nothing compared to the glory that awaits you in heaven (v. 18). The Holy Spirit prays for you in groans too deep for words (v. 26). God works for your good no matter what you endure in life (v. 28). And you're destined to look like Jesus (v. 29).

If that isn't enough, the chapter finishes with reason after reason to trust the Lord's love. With God on your side, it doesn't matter who is against you (v. 31). And there's nothing in the entire universe that can separate you from the love you get in Jesus (vv. 38–39).

PRAY IT

Lord, teach me to rely on you. I want your Spirit to work inside me. I trust your unstoppable love.

day206 july 25

READ IT

2 Chronicles 24:1–25:28, Romans 9:1–21, Psalm 89:9–13

"You rule over the surging sea; when its waves mount up, you still them."

Psalm 89:9

LIVE IT

The Bible sometimes makes you feel like you're on the outside of an inside joke. Or you're part of a whispered conversation you're sure was intended to exclude you. You can scratch your head about what the Lord intended to say through Scripture, or you can try to solve the book's puzzles.

This passage starts with words able to boost your worst day. What's not to like about a God who rules the surging sea? He flattens waves that threaten to drown you.

But what's the point about Rahab? Maybe you remember Rahab as a prostitute who bravely helped two Israelite spies escape their enemies in Joshua 2:1–24. But that's not the Rahab mentioned here, because the spelling is different in the Hebrew language used to write the Old Testament. This Rahab happens to be a symbolic name for Egypt (Psalm 87:4). So this song celebrates God crushing a nation that forced his people into slavery.

Then there's "Tabor" and "Hermon." Those names sound like long-lost great uncles, but they're actually mountains significant in Israel's history, with Hermon the likely site of Jesus' transfiguration (Matthew 17:1). These peaks show off God's enormous power.

It's easy to skip parts of the Bible you don't understand. But you can ask a pastor where to find a solid Bible dictionary. Or look for resources online. Easy digging often lets you track with the action.

PRAY IT

God, sometimes I feel stupid and bored when I don't understand the Bible. Teach me how to study your Word for myself.

READ IT

2 Chronicles 26:1–28:27, Romans 9:22–10:4, Psalm 89:14–18

> *"Righteousness and justice are the foundation of your throne; love and faithfulness go before you."*
>
> Psalm 89:14

LIVE IT

The ancient words of Psalm 89 aren't phrased in a way that naturally spill from your mouth. Even so, they make amazing statements about your God and what it's like to follow him.

Imagine all the most glamorous celebrities in the world gathered in the seats of a major stadium. Fill in the open spots with all the best-known politicians, all the most powerful military leaders, and the wealthiest people ever known. Then ask yourself this. How many of those ultra-famous people have built their lives on qualities like goodness and justice? How many exude love and loyalty to the rest of the world?

Not many. Nobody does it like your flawless God. Even the biggest humanitarians and givers to charity will eventually do something that can let you down.

This song says you're "blessed" (or "fortunate" or "happy") if you learn to praise God's perfect character and live close to him (v. 15). He gives you reason to party all day long (v. 16).

PRAY IT

God, I'm happiest when I recognize your goodness and bow to you. You show me love and loyalty no human can match.

day208 july 27

READ IT

2 Chronicles 29:1–31:1, Romans 10:5–11:10, Proverbs 18:7–16

> *"If you declare with your mouth, 'Jesus is Lord,' and believe in your heart that God raised him from the dead, you will be saved."*
>
> Romans 10:9

LIVE IT

You might get the impression from reading the apostle Paul's letter to the Romans that the Christian faith is complicated beyond the comprehension of normal human beings. Romans 10–11 actually gets tougher to track as Paul explains the place of God's Old Testament people now that Jesus has come to save people from all over the world.

Even in the midst of these difficult paragraphs, however, Paul explains your faith in a way you can memorize and hang on to forever. So look at what he says in Romans 10:9.

The message is simple. God requires people to believe wholeheartedly that Jesus rose from the dead. People make this truth clear to themselves and others when they declare that Jesus is now master of their lives. And the result of this "confession of faith" is that God saves them. He freely gives them all the benefits of being his children, starting now and lasting for all eternity.

If you ever wonder if you're truly a Christian, those words point out that faith is a lot simpler than some people say. You can reassure yourself that you truly believe and that the Lord will welcome you home to heaven. And if you aim to explain your faith to a non-Christian, Romans 3:23, 6:23, and 10:9 are phenomenal places to start.

PRAY IT

Lord, trusting you isn't complicated. I believe that you rose from the dead. I recognize that you're my Lord now and forever.

READ IT

2 Chronicles 31:2–33:20, Romans 11:11–32, Psalm 89:19–29

> *"Manasseh was twelve years old when he became king, and he reigned in Jerusalem fifty-five years. He did evil in the eyes of the LORD."*
>
> 2 CHRONICLES 33:1

LIVE IT

Hezekiah ruled as one of the godliest and most accomplished kings in the royal line of Judah. Toward the end of his life he grew proud and ignored God's kindness, but he turned back to God before he died.

Manasseh came to the throne at age twelve and committed unspeakable evil, undoing much of the good his father Hezekiah had done. He reestablished the high places, illegal worship sites built atop hills and mountains. He built altars to pagan gods and worshiped the sun and stars. He even put altars to false gods within the Lord's temple. He practiced witchcraft and turned to mediums to contact the dead on his behalf. And he burnt his children alive as sacrifices to idols (2 Chronicles 33:1–6).

When the Lord spoke up to stop these evils, Manasseh ignored him. Not until an invading army led the king away in chains with a hook in his nose did he humble himself and turn back to the Lord. He then did everything in his power to lead the nation back to worship the one true God.

No matter who you are or what you have done, the Lord always invites you to repent—to quit sinning and turn to him. Whenever you feel like you have wandered far from God, he's always eager to welcome you home.

PRAY IT

God, thanks for welcoming me back when I have run away from you. I want to rid my life of sin and follow you as best I know how.

day210 july 29

READ IT

2 Chronicles 33:21–35:19, Romans 11:33–12:21, Psalm 89:30–37

> *"Therefore, I urge you, brothers and sisters, in view of God's mercy, to offer your bodies as a living sacrifice, holy and pleasing to God—this is your true and proper worship."*
>
> Romans 12:1

LIVE IT

If you want to live all-out for the Lord, you want a convincing reason to follow. And you need to know how that happens. The apostle Paul serves up the answers in Romans 12:1–2.

Paul doesn't downplay the commitment God wants from you. He urges you to offer yourself as "a living sacrifice." If you're picturing an Old Testament sacrifice with an animal going up in smoke, you're beginning to catch the point. The Lord doesn't want you to set yourself aflame but to offer every last part of yourself to him. You do this by being "holy," or passionately dedicated. You aim to be "pleasing," looking out for what your Lord wants more than what you want.

There's only one reason for you to accept that challenge. You offer yourself "in view of God's mercy," remembering the compassion and forgiveness the Lord constantly shows you. Because Jesus died for you, now you live for him (2 Corinthians 5:14–15). This is "your true and proper worship," the only appropriate response to all he's done for you.

It's impossible to obey God without first being transformed from the inside out. When you let God "renew your mind" by changing how you think and feel, then you will know what God wants you to do. Not only will you be able to identify his will, but you will also be motivated to do it.

PRAY IT

Lord, I offer myself to you as a living sacrifice. I don't just want those to be words but real actions. Thank you for all your mercy for me.

READ IT

2 Chronicles 35:20–36:23, Romans 13:1–14, Psalm 89:38–45

> *"The other events of Josiah's reign and his acts of devotion in accordance with what is written in the Law of the LORD—all the events, from beginning to end, are written in the book of the kings of Israel and Judah."*
>
> 2 CHRONICLES 35:26–27

LIVE IT

King Manasseh of Judah wasted years committing terrible sins until he turned back to the Lord and led his kingdom away from false gods (2 Chronicles 33:1–20). But an even bigger spiritual revival soon started under King Josiah.

Josiah was just eight years old when he rose to the throne. At sixteen he began to passionately search for God, and at twenty he traveled the country to smash pagan altars. At twenty-six he set out to repair the Lord's long-neglected temple (34:3–8).

That's when the unexpected happened. As the temple is undergoing repairs, Hilkiah the priest uncovered the "Book of the Law," likely the first five books of the Old Testament, parts of the Bible that had been suppressed by evil leaders. Josiah heard God's words and wept. He grieved that people had abandoned the Lord's commands (vv. 14–21). When Josiah called together God's people, he not only read the words of the lost book but also pledged that he and the people would follow the Lord's commands (vv. 29–32).

When the kings who reigned after Josiah led the people back to sin, disaster struck and Jerusalem fell to the Babylonians. But Josiah did what he could—as long as he could—to live and lead with total devotion to the Lord. People all around you might dive into evil. But you can follow God.

PRAY IT

God, I want to obey you. And I want to help others follow you too. Don't let me go back on my commitment to you.

day212 july 31

READ IT

Ezra 1:1 – 2:67, Romans 14:1 – 18, Proverbs 18:17 – 19:2

> *"The tongue has the power of life and death, and those who love it will eat its fruit."*
>
> Proverbs 18:21

LIVE IT

You might seem tough on the outside, as if harsh words bounce right off you. But if you're like most people, hurtful words cut you like a knife.

It's no surprise that the Lord wants you to get your own mouth under control. Your tongue can do harm unlike any other part of your body. Like the apostle James says, the tongue is "full of deadly poison" (James 3:8). It "sets the whole course of one's life on fire, and is itself set on fire by hell" (v. 6).

Your words also have power to help and heal. The apostle Paul offers a convenient test for what you let past your lips. He writes, "Do not let any unwholesome talk come out of your mouths, but only what is helpful for building others up according to their needs, that it may benefit those who listen" (Ephesians 4:29).

If you never slip up in what you say, you're perfect, the master of your entire body (James 3:2). But there's really only one way to take control of your words. Jesus says, "The mouth speaks what the heart is full of" (Matthew 12:34). If you want your words to be helpful instead of hurtful, you need to let God change what goes on in your heart and mind. If you're full of his love, then his kindness will spill out in your words.

PRAY IT

Lord, help me know and experience your love so I'm changed from the inside out. Then my words will convey your compassion.

READ IT

Ezra 2:68–4:5, Romans 14:19–15:13, Psalm 89:46–52

> *"And all the people gave a great shout of praise to the LORD, because the foundation of the house of the LORD was laid."*
>
> EZRA 3:11

LIVE IT

The book of Ezra begins by announcing extraordinary news: Cyrus, king of Persia, decided to set God's people free from captivity in Babylon to return to their homeland in Judah. Cyrus acknowledged that the Lord had set him on the throne of a vast empire, and he directed the returning captives to build a temple to God in Jerusalem (Ezra 1:1–3).

The most astonishing part of this news is that more than a hundred years before Cyrus issued his decree, Isaiah prophesied that the king would give exactly that order (Isaiah 44:28). As the people traveled hundreds of miles back to their homeland, they could be sure they had God's blessing on their task.

A man named Zerubbabel led the group homeward. He and Joshua the high priest immediately set up an altar for burnt offerings and began rebuilding the temple. The people celebrated and applauded God when the foundation was complete. But enemies soon brought the work to a halt for nearly two decades (Ezra 4:5). In the meantime, everyone became preoccupied with building themselves lavish houses instead of completing the house of worship (Haggai 1:2–4).

God sets you free to live for him. But if you let opposition and distractions pull you away from his plans for you, you miss out on his best blessings. Stay on task and you'll have real reason to celebrate.

PRAY IT

God, help me press on in all the tasks you give me to do. Teach me to stay focused and finish the jobs I start.

day214 august 2

READ IT

Ezra 4:6–5:7, Romans 15:14–33, Psalm 90:1–10

> *"It has always been my ambition to preach the gospel where Christ was not known, so that I would not be building on someone else's foundation."*
>
> Romans 15:20

LIVE IT

God aims to give you ambitious dreams and concrete goals. Are you paying attention so he can show you what they might be?

The apostle Paul knows he is called to preach almost as soon as Jesus flashes a blinding light from heaven and drops the bad-tempered man to the ground. Paul immediately begins to tell the Jews that Jesus is God's Son (Acts 9:1–22). A while later he consciously chooses to take the message about Jesus to non-Jews (13:46). Somewhere along the way he develops a passion to preach Jesus in places the Lord was totally unknown.

The Bible presents countless people who are surprised by God's plan for their lives. Abraham hears a message from the Lord to pack up his family and journey to an unknown place (Genesis 12:1). Moses encounters God at a burning bush, where he's handed the task of leading an enormous multitude of slaves to freedom (Exodus 3:1–15). Ruth finds her destiny after her husband dies (Ruth 1:1–18). And Esther discovers her lifesaving mission after winning a beauty pageant to become queen of Persia (Esther 4:14).

As you study the lives of these believers, you discover what drives their ambition. They shift their focus off themselves to what the Lord wants them to do. They find their ultimate happiness in completing the tasks he gives them. They let God give them one-of-a-kind dreams. Even the most extreme stories here started when someone let God use them for his glory: God gave you gifts and a dream as well—keep your eyes open for where he wants to lead you.

PRAY IT

Lord, show me what you want me to do with my life—right now and as I take steps toward my future. I dream of serving you.

READ IT

Ezra 6:1–7:10, Romans 16:1–27, Psalm 90:11–17

> *"Then the people of Israel— the priests, the Levites and the rest of the exiles— celebrated the dedication of the house of God with joy."*
>
> EZRA 6:16

LIVE IT

God's people finally had a real reason to celebrate. Their work on the temple got off to a nice start, then stalled. Two decades later they had pushed through every kind of opposition. Now their job was done.

Opposition to building the temple began when Judah's neighbors heard about the project. Their offer of assistance sounded good at first, but these sly enemies weren't part of God's people. They had been forcibly resettled in the land just as the people of Judah had been taken captive to Babylon. To them the Lord was merely one of many gods. They didn't even know his proper name, Yahweh (Ezra 4:1–5).

Their opposition made the people afraid to build, and their complaints to a new king, Artaxerxes, forced the work to stop altogether. Only when the prophets Haggai and Zechariah came on the scene did work begin again (5:1–3). They stood up for their right to rebuild the temple, convincing yet another king, Darius, to let them proceed. Darius even stepped up and paid for the project from his royal treasury, supplying everything needed for the task.

When you set your mind on serving God, he will ensure you accomplish his plans. Yet his help doesn't mean you won't face ferocious opposition. If you give up at the first sign of trouble, you might never know what he can accomplish through you.

PRAY IT

God, you know all the things that can make me afraid to keep serving you. I count on you to help me finish everything you ask me to do.

day216 august 4

READ IT

Ezra 7:11 – 8:14, 1 Corinthians 1:1 – 17, Proverbs 19:3 – 12

> *"I appeal to you, brothers and sisters, in the name of our Lord Jesus Christ, that all of you agree with one another in what you say and that there be no divisions among you, but that you be perfectly united in mind and thought."*
>
> 1 CORINTHIANS 1:10

LIVE IT

Jesus had you in mind as he prayed just hours before he went to the cross. In John 17 he asks his Father to show off his glory. He asks for protection for his disciples, people who walked with him on earth. Then he pleads that you and every other believer would experience total unity. Only then will the rest of the world be convinced his love is real (vv. 1 – 26).

Around two decades after Jesus utters this prayer, the apostle Paul saw divisions threatening to split up the church in Corinth. Some in Corinth claimed loyalty to him, their founding pastor (Acts 18:1 – 8). Others preferred Apollos, an intellectual speaker, or Peter, who emphasized Jewish ministry. Some claimed to follow only Jesus, but those spiritual-sounding people likely considered themselves superior to others. Paul told everyone to get rid of these factions and regroup around the gospel, the message of what Jesus accomplished on the cross.

Churches are famous for being rife with petty bickering and divisions, bad habits that infect not only adults but youth. If you cut yourself off from other Christians, you won't grow into the maturity God has in store for you. If you cause fights and factions within your church or youth group, the Lord takes serious offense. Get to work and figure out how to get back together with your Christian sisters and brothers.

PRAY IT

Lord, I need friends who follow you. Don't let petty issues split us up. We want to experience the unity you expect us to enjoy.

READ IT

Ezra 8:15–9:15, 1 Corinthians 1:18–2:5, Psalm 91:1–8

> *"For the message of the cross is foolishness to those who are perishing, but to us who are being saved it is the power of God."*
>
> 1 Corinthians 1:18

LIVE IT

God wants you and his people to unite around more than having a good time together. Or a particular style of dazzling music. Or a reputation for tradition or influence or hipness that spreads far and wide. The one factor that brings every Christian together is Jesus dying on the cross and rising from the dead.

The apostle Paul just told the Corinthian believers to get over their divisions. He now explains what holds them together. Some people in that culture (and in their church) wanted brilliant explanations of God. These Greek-influenced people valued intellectual arguments, and to them the story of a Savior dying on a cross didn't make sense. Other people in Corinth (and in their church) demanded miraculous signs to prove they should follow Jesus. These people valued their traditions above all else, and to them the cross was unimaginably shameful.

Paul urged both groups to accept the cross as God's solution to human sin. Only the death of Jesus provides a way back to God. The message of the cross might sound foolish, but it's the means God uses to save people (Romans 1:16).

The Lord doesn't want you to be empty-headed, and sometimes he does perform miracles to demonstrate his power. But above all he wants you to hold tight to the news of the cross. It's how he makes you his friend.

PRAY IT

God, the cross is the only way I can get right with you. Sometimes it doesn't make sense to me, but you're wiser than all of us put together.

day218 august 6

READ IT

Ezra 10:1–44, 1 Corinthians 2:6–16, Psalm 91:9–16

> *"'Because he loves me,' says the* Lord*, 'I will rescue him; I will protect him, for he acknowledges my name.'"*
>
> Psalm 91:14

LIVE IT

Ever feel like you need divine protection? The soaring words of Psalm 91 will make you feel like you're wearing a bulletproof jumpsuit.

Notice where this song starts. You experience calm when you make the Lord your shelter (v. 1). Then the Lord makes amazing promises to guard you. He saves you from cunning traps and deadly diseases (v. 3). You find protection in the Lord like a chick hides under its mother's wings (v. 4). You don't have to fear enemies that stalk by night or epidemics that strike by day (vv. 5–6). Even if ten thousand bodies drop dead at your side, you have nothing to fear (v. 7).

When you count on God as your refuge, disasters can't overtake you (vv. 9–10). The Lord tells his angels to guard you wherever you go and lift you out of danger (v. 12). You dance on cobras and sharp-toothed beasts (v. 13).

Nothing in this song promises to remove you from the swirl of evil going on all around you. And Jesus himself knew not to take God for granted or push the limits of his protection (Matthew 4:5–7). The end of this song offers you the Lord's ultimate protection. One day he will show you his salvation, bringing you home to live forever in heaven.

PRAY IT

God, protect me from evils that threaten to do me in. I trust you to be my shelter. I feel calm when I rest next to you.

READ IT

Nehemiah 1:1 – 2:20, 1 Corinthians 3:1 – 23, Psalm 92:1 – 15

> *"Those who survived the exile and are back in the province are in great trouble and disgrace. The wall of Jerusalem is broken down, and its gates have been burned with fire."*
>
> Nehemiah 1:3

LIVE IT

Almost a century after captives returned from Babylon to rebuild God's temple in Jerusalem, Nehemiah receives an urgent message from home. He discovers the returnees are still struggling to survive, with the holy city's protective walls flattened and its thick gates burned.

Nehemiah weeps at this news. For days he grieves and goes without food. Then he prays. He reminds his awesome God of his loving care. He begs God to pay attention to his words. He confesses wrongs done by him and the entire nation. Then he pleads with the Lord to keep his promises to protect his people.

Nehemiah serves as the king of Persia's trusted cupbearer, the guy who samples royal food and drink to ensure it isn't poisoned. He lives hundreds of miles from Jerusalem, yet he refuses to forget about far-off troubles. He seeks help from his powerful boss, then travels in secret to Jerusalem. He surveys the damage and gathers his fellow citizens to reconstruct the wall.

This smart and compassionate man demonstrates steps you can take to make a difference in your hurting world. Start with prayer, make a plan, and then do your part. You can press the Lord to solve the problem, then do everything in your power to work hard and rally others to the cause. You won't accomplish anything if you pray and then stop. Dig in and get things done.

PRAY IT

God, give me a heart that grieves with you for tragedies I see all around me. I count on you to act. And I won't walk away from the problem.

day220 august 8

READ IT

Nehemiah 3:1–4:23, 1 Corinthians 4:1–21, Proverbs 19:13–22

> *"Discipline your children, for in that there is hope; do not be a willing party to their death."*
>
> Proverbs 19:18

LIVE IT

Parents aren't all that tough to understand. Just try to look at yourself through their eyes. What do they see—and hope to see? Then try taking a few mental steps in their shoes. What are they responsible for—at home, at work, and in raising you?

God gives parents a staggering opportunity. He commands them to nurture children to know him well and thrive in every part of life. The Bible tells parents to "start children off on the way they should go," so that "even when they are old they will not turn from it" (Proverbs 22:6). They should train you to follow God's commands, talking about them "when you sit at home and when you walk along the road, when you lie down and when you get up" (Deuteronomy 6:7). God expects them to bring you up "in the training and instruction of the Lord" (Ephesians 6:4).

The Lord knows that parents aren't perfect. They discipline you the best they know how (Hebrews 12:10). After all, guiding and correcting you is their only good option. If they don't discipline you, they risk watching you walk off a cliff, hurting yourself spiritually, emotionally, physically, or morally.

You have a choice today to work with your parents or against them. When you let them do their job, you avoid doing yourself harm that will do you in.

PRAY IT

God, sometimes I struggle with my parents. Help me understand the job you give them. Help me live up to what they teach me.

READ IT

Nehemiah 5:1 – 7:3, 1 Corinthians 5:1 – 13, Psalm 93:1 – 5

> *"When all our enemies heard about this, all the surrounding nations were afraid and lost their self-confidence, because they realized that this work had been done with the help of our God."*
>
> Nehemiah 6:16

LIVE IT

Jerusalem's residents got to work as soon as Nehemiah persuaded them it was possible to rebuild the protective wall that ringed the city. Even when they endured fierce opposition, they didn't stop until they were done.

Don't skip over key details of this divine construction project. Right from the start the builders face ridicule and lies (Nehemiah 2:19). People take responsibility for specific portions of the job (3:1 – 32). A few popular people refuse to lift a finger to help (v. 5). When enemies mock, workers pray (4:1 – 5). Because almost everyone decides to work hard, the wall quickly reaches half its height (v. 6).

Those problems and solutions fit any job you will ever do. And there's more. When enemies threaten to attack, the people think smart, both praying to God and posting a guard night and day (v. 9). The builders depend on the Lord for protection and strength (v. 14). When the wall is finished, everyone near and far knows only God could have powered their work.

The book of Nehemiah is all about seeing a problem, getting a God-sized solution, and working hard to finish the task. Don't think you can accomplish that kind of job on your own. No matter what tasks you need to get done today, God wants you to lean on him for power and encouragement.

PRAY IT

Lord, you know the tasks piled on me right now. I want to work hard, and I need your support. Give me everything I need to get the job done.

day222 august 10

READ IT

Nehemiah 7:4–8:18, 1 Corinthians 6:1–20, Psalm 94:1–11

> *"If any of you has a dispute with another, do you dare to take it before the ungodly for judgment instead of before the Lord's people?"*
>
> 1 Corinthians 6:1

LIVE IT

You probably haven't ever taken a friend to court, suing to solve a conflict. But you likely have carried a fight into the court of public opinion, telling everyone about your issue and trying to win them to your side.

The apostle Paul had no patience with Christians who sued each other in Roman courts presided over by pagan judges. Those judges "scorn" or "regard as worthless" any faith in Jesus or obedience to his commands. Paul orders believers to settle their conflicts among themselves. By resorting to court they displayed their own lack of wise maturity. It would be better to let themselves be wronged than show off their ignorance among unbelievers.

Jesus taught a solid way to solve disputes. When someone has wronged you, go straight to that person one-on-one and gently point out what he or she did wrong. If that fails, bring along a mature helper, not to gang up on your opponent but to assist you in talking things through. If you still haven't solved your issue, appeal to someone in authority. And if that step doesn't fix a serious conflict, you might need to take a time out from that relationship (Matthew 18:15–17).

As a follower of Jesus you don't score points with anyone when you don't deal well with conflict. Fights aren't your chance to win big. They give you an opportunity to show God's wisdom, love, and grace to people who wrong you.

PRAY IT

Lord, train me to show others the love you show me. I want to solve conflicts your way.

READ IT

Nehemiah 9:1–37, 1 Corinthians 7:1–16, Psalm 94:12–23

"On the twenty-fourth day of the same month, the Israelites gathered together, fasting and wearing sackcloth and putting dust on their heads."

NEHEMIAH 9:1

LIVE IT

A few weeks before the scene in Nehemiah 9, the people of Israel assembled in a public square. They asked Ezra the priest to bring out the Book of the Law, the early Old Testament books that recorded all of God's commands. Everyone old enough to understand listened attentively as he read from dawn until noon (Nehemiah 8:1–3).

Other leaders explained Ezra's words so no one would be confused about the Lord's expectations. As the people listened, they began to weep. Nehemiah told the people not to cry but to celebrate their great God. "The joy of the LORD is your strength," he said (v. 10).

But now the people gather again. They go without food, put on rough clothes, and cover their heads with dust—all signs of mourning. They worship the Lord, but they also pour out the grief that overwhelms their hearts. They realize God always keeps his promises to them. He's gracious and compassionate, rich in love. He provides for their physical needs and drives out their enemies. Yet the people admit they have sinned against him again and again.

The Lord enjoys when you celebrate his awesome greatness. But there are times to feel sorrow for what you do wrong. Pour out your heart to God and admit where you fail. When you confess your sins, you can be sure the Lord forgives them (1 John 1:8–9).

PRAY IT

God, I'm sad about my sins. I'm tired of the way I hurt myself, other people, and you. Thanks for forgiving me and making me right with you.

day224 august 12

READ IT

Nehemiah 9:38 – 11:21, 1 Corinthians 7:17 – 35, Proverbs 19:23 – 20:4

> *"Sluggards do not plow in season; so at harvest time they look but find nothing."*
>
> Proverbs 20:4

LIVE IT

You don't want a teacher writing "sluggard" across the top of an essay. You definitely don't want a boss scrawling anything that ugly on a job review. The word "sluggard" derives from the "slug," a shell-free snail that oozes exceedingly slowly across leafy plants.

The book of Proverbs isn't short on wisdom about working hard. Your dreams need to be grounded in reality: "Those who work their land will have abundant food, but those who chase fantasies have no sense" (12:11). Big talk won't earn you a living: "All hard work brings a profit, but mere talk leads only to poverty" (14:23). You need to work for what you want: "A sluggard's appetite is never filled, but the desires of the diligent are fully satisfied" (13:4).

Proverbs 20:4 isn't hard to figure out. If you don't put seed in the ground at the right time, you won't reap a harvest. Or if you don't study, you won't succeed when you're tested. Or if you don't work on a big project in pieces, you will never get it done.

God didn't create you to sit around and do nothing. He designed you to work hard at everything he plans for you to do. Like Ephesians 2:10 says, "For we are God's handiwork, created in Christ Jesus to do good works, which God prepared in advance for us to do."

PRAY IT

God, teach me to plan my work and work my plan. I want to accomplish everything you have prepared for me to do.

READ IT

Nehemiah 11:22–12:47, 1 Corinthians 7:36–8:13, Psalm 95:1–11

> *"Today, if only you would hear his voice, 'Do not harden your hearts as you did at Meribah, as you did that day at Massah in the wilderness."*
>
> PSALM 95:7–8

LIVE IT

Meribah wasn't one of the Israelites' finest moments. Neither was Massah. In this song God speaks firsthand and tells you not to repeat the mistakes of his ancient people.

"Meribah" literally means "rebellion," and it refers to an episode of open revolt against God. After the Lord set his people free from slavery in Egypt (Exodus 12:31–42), he brought them to the edge of the land he had promised them long before. Twelve spies surveyed the new homeland and agreed it was impressive. But ten of those spies argued the inhabitants of the land were too powerful to conquer. They persuaded the people not to enter the land. When the masses rebelled against the Lord, he sentenced the entire generation to wandering in the desert until death (Numbers 32:1–13).

"Massah" and "meriban" was a wilderness site where the Israelites complained of dire thirst. God instructed Moses to speak to a rock and cause water to spring up. When Moses disobeyed and instead struck the rock with his staff, he too was banned from entering and enjoying the Promised Land (Numbers 20:2–13).

To be "hard-hearted" means you ignore God's voice and fight his instructions. It's when you disobey an obvious Bible command or block out the Holy Spirit's whisper pointing you the right way to go. You end up pushing God away and detouring from his best plans for you.

PRAY IT

Lord, I want to listen carefully for your voice and act on your commands. Teach me to obey you as soon as I hear you.

day226 august 14

READ IT

Nehemiah 13:1 – 31, 1 Corinthians 9:1 – 18, Psalm 96:1 – 13

> *"Am I not free? Am I not an apostle? Have I not seen Jesus our Lord? Are you not the result of my work in the Lord?"*
>
> 1 CORINTHIANS 9:1

LIVE IT

The apostle Paul cheerfully sacrificed for others. He told the Colossians "I rejoice in what I am suffering for you" (Colossians 1:24). He endured endless hardships to tell the world about Jesus (2 Corinthians 11:16 – 33). But he wasn't happy getting abuse by Christians who knew better.

The Corinthians weren't an easy group to lead. They lived in a sophisticated city of nearly half a million residents from across the empire. Corinth was the most important business center in Greece and host to the Isthmian games, a competition equal to the ancient Olympics. Pagan religions flourished, complete with rampant ritual prostitution.

Paul started the church in Corinth, and he stayed in the city for eighteen months (Acts 18:1 – 11). But even his rigorous teaching couldn't change the people overnight. They struggled with pride and divisions (1 Corinthians 1:10 – 2:5) as well as sexual sin (6:15 – 19). When Paul writes this letter a couple of years after his time with them, they question his credentials and his right to be paid for preaching. He defends himself and calls out their insulting behavior.

Living all-out for God doesn't mean you need to put up with abuse from others, especially other believers. Like Jesus said, you can go and gently show others their sin (Matthew 18:15 – 19). And his words here remind you to respect people who teach you about God.

PRAY IT

Lord, show me how to deal with people who treat me badly. And I want to give respect to people who dedicate their lives to serving you.

READ IT

Esther 1:1–2:18, 1 Corinthians 9:19–10:13, Psalm 97:1–12

> *"Now the king was attracted to Esther more than to any of the other women.... So he set a royal crown on her head and made her queen instead of Vashti."*
>
> Esther 2:17

LIVE IT

No one expects to find a beauty pageant in the middle of the Bible, yet that's the scene at the start of the famous story of Esther.

King Xerxes of Persia ruled an empire stretching from India to Sudan. He threw nonstop parties to entertain leaders from across his kingdom. One day he commanded his wife, Queen Vashti, to flaunt her beauty for his drunken male guests, and she refused. To ensure that other wives wouldn't disrespect their husbands, the king arranged a beauty pageant to choose a new queen.

Esther is a young woman gathered to the king's harem. She received a year of spa treatments to impress the king. When she won Xerxes' heart and everyone's favor, the king made her the new queen. And by the time the story ends, Esther will prove she has even more brains than beauty.

The Bible isn't down on physical attractiveness, but it also doesn't let good looks take top place. It says to boast about your powerful God instead of your own brute strength (Jeremiah 9:23). It advises that real beauty comes not from clothes and accessories but from inner character, a message that applies to both girls and guys (1 Timothy 2:8–10). It cautions that outward appeal won't last but that respect for God keeps its value forever (Proverbs 31:30).

God doesn't say you have to go around looking ugly. But your heart is in the wrong place if that's what matters most to you.

PRAY IT

God, I value what you value. Looks aren't everything. Living for you is infinitely more important.

day228 august 16

READ IT

Esther 2:19–5:14, 1 Corinthians 10:14–11:1, Proverbs 20:5–14

> *"So whether you eat or drink or whatever you do, do it all for the glory of God."*
>
> 1 Corinthians 10:31

LIVE IT

You can spend the rest of your life studying the Bible and still not grasp everything there is to know. But the biggest of the Lord's big commands aren't tough to remember.

God wants you to love him above everything else and love people almost as much. Jesus says, " 'Love the Lord your God with all your heart and with all your soul and with all your mind.' This is the first and greatest commandment. And the second is like it: 'Love your neighbor as yourself' " (Matthew 22:37–39). That's the *Great Commandment.*

Jesus wants you to be part of telling the world about him. He says, "Therefore go and make disciples of all nations, baptizing them in the name of the Father and of the Son and of the Holy Spirit, and teaching them to obey everything I have commanded you" (Matthew 28:19–20). That's the *Great Commission.*

And the apostle Paul gives you one more unforgettable command. It's a test that tells you moment-by-moment if you're fully on track with the Lord. He writes, "Whatever you do, do it all for the glory of God" (1 Corinthians 10:31). There's no special name for that verse, but it tells you to always put God first. Whatever situation you're in, you glorify him by striving to show off his greatness. You aim to honor him in every thought, word, and action.

PRAY IT

God, forgive me when I don't live to show off your greatness. I'm making it my goal to honor you.

READ IT

Esther 6:1–8:17, 1 Corinthians 11:2–34, Psalm 98:1–9

> *"For how can I bear to see disaster fall on my people? How can I bear to see the destruction of my family?"*
>
> Esther 8:6

LIVE IT

Plenty of action has swept by since Esther won the role of queen in a royal beauty pageant.

Not long after Esther rose to the throne, her elder cousin Mordecai courts trouble for refusing to bow to an arrogant government official named Haman. In a fit of revenge, Haman plots to kill not just the disrespectful Mordecai but all his people (Esther 3:5–6). Mordecai and the Jews weep and wail at their impending death, and he pleads with Esther to bring the matter to the attention of the king. Xerxes doesn't yet realize his young queen was born to the people his own edict allows to be killed. Yet Esther protests that she can't approach the king without being called into his presence, as entering without permission is an offense that carries a sentence of death. (4:1–11).

Esther faces a choice to brave the king's wrath and put her life on the line for the sake of her people. Mordecai warns that Esther won't escape the slaughter even if she hides her true identity, and he suggests God has made her queen "for such a time as this" (v. 14).

You might never face a situation where you have to risk your life or physical safety for the sake of your family or people. But if you know what you're willing to die for, you know what's worth living for.

PRAY IT

God, I want to live for everything that's truly important—for you, for people, and for causes you care about.

day230 august 18

READ IT

Esther 9:1 – 10:3, 1 Corinthians 12:1 – 26, Psalm 99:1 – 9

> *"There are different kinds of gifts, but the same Spirit distributes them.... Now to each one the manifestation of the Spirit is given for the common good."*
>
> 1 Corinthians 12:4, 7

LIVE IT

You're awesomely gifted, and you might not even know it. Your God makes you and every other believer an unbreakable promise to endow you with special spiritual abilities.

Back at the start of this letter, the apostle Paul called out the bitter fights brewing between various groups in the church in Corinth. They made all kinds of excuses for their opinions and divisions (1 Corinthians 1:10 – 17, 3:1 – 4). Now Paul gives the believers a reason to pull together.

Paul starts off by saying he doesn't want the Corinthians to be ignorant about "the gifts of the Spirit" (12:1). These signs of God's working in and through people can look radically different, but they all flow from the same Holy Spirit. Some people might have unmatched wisdom. Others have abilities that look clearly supernatural, like the gift of prophecy. Still others have gifts that look a lot like everyday natural talents. Paul says more about these gifts in Romans 12:3 – 8 and Ephesians 4:7 – 16.

God gives you a crucial gift for the benefit of everyone around you inside the church and out. When you and other Christians each use the abilities God puts inside you, everyone grows up spiritually. But if anyone looks down on others or thinks their own gift is unimportant, everyone suffers. It's like a body missing a part. You can't survive without others, and they can't survive without you.

PRAY IT

Lord, show me my gifts and help me learn how to put them to work. I want to use my gifts to help others grow.

august 19

day231

READ IT

Job 1:1–3:26, 1 Corinthians 12:27–13:13, Psalm 100:1–5

> *"Naked I came from my mother's womb, and naked I will depart. The LORD gave and the LORD has taken away; may the name of the LORD be praised."*
>
> JOB 1:21

LIVE IT

The man Job (rhymes with "robe") ranks near the top of any list of the Bible's most prominent people. His story was probably written in King Solomon's era, and his reputation as "the greatest man among all the peoples of the East" (Job 1:3) likely locates him in the ancient land of Edom. But the Bible's account of Job's suffering intrigues people in every time and place.

Satan was conversing with the Lord when he suggested that Job lived uprightly only because the Lord filled his life with so many blessings. God agreed to let Satan prove his point by testing Job. Soon fire and marauders destroyed Job's wealth. Wind killed his children. Oozing sores afflicted his body from head to toe.

Whether blessings come or go, Job still trusted God, even though his wife told him to curse the Lord and die. When three friends showed up, they barely recognized him. They sat with him and wept night and day for a week, unable to say anything because of Job's horrible pain. When they finally spoke, their words weren't exactly comforting.

The book of Job helps you think through tough issues like why good people suffer. It teaches you what to say—or not say—to hurting friends. In the end you find that questions about good and evil aren't always easy to answer. But you can be sure that no matter what you suffer, the Lord is worth trusting.

PRAY IT

God, I don't understand why good people suffer. But I trust that your love for me never stops.

day232 august 20

READ IT

Job 4:1 – 7:21, 1 Corinthians 14:1 – 19, Proverbs 20:15 – 24

"A gossip betrays a confidence; so avoid anyone who talks too much."

PROVERBS 20:19

LIVE IT

Sharing a secret fact or feeling is like handing others an enormous diamond. It's natural for them to gleefully pull it out, check it over, spin it around, and show it off. Trust yourself to the wrong person, and your hidden gem soon goes on public display.

Proverbs 20:19 might sound harsh when it advises you to stay clear of people who endlessly chatter, but it makes complete sense. People with mouths in constant motion are sure to make trouble, because the more words they spill, the more likely they will say something meant to be kept private. Even if you swear a mouthy person to secrecy, sooner or later the rest of the world ends up hearing a secret you thought was safe.

Maybe you're the one with a nonstop mouth. It's almost impossible not to become a gossip, a person who betrays other people's confidence. When you pass along things you shouldn't, you're sure to face rage. Like Proverbs 13:3 says, "Those who guard their lips preserve their lives, but those who speak rashly will come to ruin."

God says, "Everyone should be quick to listen" and "slow to speak" (James 1:19). If you practice listening more than you talk, you won't often share things you shouldn't. When you care more about paying attention to people than trying to rule a conversation, you have less opportunity to spread what someone trusted you to keep safe.

PRAY IT

God, teach me to listen more than I talk. Alert me when I'm about to say something meant to be private.

READ IT

Job 8:1–10:22, 1 Corinthians 14:20–40, Psalm 101:1–8

> *"Does God pervert justice? Does the Almighty pervert what is right? When your children sinned against him, he gave them over to the penalty of their sin."*
>
> Job 8:3–4

LIVE IT

At the start of Job's story his friends couldn't have been more helpful. They rush to his side. They weep at his pain. They stay close with a man whose only relief is scraping open sores with a slice of broken pottery. And they don't try to give quick and easy answers to a situation too bad for words. Counselors call this "being present" for people.

Then the three friends open their mouths. Their arguments sound impressive, but they give their hurting friend messed-up advice. Eliphaz speaks first, arguing that Job must have purposely sinned to deserve such pain. Bildad commands Job to stop questioning God. And Zophar orders Job to repent—to quit sinning and turn to God. These three men each speak three times during the book. Job counters their arguments each time.

Eliphaz, Bildad, and Zophar all mistakenly argue that bad things always happen as a result of someone's sin. Because Job faces terrible pain, they think he must have committed terrible sins. The more Job protests his innocence, the more they continue to heap guilt on him.

You know the inside scoop on Job: God knows Job is a good man. Even Satan realizes Job's righteousness. Job is undergoing a spiritual test, but none of the humans in the story can see that. People can try with all their might to figure out pain and suffering, but only the Lord knows the whole truth.

PRAY IT

God, I want to understand why bad things happen to me and other people. But you're the only one who ever knows everything.

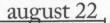

day234 august 22

READ IT

Job 11:1 – 14:22, 1 Corinthians 15:1 – 34, Psalm 102:1 – 11

> *"For what I received I passed on to you as of first importance: that Christ died for our sins according to the Scriptures, that he was buried, that he was raised on the third day according to the Scriptures."*
>
> 1 Corinthians 15:3 – 4

LIVE IT

If you're looking for a tight way to remember what you believe as a Christian, this passage is it. The apostle Paul sums up the core truths of your faith.

Paul starts by declaring he didn't make up any of what he's about to say. He received this package of truths both from Old Testament prophets who foresaw Jesus's arrival and from New Testament eyewitnesses to the Lord's birth, life, death, and resurrection.

Then Paul unfurls facts you don't want to forget. Jesus died for your sins, which was predicted in passages like Isaiah 53:8 – 10. His death wasn't a prank or an illusion, and no one in those days argued that his lifeless body wasn't buried. After three days Jesus rose from the dead, as foretold in the Lord's own promise in Matthew 12:40.

Eyewitnesses guarantee that Jesus's resurrection was a real event. He appeared to Peter (Cephas), his closest followers, and his half-brother, James. Paul was the last person to see Jesus back from the dead (Acts 9:1 – 5). And the resurrected Jesus once appeared to a crowd of more than five hundred people. Paul mentions that most of these people were still living, so his readers could check the facts for themselves (1 Corinthians 15:6).

You don't have to wonder about what you believe. God lays out the basic facts for you and everyone else to examine.

PRAY IT

God, sometimes I feel lost in all the Bible's facts and commands and details. You make clear what's most important.

august 23 **day235**

READ IT

Job 15:1–18:21, 1 Corinthians 15:35–49, Psalm 102:12–17

> *"So will it be with the resurrection of the dead. The body that is sown is perishable, it is raised imperishable; it is sown in dishonor, it is raised in glory; it is sown in weakness, it is raised in power."*
>
> 1 CORINTHIANS 15:42–43

LIVE IT

You might not plan much beyond the next minute, day, or week. Even if you like to dream about what the rest of your life might bring, it's mind blowing to ponder what lies on the other side of your own death. Yet one thing is sure: God has a heavenly body in store for you.

Jesus made clear that his followers will live forever. Some of the Bible's most famous words say that whoever believes in Jesus "shall not perish but have eternal life" (John 3:16). Jesus said that anyone who has faith in him has already "crossed over from death to life" (5:24). Jesus pointed out his own power to raise the dead when he called himself "the resurrection and the life" (11:25).

Paul admits you might have a tough time making sense of what your body will be like when you come back to life. But he says your body will be "imperishable" or permanently indestructible, full of "glory" and "power" (1 Corinthians 15:42–43). You will possess a "spiritual body" unlike the physical shell you occupy right now (v. 44).

That's a splendor you can barely begin to understand. Whatever your heavenly body is like, it will resemble Jesus more than ever, showing off "the image of the heavenly man" (v. 49).

PRAY IT

God, I know you will raise me to life after I die. I can't grasp what my body will be like, but I trust you to make it better than anything I can ever imagine.

day236 august 24

READ IT

Job 19:1 – 21:34, 1 Corinthians 15:50 – 16:4, Proverbs 20:25 – 21:4

"The glory of young men is their strength, gray hair the splendor of the old."

PROVERBS 20:29

LIVE IT

Look at your face in the mirror, then picture yourself with wrinkled skin. It sags under your eyes, across your cheeks, and beneath your chin. Imagine your forehead with deep creases from worry and surprise. Your mouth is ringed by lines from a lifetime of smiles. Top off your self-portrait with a head full of silver hair. Now tell yourself you're beautiful.

You're engulfed by a culture that loves everything young. People prefer to be smooth and strong rather than saggy and weak. They would rather run all-out than shuffle along. When you're at a point in life where you're closer to getting your driver's license than getting it taken away, why should you care?

Old people have experience you can only begin to grasp. The Lord promises to teach you as long as you live (Psalm 71:17). He will be your God until your last breath (Isaiah 46:4). So the older you get, the wiser you become. Like Job 12:12 asks, "Is not wisdom found among the aged? Does not long life bring understanding?"

God puts older people in your life to instruct and guide you. Yet you'll miss out on all their insights if you don't value them enough to pay attention. Do like Leviticus 19:32 says: "Stand up in the presence of the aged, show respect for the elderly and revere your God."

PRAY IT

Lord, I won't ignore the older and elderly people you bring into my life. Use them to teach me things I don't even know I need to learn.

august 25

day237

READ IT

Job 22:1 – 24:25, 1 Corinthians 16:5 – 16:24, Psalm 102:18 – 28

> *"Is it for your piety that he rebukes you and brings charges against you? Is not your wickedness great? Are not your sins endless?"*
>
> Job 22:4 – 5

LIVE IT

As if it isn't bad enough that Job had to put up with the loss of everything that mattered to him — his family, riches, and health — he now had to listen to his so-called friends pelt him with lies.

Eliphaz, Bildad, and Zophar all started with a wrong assumption that life's painful experiences are the Lord's payback for wrongdoing. They thought God automatically and instantly sent consequences for sin. In their eyes someone's suffering was therefore undeniable proof of their evil behavior.

Jesus himself debunks that way of thinking. He points out that all people do wrong and will one day die if they don't repent — if they don't quit sinning and turn to God. But experiencing a disaster doesn't make someone more guilty than anyone else (Luke 13:1 – 5).

Since the start of this book, Job has protested his innocence. When Eliphaz can't spot anything Job has done wrong, he makes up false accusations. He says Job has cheated the poor, refused to feed the hungry, and mistreated orphans (Job 24:7 – 10).

When people decide to make you a target, you often can't shut them up. If they can't find a fault to pick at, they invent one. Your only real choice in that situation is to do what Job did. You keep trusting God (Psalm 25:1 – 2). Keep believing in yourself (17:3). And keep doing right (1 Peter 3:8 – 17).

PRAY IT

God, you know all my good points and all the ways I struggle. Help me stand strong when people pick on me.

day238 august 26

READ IT

Job 25:1–29:25, 2 Corinthians 1:1–11, Psalm 103:1–12

> *"Praise be to . . . the God of all comfort, who comforts us in all our troubles, so that we can comfort those in any trouble with the comfort we ourselves receive from God."*
>
> 2 Corinthians 1:3–4

LIVE IT

The last thing you want to hear when you suffer any kind of pain is that "God always makes good come out of a bad situation." Those words can sting if you say them right away to a hurting friend. But that doesn't mean they're not true.

The apostle Paul knew all about pain. He tells his friends in Corinth he doesn't want them to be ignorant of the troubles he faced in Asia, which is part of modern-day Turkey. While Paul doesn't spill the details here, he might be talking about a riot in Ephesus that nearly killed him (Acts 19:23–41). Paul felt so much pressure he didn't think he could survive. He wasn't even sure he wanted to live.

During that time of awful suffering Paul mastered a couple of lessons. He discovered he could rely on God instead of himself. And he grew confident the Lord was powerful enough to rescue him again and again.

When Paul looks back at the comfort God gave him in the midst of his trouble, he realizes he can help others by passing along the same comfort he received from God. Like you or your hurting friends, he needed time to think that through. In the end, something good came out of his unbearable pain.

Don't ever waste the compassion you feel from the Lord when you suffer. Don't forget to pass along the comfort you get from him.

PRAY IT

God, you help me when I'm down and ache deep inside. Teach me how to show others the care you show me.

august 27

day239

READ IT

Job 30:1–32:22, 2 Corinthians 1:12–22, Psalm 103:13–22

"As a father has compassion on his children, so the LORD has compassion on those who fear him; for he knows how we are formed, he remembers that we are dust."

PSALM 103:13–14

LIVE IT

The Bible speaks truth even when it might not feel good. It lets you spot the real you even if the picture isn't pretty. But there's always a sweet upside to seeing things as they really are. Like the fact that you're dust.

You might think being "dust" means you're ugly and worthless, a clump of fuzz living under your bed, hiding until it gets swept away. Yet that's not the message the Lord wants you to hear. He aims to make the point that you're formed from the stuff of the earth, and one day your body will disappear. Genesis 3:19 even fills out the details. It says, "Dust you are, and to dust you will return."

Calling you "grass" makes the same point. You're like desert grass that quickly grows and withers. Or you're like "a flower of the field" whose beauty blows away in a blast of hot wind.

God knows all this, but there's an upside. Because he realizes you and all human beings are frail and temporary, he cradles you with huge compassion. He doesn't treat you like your sins deserve (Psalm 103:10). His love for you is as everlasting and far-reaching as his own kingdom.

You might think you will last forever. You won't. Yet even in all your dustiness God values you like a priceless treasure. You can count on his compassion today and always.

PRAY IT

God, I'm weaker than I want to admit and someday my body will die. Thank you for your love that lasts forever.

day240 august 28

READ IT

Job 33:1–34:37, 2 Corinthians 1:23–2:11, Proverbs 21:5–16

> *"When a mocker is punished, the simple gain wisdom; by paying attention to the wise they get knowledge."*
>
> PROVERBS 21:11

LIVE IT

You get smart learning from others' mistakes. It's their pain, your gain. You can also grow wise studying others' successes. It's win-win for everyone. Either way, you have to pay attention in order to learn.

Some of the Bible's biggest cries of confusion come when bad people appear to get away with committing evil acts. The prophet Habakkuk asks God, "Why do you make me look at injustice? Why do you tolerate wrongdoing?" (Habakkuk 1:3). Asaph struggles when he sees "the prosperity of the wicked," people who never seem to struggle at anything (Psalm 73:3–4). Habakkuk and Asaph both found that the world suddenly made sense when God put a stop to evil, using other nations to punish the wicked people of Israel and Judah.

It's tempting to applaud when bad people get what they have coming. But it's better to just step back and learn the lessons they refused to master. A "mocker" is someone who sneers at God's commands. When a mocker faces punishment, even someone who has no sense at all can take note of the consequences of evil. Seeing those consequences gives you one more reason to avoid sin.

The real trick is to see through what looks like the success of evil people and spot those consequences even before they arrive. If you can foresee the bad results of disobeying the Lord, you stay smart. No one will be able to lure you into doing anything stupid.

PRAY IT

God, help me not be jealous of people who seem to get away with doing wrong. Help me learn from their mistakes.

READ IT

Job 35:1 – 37:24, 2 Corinthians 2:12 – 3:6, Psalm 104:1 – 18

"Unlike so many, we do not peddle the word of God for profit. On the contrary, in Christ we speak before God with sincerity, as those sent from God."

2 Corinthians 2:17

LIVE IT

Your life is on the line whenever you pick a hero. And the apostle Paul dared you to live differently from almost everyone around you when he said, "Follow my example, as I follow the example of Christ" (1 Corinthians 11:1).

The believers in Corinth knew Paul up close. He started their church, then hung around to teach them everything he could about Jesus (Acts 18:1 – 17). He spent much of his first letter to the Corinthians defending his qualifications to lead them and hold them accountable to obeying Christ. That theme continues as he writes them this second letter.

Paul says he's unlike so many of the religious teachers demanding his old friends' attention. He doesn't preach about Jesus to make money, using God for personal gain. He teaches about Jesus with "sincerity," pure motives that look out for their good. And he offers proof that he's sent from God. The Corinthians themselves are his ultimate recommendation. Their transformed lives are the result of Paul's solid work.

God wants you to be on guard when you pick spiritual teachers and other role models. Whether you're listening to pastors, youth workers, writers, musicians, or anyone else, they should all meet Paul's high standards. They shouldn't do the Lord's work from selfish motives. They must have your best interests in mind. And their efforts should bring righteous results. When you find heroes like that, you can dare to live like them.

PRAY IT

Lord, give me spiritual mentors worth imitating. Help me spot fakes and find authentic people I can trust.

day242 august 30

READ IT

Job 38:1–40:2, 2 Corinthians 3:7–18, Psalm 104:19–30

> *"Then the LORD spoke to Job out of the storm. He said: 'Who is this that obscures my plans with words without knowledge?'"*
>
> Job 38:1–2

LIVE IT

At first Eliphaz, Bildad, and Zophar won't stop talking. After their longwinded speeches fail to persuade Job to drop his defenses and quit complaining about God, young Elihu chimes in, angry that his elders can't silence one pitiful man (Job 32:3). As these four men take turns speaking throughout the book, Job answers them point by point.

Suddenly it's the Lord's turn to speak, and you catch right away he isn't happy with all the words these guys have spoken. After Job has uttered countless questions for God, now it's God's turn to probe Job.

Job shrinks as the Lord hits him with impossible questions. This troubled man wasn't around when God laid the earth's foundations (38:4). He doesn't tell the stars when to move (v. 31). The creatures of the earth don't serve him (39:27). When the Lord invites Job to answer, Job realizes he has nothing left to say (40:1–5). He concludes that God knows everything and can do anything (42:1–6). When Job repents, the Lord restores everything Job had lost (vv. 7–17).

God welcomes your big questions. He listens to your complaints. He hears your agonizing cries. But he won't settle for anything less than your total respect. Even when you can't understand everything life throws at you, God is in control. He always cares.

PRAY IT

God, I will never completely understand why bad things happen to me or other people. I choose to trust you no matter what I face.

READ IT

Job 40:3–42:17, 2 Corinthians 4:1–18, Psalm 104:31–35

> *"But we have this treasure in jars of clay to show that this all-surpassing power is from God and not from us."*
>
> 2 Corinthians 4:7

LIVE IT

Clay was everywhere in the ancient world. It was shaped into bricks and stacked into buildings. Clay seals stamped by signet rings proved ownership of crafts and homes, possibly even Jesus's tomb (Matthew 27:66). Clay formed a writing surface that could be hardened by the sun or the heat of a kiln. And all kinds of pottery were formed from clay, creating lamps, vases, dishes, and cooking pots.

Clay jars were common vessels found in every home. They were highly useful but easily broken. They weren't worth much. Archaeological digs around the world frequently unearth shattered jars in garbage pits.

So everyone knew what the apostle Paul meant when he compared himself to a clay jar. There was nothing special about him, an everyday container. But he held a treasure inside, the message about Jesus. God decided to use fragile clay vessels to carry the good news about Jesus to demonstrate that the real power comes only from him.

Paul doesn't feel bad about being a pot that easily cracks, and neither should you. God sends you to carry the message about Jesus to your world, and often that isn't easy. But don't lose heart. Even if you feel ready for the trash bin, God renews you every day. You can be hard pressed, but ultimately you won't be crushed. You might feel confused, but you don't have to despair. Even if you're struck down, you won't be destroyed.

PRAY IT

Lord, send me out to tell others about you. You're the real treasure I want people to see.

day244 september 1

READ IT

Ecclesiastes 1:1 – 3:23, 2 Corinthians 5:1 – 10, Proverbs 21:17 – 26

> *" 'Meaningless! Meaningless!' says the Teacher. 'Utterly meaningless! Everything is meaningless.' "*
>
> Ecclesiastes 1:2

LIVE IT

At first glance Ecclesiastes reads like a depressing note from a friend who spends too much time wallowing in dark thoughts. Read further and deeper, however, and soon you find that the book's gloomy backdrop makes God stand out even better and brighter.

The start of the book credits this piece of writing to "the Teacher," the son of David ruling in Jerusalem. That's Solomon, renowned as the wisest person who ever lived (1 Kings 4:29–34). The book tells the story of how the teacher goes on a hunt to find meaning in a world where everything is "meaningless," or "utterly empty" or "totally absurd." First he studies hard, but he decides wisdom is meaningless. He tests all kinds of pleasure and uses his riches to buy whatever he wants, but he ends up empty. He works hard, but he feels his toil is absurd. He gains riches, but he still feels poor.

As the Teacher tells his story and teaches, he captures frustrated feelings you might be afraid to say out loud. He says things that sound like poetry and lyrics, like Ecclesiastes 3:1 – 8, turned into a hit by the classic band the Byrds.

As you read this book, watch for the one thing that the Teacher never calls meaningless: the Lord and his commands. However pointless life might feel, God always gives you purpose.

PRAY IT

God, thanks that I can speak up to you when I feel frustrated by the pointless grind of life. I need you to make my days meaningful.

READ IT

Ecclesiastes 4:1 – 6:12, 2 Corinthians 5:11 – 6:2, Psalm 105:1 – 11

> *"And he died for all, that those who live should no longer live for themselves but for him who died for them and was raised again."*
>
> 2 Corinthians 5:15

LIVE IT

Homework will always be a chore until you decide you like to learn. Sports drills always get old if you don't fall in love with your game. In a similar way, living all-out for God won't ever happen freely and easily until something changes inside you.

As soon as you become a Christian, the Lord makes you a "new creation" (2 Corinthians 5:17). He forgives you and begins making you over. When that happens, his love begins to take over your heart. The more you experience that amazing love and grasp the awesome fact that Jesus died and rose for you, the more motivated you are to live for him.

That's what the apostle Paul means when he says, "Christ's love compels us" (v. 14). Christ's love inside you propels you from the inside out. You follow Jesus wholeheartedly because of what he's done for you. You obey because you want to, not because you have to.

Living all-out for God isn't about you trying harder or needing someone to force you to be spiritual. Your head might be convinced that following Jesus is the best way to live, but there might be times you aren't so sure. Wanting to please Christians you respect might energize you for a while, but that wears off. Love from the heart will keep you chasing Jesus for the rest of your life.

PRAY IT

Lord, you died for me so I can live for you. Help me to understand your love. Change me from the inside out so I want to follow you.

day246 september 3

READ IT

Ecclesiastes 7:1–9:12, 2 Corinthians 6:3–7:1, Psalm 105:12–22

> *"Do not be yoked together with unbelievers. For what do righteousness and wickedness have in common? Or what fellowship can light have with darkness?"*
>
> 2 Corinthians 6:14

LIVE IT

The religious leaders who battled Jesus often criticized his choice of friends. He hung out with obvious sinners like prostitutes and tax collectors, people the religious folks shunned in order to stay spiritually pure. Jesus retorted that he came like a doctor to help the sick. He said, "For the Son of Man came to seek and to save the lost" (Luke 19:10).

You wouldn't be a Christian if you didn't realize you need help. But now that you know Jesus, you're missing the point if you cut yourself off from people who still disrespect God or don't join you in following Jesus. He gives you the privilege of showing them the same love he would if he were standing in your shoes.

Jesus could hang out with even the wildest and worst evildoers without getting pulled into their sin. But that's a problem for you, because you're not Jesus. It's possible to get "yoked" to people who don't know Jesus, lashed together like a couple of cattle plowing a field. Instead of you pulling that person toward God, they can pull you into trouble.

Christians often point to 2 Corinthians 6:14 to prove you shouldn't date or marry a non-believer. That's a solid application of this Bible truth. But these words also alert you to rethink any relationship that drags you away from God.

PRAY IT

God, point out my relationships that don't help me follow you. Help me find ways to lead people toward you instead of me getting yanked away from you.

READ IT

Ecclesiastes 9:13–12:14, 2 Corinthians 7:2–16, Psalm 105:23–36

> *"Remember your Creator in the days of your youth, before the days of trouble come and the years approach when you will say, 'I find no pleasure in them.'"*
>
> ECCLESIASTES 12:1

LIVE IT

The Teacher tried everything and said it was all meaningless. "I have seen all the things that are done under the sun," he says. "All of them are meaningless, a chasing after the wind" (Ecclesiastes 1:14).

But not everything in life feels utterly absurd.

The Teacher finds pleasure in simple things. He says, "A person can do nothing better than to eat and drink and find satisfaction in their own toil. This too, I see, is from the hand of God, for without him, who can eat or find enjoyment?" (2:24–25). The Teacher also recognizes God blesses his followers. He declares, "To the person who pleases him, God gives wisdom, knowledge and happiness" (v. 2:26). And the Teacher realizes love brings meaning to life. He says, "Enjoy life with your wife, whom you love" (9:9).

The last pages of this book reveal the Teacher's ultimate answers to his quest for meaning. He instructs you first of all to remember God when you're still young. That's not telling you just to think about the Lord once in a while but to act every day on what you already know. And then the Teacher announces your core duty. You're to give God the respect he deserves and keep all his commands, because he's the one thing you can count on to give your life meaning (12:13).

PRAY IT

Lord, I can't always figure out the deep mysteries of life. But I have made up my mind to live for you.

day248 september 5

READ IT

Song of Solomon 1:1 – 4:16, 2 Corinthians 8:1 – 15, Proverbs 21:27 – 22:6

> *"Your hair is like a flock of goats descending from the hills of Gilead. Your teeth are like a flock of sheep just shorn, coming up from the washing. Each has its twin; not one of them is alone."*
>
> Song of Solomon 4:1 – 2

LIVE IT

Some day you might want to take a stab at writing love poetry, but it's not likely to come out sounding like the Song of Solomon. This tale of love celebrates human affection with imagery and honesty that might catch you by surprise.

Some readers see this book as a picture of God's love for his people. They say it honors the love between God and his Old Testament people, the Israelites, or the love shared by Jesus and his New Testament people, the church. But the most obvious way to interpret these words is simple and straightforward. They picture a man and woman who are crazy about each other.

This book doesn't hide the passion that flows between the author and a young country girl. You quickly learn that the Bible isn't bashful about physical love. After all, God created man and woman to bond in heart, mind, and body. Adam saw Eve and thought she was perfect, and the Lord planned right from the start that husband and wife would become "one flesh" (Genesis 2:24). That first couple felt no shame in being naked (v. 25).

The Song of Solomon makes an unmistakable push for purity, waiting for sexual intimacy until marriage. Solomon's bride kept herself pure as she grew up (Song of Solomon 8:8 – 10). And the book challenges you to "not arouse or awaken love" until God's right time (2:7).

PRAY IT

God, you designed human love. Help me stay pure for you and my future spouse. I trust you enough to obey your commands.

READ IT

Song of Solomon 5:1 – 8:14, 2 Corinthians 8:16 – 9:5, Psalm 105:37 – 45

> *"For he remembered his holy promise given to his servant Abraham. He brought out his people with rejoicing, his chosen ones with shouts of joy."*
>
> Psalm 105:42 – 43

LIVE IT

The story of God rescuing his people from slavery in Egypt is big. The "Exodus" is as significant to the Old Testament as the death and resurrection of Jesus are to the New Testament. Exodus 1 – 15 tells the full story of this great escape, but reminders of this epic event pop up throughout the Bible.

Psalm 105 starts by telling you to "Give praise to the Lord, proclaim his name; make known among the nations what he has done" (Psalm 105:1). Then it takes you on a historical tour of all the miracles he accomplished for the Israelites. The song recalls the promises God made to Abraham ... Joseph's rise to power ... the conspiracy among the Egyptians to enslave the Israelites ... the plagues that set his people free ... how the Lord led and fed his people in the desert.

God did powerful things to rescue his people from slavery. But there's a detail you don't want to overlook. The Exodus came about because the Lord made a promise. God told the patriarch Abraham to leave his home, vowing to give him a bountiful land (Genesis 12:1) and a family as numerous as the stars (15:5). While Abraham likely didn't expect the promise to take so long, or to take place under those circumstances, everything he was promised did come to pass, including his descendents receiving a country of their own after forty additional years.

When the Lord makes you a promise, he does whatever it takes to make it come true. He gives you reasons to praise him. He acts in astonishing ways to make you smile.

PRAY IT

God, I trust you to keep all of your promises to me. You never lie to me or trick me. You do whatever it takes to keep your word.

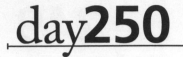

day250 september 7

READ IT

Isaiah 1:1–2:22, 2 Corinthians 9:6–15, Psalm 106:1–15

> *"Each of you should give what you have decided in your heart to give, not reluctantly or under compulsion, for God loves a cheerful giver."*
>
> 2 Corinthians 9:7

LIVE IT

You buy cookie dough from the soccer team. You pledge dollars to a friend trekking to fight cancer. You purchase a car wash coupon from the choir, and you don't even own a car.

God applauds generosity, especially when you give to people who are facing genuine hardship. The Lord doesn't just want you to have warm feelings toward the poor. He challenges you to put your money where your mouth is. Like 1 John 3:17–18 says, "If anyone has material possessions and sees a brother or sister in need but has no pity on them, how can the love of God be in that person? Dear children, let us not love with words or speech but with actions and in truth."

The New Testament gives details about a significant example of group generosity. As the apostle Paul traveled the Mediterranean on his third mission trip, he requested money for impoverished believers in Jerusalem (Romans 15:25–28). He praises the people of northern Greece for their gifts (2 Corinthians 8:15), and urges the Corinthians to be just as generous (8:16–9:5).

Paul applies gentle pressure for the Corinthians to give, explaining why it's the right thing to do. But God doesn't squeeze you to give. He would rather have you grapple with real needs, make up your mind how much to give, then give from the heart.

PRAY IT

God, help me find causes worth my support. I want to give with a smile to people and places that matter most to you.

READ IT

Isaiah 3:1–5:7, 2 Corinthians 10:1–18, Psalm 106:16–31

> *"Then they despised the pleasant land; they did not believe his promise. They grumbled in their tents and did not obey the LORD."*
>
> PSALM 106:24–25

LIVE IT

Suppose someone says a million dollars is buried in your yard. Unless you know your family abode was once owned by pirates or gangsters, the idea sounds preposterous. But if you believe the word of someone who claims to know the whereabouts of a tidy fortune, you won't let anything stop you from digging.

Psalm 106 tells of sad episodes where the ancient Israelites don't believe the Lord. They rebel as soon as God sets them free from slavery (Psalm 106:7). When the Lord dries up the Red Sea to let them escape the Egyptian army, they trust his promises for a while. But they soon forget his powerful acts and detour from his plan (v. 13).

Psalm 106 goes on to describe a couple of particularly awful instances of rebellion. Right when God is giving Moses his most important commandments, the people bow to a golden calf (Exodus 32:1–35). When he brings them up to the edge of the Promised Land, they refuse to enter (Numbers 13:26–14:45).

This song starts and ends with praise for the Lord's goodness and love, but the middle is full of the people's repeated failures. And there's one thing behind all those catastrophes. When God swears to give them incredible blessings, "they did not believe his promise" (Psalm 106:24).

If you struggle to follow God, maybe you don't really trust his promises to you. If you don't choose to rely on his word, his commands will always sound crazy.

PRAY IT

God, help me to trust what you say. I aim to listen to your warnings and lean on your promises.

day252 september 9

READ IT

Isaiah 5:8 – 8:10, 2 Corinthians 11:1 – 15, Proverbs 22:7 – 16

> *"In the year that King Uzziah died, I saw the Lord, high and exalted, seated on a throne; and the train of his robe filled the temple."*
>
> Isaiah 6:1

LIVE IT

Most people who plan to go to heaven don't know much about it. It's not as if every page of the Bible talks about the place God dwells, so passages that fill in the details should get your prime attention.

The start of the book of Isaiah spells out exactly when and where the prophet Isaiah spoke for the Lord. He brings messages from God to the southern kingdom of Judah "during the reigns of Uzziah, Jotham, Ahaz and Hezekiah" (Isaiah 1:1), which spanned from 792 to 699 BC.

Isaiah doesn't set out to be a mouthpiece for God. In the year King Uzziah dies, he peers into God's throne room. He must have been shocked at the sight of six-winged angels, called "seraphim," flying above the Lord. Their temple-rattling voices keep saying the same thing over and over: "Holy, holy, holy is the Lord Almighty; the whole earth is full of his glory" (6:3).

This passage doesn't really say what heaven looks like. But it's a place where God's servants constantly admire his total purity. They can't stop talking about his holiness. And in that throne room God reaches out, cleanses Isaiah, and assigns him the job of prophet.

You won't likely travel to heaven for a long time. But God forgives you right now. He wants to commission you. So ask him right now how he wants you to serve him.

PRAY IT

Lord, you forgive me. You send me to do your work in the world. Show me how and where you want me to serve you.

READ IT

Isaiah 8:11–10:19, 2 Corinthians 11:16–33, Psalm 106:32–39

> *"I have worked much harder, been in prison more frequently, been flogged more severely, and been exposed to death again and again."*
>
> 2 Corinthians 11:23

LIVE IT

When you read this passage you might wonder if the apostle Paul is posing as a tough guy, looking to score bragging rights for all his intense suffering for Jesus. But he's actually backing up his qualifications to speak for God.

Remember that at the start of 1 Corinthians, some believers in Corinth already favor other teachers more than Paul (1 Corinthians 1:10–17). They challenge his leadership (4:14–21). Now the situation has grown even more grim. Some say Paul is inferior to some "super-apostles" who look and sound more polished (2 Corinthians 11:5). Paul argues that these super-apostles are shallow at best. They're actually fakes who pretend to serve Christ. They resemble their master, Satan, who "masquerades as an angel of light" (v. 14).

Paul lists all the ways he's paid for preaching the message of Jesus, arguing that his suffering proves he's an authentic servant of God. The book of Acts reports a few of these specific events, like a stoning at Lystra (Acts 14:19) and a beating with rods in Philippi (16:22–23). It's clear Paul suffered far more than what Acts reveals.

Paul isn't merely offering proof of his authority for ancient readers. His words demonstrate why you can trust him. And when you suffer for your faith, you too prove you're truly on the Lord's side (1 Peter 1:6–9).

PRAY IT

God, I'm awed at what Paul suffered to serve you. I want to learn from your real servants. I want to stand up for you whatever the cost.

day254 september 11

READ IT

Isaiah 10:20 – 13:22, 2 Corinthians 12:1 – 10, Psalm 106:40 – 48

> *"Three times I pleaded with the Lord to take it away from me. But he said to me, 'My grace is sufficient for you, for my power is made perfect in weakness.'"*
>
> 2 Corinthians 12:8 – 9

LIVE IT

When you feel weak, you don't feel strong. Obvious, right? Not to the apostle Paul, who learned the hard way how the Lord turns weakness into strength.

Paul just finished describing his intense sufferings as a preacher of the good news about Jesus, everything from floggings to jail time to getting tossed overboard and washed ashore. As he continues to defend his credentials as God's spokesperson, he reveals that the Lord has given him startling visions. He's being modest when he says "I know a man who ..." then talks about being caught up into heaven. Paul found himself in paradise, where he heard things too wonderful to tell.

Paul says God wanted to make sure he didn't boast about these "surpassingly great revelations," so the Lord allowed him to be tormented by "a thorn in the flesh" (2 Corinthians 12:7). No one knows exactly what Paul suffered, but theories range from an eye problem to persistent enemies. Whatever "the thorn" is, no amount of pleading takes it away.

When you feel like you have your life together, you might forget to depend on God. As soon as you feel beat up, you discover reasons to turn to him. So while your weak points might annoy you, they remind you to keep counting on God. Let the Lord's kindness carry you, and you will discover your weakness amounts to nothing compared to his strength.

PRAY IT

God, you are bigger than any of my weak spots. Teach me to be patient when I feel powerless. I need you.

READ IT

Isaiah 14:1–16:14, 2 Corinthians 12:11–21, Psalm 107:1–9

> *"You said in your heart, 'I will ascend to the heavens; I will raise my throne above the stars of God.'"*
>
> Isaiah 14:13

LIVE IT

Tucked into Isaiah's prophecies against Babylon and its king comes a section many Bible students say vividly portrays Satan.

To see their logic you need to back up to Isaiah 13, where Isaiah begins a speech against Babylon, the empire that will ultimately defeat the southern kingdom of Judah and drag many of its inhabitants into captivity (2 Kings 25:1–21). In chapter 14, Isaiah begins to taunt the king of Babylon, who sought to rule the world (vv. 3–4).

No one doubts that Isaiah is speaking to the human ruler of an evil empire. But his words also seem to mean something more. Isaiah 14:12 says this person has "fallen from heaven." That's a figure of speech for being ejected from a high political position, but Jesus used it to describe the devil (Luke 10:18). Isaiah 14:12 also calls this person "the morning star," a poetic Hebrew name for the devil. This person tries to ascend to heaven and replace God, and his outrageous action sends him "down to the realm of the dead, to the depths of the pit" (v. 15).

While this passage doesn't explicitly name Satan, it at least illustrates how he operates. Whenever any of us try to put ourselves above the Lord, we imitate the devil's arrogance. If you think you're more important or intelligent than God, watch out.

PRAY IT

God, you're so high above me. I won't pretend I can take your place. I choose to submit to you in every way.

day256 september 13

READ IT

Isaiah 17:1 – 19:25, 2 Corinthians 13:1 – 14, Proverbs 22:17 – 27

> *"Do not make friends with a hot-tempered person, do not associate with one easily angered, or you may learn their ways and get yourself ensnared."*
>
> Proverbs 22:24 – 25

LIVE IT

That "hot-tempered person" in Proverbs 22:24 might sound like someone you know. Maybe even you. Hanging out with a friend with a short fuse puts you in danger of deadly blow-ups.

The Bible doesn't say all anger is wrong. Ephesians 4:26 says, "In your anger do not sin," showing that anger and sin are two different things. Yet it hints that anger often leads to sin. So the Bible says to not let anger burn but to sort out issues quickly (v. 26). If you don't, you give Satan entry to your life (v. 27). The Bible also points out that human anger doesn't produce the good lives God wants (James 1:20). It says there are times when it's wise to overlook wrongs done to you rather than get angry (Proverbs 19:11).

People with anger management issues aren't any better or worse than everyone else in the sins they struggle to overcome. But they do require careful handling. Proverbs 22:24 literally calls an angry person "a man of heat." Getting too close can get you burned. Anger acts like fire, with bad tempers leaping from person to person like flames spread across dry grass.

Anger isn't just a personality issue. God wants you to get rid of it, along with bitterness and rage (Ephesians 4:31). He aims for you to deal kindly and patiently with others, just like he puts up with you (v. 2).

PRAY IT

God, help me get rid of anger and treat people like you treat me. Show me how I can help family and friends get over their anger.

READ IT

Isaiah 20:1–23:18, Galatians 1:1–24, Psalm 107:10–22

> *"Am I now trying to win the approval of human beings, or of God? Or am I trying to please people? If I were still trying to please people, I would not be a servant of Christ."*
>
> Galatians 1:10

LIVE IT

You know God should come first in your life. Yet almost anything can push him out of the top spot. Sometimes it's possessions, being owned by your stuff and always craving more. Or it might be activities, getting so busy that God gets bumped from your schedule. But often it's people who take God's place.

The book of Galatians is one of the apostle Paul's most potent letters. It's written to Christians living in a region that's now central Turkey. Just a few sentences into his note, Paul accuses the Galatians of abandoning Jesus for a different message, one that puts them at risk of going to hell. False teachers are defying the truth that God saves people because of his kindness when they believe in Jesus, not because they do good works (Ephesians 2:8–9). These frauds say Christians have to follow Old Testament rituals like circumcision to get right with the Lord.

Paul bluntly announces that he deserves God's curse if he ever preaches anything except the real facts about Jesus. And he reveals the secret of his willingness to stand up for truth: He doesn't care what anyone else thinks.

It's impossible to keep following Jesus if people's opinions matter to you more than what God wants. Sometimes you can make both God and people happy. But sometimes you can't. Then whose voice are you going to listen to?

PRAY IT

God, I care a lot about what other people think. Show me when I let their voices come through louder than yours.

day258 september 15

READ IT

Isaiah 24:1 – 26:21, Galatians 2:1 – 10, Psalm 107:23 – 32

> *"You will keep in perfect peace those whose minds are steadfast, because they trust in you."*
>
> Isaiah 26:3

LIVE IT

The prophet Isaiah had the tough job of delivering news of ultimate doom. He says, "See, the Lord is going to lay waste the earth" (Isaiah 24:1). The message doesn't stop there. Because of human sin, destruction strikes everyone on earth. But people who rely on him escape. They see God's perfect faithfulness (25:1). The Lord wipes tears from their faces (v. 8). People feel relief when they count on him to save them (v. 9).

Then comes news you can use right now. Isaiah says, "Trust in the Lord forever, for the Lord, the Lord himself, is the Rock eternal" (26:4). When you trust in God, there's a mindboggling result. He keeps you in "perfect peace" (v. 3). "Peace" is a major Old Testament word meaning rest, completeness, and well-being in every part of you.

That peace is a gift you enjoy when your mind is "steadfast," not wavering in your commitment to God or your belief in him. It's the same promise the Lord makes later when he commands you "do not be anxious about anything" but instead "present your requests to God." When you do, "the peace of God, which transcends all understanding, will guard your hearts and your minds in Christ Jesus" (Philippians 4:6 – 7).

Trust God. His calm can carry you through anything. He gives you the kind of peace you can only get from him.

PRAY IT

God, I trust you to care for me in everything I face. You're my eternal Rock. Keep me in your perfect peace.

september 16 **day259**

READ IT

Isaiah 27:1 – 28:29, Galatians 2:11 – 3:9, Psalm 107:33 – 43

> *"He turned the desert into pools of water and the parched ground into flowing springs; there he brought the hungry to live."*
>
> Psalm 107:35 – 36

LIVE IT

God knows what you need exactly when you need it. He works his wonders at precisely the right time. He constantly gives you specific reasons to give thanks for his unfailing love. That's the point of Psalm 107.

Psalm 107 looks like the previous two psalms in a same-but-not-the-same sort of way. Each song recites a story. Psalm 105 recaps the Israelites' miraculous escape from slavery in Egypt. Psalm 106 helps you learn the lessons of their most rebellious moments. And Psalm 107 thanks the Lord for redeeming his people, releasing them from all kinds of everyday hardships.

Psalm 107 shows how God thunders to the rescue of people with real-life needs. He satisfies hungry and thirsty desert wanderers (v. 4). He breaks the chains of captives held in darkness (v. 14). His wise words heal the foolish (v. 20). He stills storms to a whisper (v. 29) and pumps the desert full of life-giving pools (v. 35). He multiplies a decimated nation (v. 39).

You might not notice that God does good things for you all the time, but you can be sure that everything sweet comes from him. When you spot him acting on your behalf, make sure you stop and "give thanks to the Lord for his unfailing love and his wonderful deeds for mankind" (v. 31).

PRAY IT

God, thanks for all your great everyday gifts. You meet my needs in ways I forget to notice. I'm grateful for your unfailing love.

day260 september 17

READ IT

Isaiah 29:1–30:18, Galatians 3:10–3:25, Proverbs 22:28–23:9

> *"These people come near to me with their mouth and honor me with their lips, but their hearts are far from me."*
>
> Isaiah 29:13

LIVE IT

God sees through people. He knows your thoughts before you think them, your words before you speak them, and your actions before you do them. So no one fools the Lord with fake religion.

No human habit disturbs God more than spiritual hypocrisy. Jesus, for example, aims his fiercest words at people who make faith a sham. He compares them to freshly painted tombs. They look tidy on the outside, but inside they're full of dead bones (Matthew 23:27).

In Isaiah 29 God speaks bluntly to "Ariel," a symbolic name for David's royal city of Jerusalem. The Lord watches his people complete yet another yearly cycle of religious festivals. They obey the rituals he commanded in the Old Testament. Yet he knows nothing is as it seems.

Everything his people say and do looks deeply spiritual on the outside, but God sees the inside. People say the right things, but their hearts aren't in it. They utter praise-filled words, but they don't truly love him. The just go through the motions, carrying out human traditions passed down for generations.

The Lord wants every part of your friendship with him to be authentic, for your inner devotion to match your outward words and actions. He's not looking for you to put yourself in a frenzy of hyped-up feelings, but he does want you to fully commit your heart and mind to him.

PRAY IT

Lord, call me out when I don't live up to my words. Make my relationship with you real inside and out.

september 18 **day261**

READ IT

Isaiah 30:19–32:20, Galatians 3:26–4:20, Psalm 108:1–5

"There is neither Jew nor Gentile, neither slave nor free, nor is there male and female, for you are all one in Christ Jesus."

GALATIANS 3:28

LIVE IT

Your world is full of boxes. Big ones. Tiny ones. Popular boxes. Odd boxes. Most people want to put others in one of these containers and never let them out. That's not how Jesus works. He breaks down every category and label that walls us off from each other.

The apostle Paul lived in a culture that strictly divided people based on race or ethnicity, like Jews and Gentiles. They were alienated because of their social and economic status, whether they were slaves or free citizens. They were cut off based on sex, their distinction as male and female. These differences dictated who was a friend or an enemy. They dictated who you could hang out with. They might give you power to dominate another person, even to the point of ownership.

Jesus demolished those categories and the rules that came with them. He tore down the wall between Jew and Gentile (Galatians 2:1–3:29, Romans 11:11–24). People from every tribe can follow him (Revelation 5:9). He made friends with every kind of people, seeing them as more than their popularity, wealth, or sex (Luke 15:1–2, John 4:7–9).

When you put your trust in Jesus, you join God's family. That connection doesn't make human distinctions disappear or do away with anyone's uniqueness. But Jesus makes differences between us less important. Because of him you can make friends outside any box.

PRAY IT

God, help me see that people are more than categories and labels. Because of you I can learn to get along with anyone.

day262 september 19

READ IT

Isaiah 33:1 – 35:10, Galatians 4:21 – 5:6, Psalm 108:6 – 13

> *"And a highway will be there; it will be called the Way of Holiness; it will be for those who walk on that Way."*
>
> Isaiah 35:8

LIVE IT

"Holiness" is God's awesome trait that combines "separation" and "brightness" to describe his unique glory. His holiness means he's completely pure and without fault. This passage from the prophet Isaiah says the Lord has plans for you to trek along his holy highway.

Ancient peoples built vast transportation systems, including a quarter million miles of roadways crossing the Roman Empire, but no one ever put down pavement across the shifting sands of vast deserts. God decides to change that. He promises to make the wilderness burst into bloom, with glory that causes it to shout for joy (Isaiah 35:1 – 2). He will transform burning sand into pools and let springs bubble up from thirsty ground (vv. 6 – 7).

Across this new landscape God lays down a "Way of Holiness." The path refers in part to the physical highways worshipers followed on their way to religious feasts at the temple in Jerusalem. God also had a broader idea in mind. For you to "walk on that Way" means you go around "doing holiness" and following God's path of right behavior.

Some people won't step foot on that path. But for you and God's people, "the redeemed," it's smooth pavement. When you walk today in the purity God intends for you, "sorrow and sighing will flee away," and "everlasting joy" will take you by surprise (v. 10). Others will chase down other paths, but this is the route you want to hike.

PRAY IT

Lord, I choose to live completely committed to you today. I want to be pure and walk your holy path.

READ IT

Isaiah 36:1–37:38, Galatians 5:7–26, Psalm 109:1–20

> *"But the fruit of the Spirit is love, joy, peace, forbearance, kindness, goodness, faithfulness, gentleness and self-control. Against such things there is no law."*
>
> Galatians 5:22–23

LIVE IT

You can't force yourself to grow spiritually any more than you can make an apple sprout from your fingertip. Only staying tightly connected to God gets good things growing in your life.

Human beings don't naturally produce high-quality traits. The apostle Paul says the "acts of the flesh" are obvious. They're things like sexual immorality, hatred, selfish ambition, and envy (Galatians 5:19–21).

But Paul also explains the results you can expect to see when God goes to work in your life. "Love" is sacrificial actions on behalf of others. "Joy" means a deep happiness that doesn't depend on your situation, and "peace" is an inner calm. "Patience" is the ability to put up with others, and "kindness" is the compassion God shows you. "Goodness" is active generosity. "Faithfulness" is reliability, "gentleness" is freedom from bad anger, and "self-control" means you don't give in to sin.

You can struggle on your own to make those huge qualities happen in you—and fail—or you can rely on the Holy Spirit to develop them naturally. As you "walk by the Spirit" (v. 16), his love, encouragement, and direction change you step by step.

The secret to real growth is that life-altering connection. Like Jesus once said, "I am the vine; you are the branches. If you remain in me and I in you, you will bear much fruit; apart from me you can do nothing" (John 15:5).

PRAY IT

Lord, I want to live close to you. Change me through your Holy Spirit's power working inside me.

day264 september 21

READ IT

Isaiah 38:1 – 40:31, Galatians 6:1 – 18, Proverbs 23:10 – 18

> *"Carry each other's burdens, and in this way you will fulfill the law of Christ. . . . Each one should carry their own load."*
>
> GALATIANS 6:2, 5

LIVE IT

There's nothing more aggravating than toiling alone on a group project or making up for slacking coworkers. There's also nothing better than giving someone just the right boost exactly when they need it most.

The apostle Paul gives exceedingly wise advice, but at first glance his words make no sense. Out of one side of his mouth he says, "carry each other's burdens" (Galatians 6:2). Out of the other he says, "each one should carry their own load" (v. 5). So when should you step in and help? Or when do you let others carry their own weight?

The answer lies in Paul's word choices. The word "burdens" (v. 2) means "heavy burdens," like rocks so large no one can possibly lift them alone. That weighty cargo needs to be hoisted by a group. The second word, "load" (v. 5), refers to a daypack carried by a soldier. It meant the essential personal responsibilities a person needs to carry alone.

You're not helping others if you pick up their right-sized loads, like their part of a project at school. But you're heartless if you don't help lift problems so enormous they crush people who try to carry them solo. Ask God to help you see the difference, and you will know the right time to give help — or when it's right to ask for help yourself.

PRAY IT

Lord, show me when it's time to give help or back off. Teach me to carry my own responsibilities and not to be embarrassed when I need others' help.

READ IT

Isaiah 41:1–42:25, Ephesians 1:1–23, Psalm 109:21–31

> *"Here is my servant, whom I uphold, my chosen one in whom I delight; I will put my Spirit on him, and he will bring justice to the nations."*
>
> Isaiah 42:1

LIVE IT

If the Bible could do a dramatic drum roll, it would start in Isaiah 42. It's the beginning of several impressive revelations of a unique servant of God. These intriguing passages point to Jesus hundreds of years before he arrives on earth.

Four "servant songs" describe this servant in Isaiah 42:1–9, 49:1–7, 50:4–9, and 52:13–53:12. The first introduces the Lord's chosen servant. Some of the descriptions you read there could apply to any representative of God, including the prophet Isaiah. Other points appear to describe God's plan to show off his glory through the nation of Israel. But as you read these words it's hard not to see a picture of Jesus.

God promises to put his Spirit on this servant, a pledge that comes true in Matthew 3:16–17 when the Spirit floats down like a dove and lands on Jesus. God says his servant will be his new "covenant" or "agreement" (Isaiah 42:6) with everyone on earth, a claim Jesus made about himself in Luke 22:20 and fulfilled when he died on the cross for the sins of every human being.

As you read these servant songs throughout the next dozen chapters of Isaiah, you get to know a deep side of Jesus. He's someone you can't help but like. He's a hero who inspires your total admiration. He's a Savior absolutely worth following.

PRAY IT

Lord, I want to meet Jesus in these Old Testament words. Show me the servant who came to save me and all humankind.

day266 september 23

READ IT

Isaiah 43:1–44:23, Ephesians 2:1–22, Psalm 110:1–7

"For it is by grace you have been saved, through faith—and this is not from yourselves, it is the gift of God—not by works, so that no one can boast."

Ephesians 2:8–9

LIVE IT

There's nothing complicated about God's plan to save people through Jesus. John 3:16 says, "For God so loved the world that he gave his one and only Son, that whoever believes in him shall not perish but have eternal life."

That straightforward truth might not settle all your questions about how you become a Christian. Maybe it sounds too easy to be true. It might leave you wondering if you have to do anything more to get on God's good side.

Ephesians 2:8–9 is one of the Bible's key passages for explaining exactly how the Lord "saves" you, the process where he forgives all your wrongdoing, breaks sin's power to control you, and puts you on a path to your forever home in heaven.

The apostle Paul says everything starts with "grace," God's decision to show you kindness you don't deserve. His grace saves you "through faith," your belief that Jesus is God's Son and the one who died on the cross to pay the penalty for your sins. Getting saved is "not by works," the good acts you might do to try to impress him. Salvation is a total gift, so you have no reason to brag about it.

The Lord saves you by grace through faith to prove his love and to show everyone his phenomenal power. You can trust your life to these facts from God's reliable Word.

PRAY IT

God, thank you that I become your friend because of your grace—your kindness I don't deserve. I trust Jesus to be my Savior.

READ IT

Isaiah 44:24–46:23, Ephesians 3:1–21, Psalm 111:1–10

> *"And I pray that you, being rooted and established in love, may have power, together with all the Lord's holy people, to grasp how wide and long and high and deep is the love of Christ."*
>
> EPHESIANS 3:17–18

LIVE IT

Think big about what it would be like for you and your friends to live utterly tight with the Lord. Then borrow the apostle Paul's words in Ephesians 3:14–21 and pray them for yourself and everyone you know.

Paul starts Ephesians 3 by explaining the Lord's goal to bind his Old Testament people together with the Gentiles, non-Jews. It's part of his astonishing plan to let everyone get close to him (Ephesians 3:12).

Paul willingly suffers to spread this news far and wide, and the message makes him burst into prayer. He kneels to God and pleads for blessings beyond your most outrageous dreams. He asks that you would experience Jesus living inside you through the Holy Spirit, making you mighty with every kind of power. He wants your life to be built on love and for you to never stop trying to grasp the limitless size of God's care. This love is so enormous you can never completely understand it, but it makes you overflow with a fullness as big as God.

There's more. Your God plans to wield his power to accomplish more than you can ever ask or even imagine. He will bring glory to himself by everything he does in and through you.

Don't settle for a small faith that doesn't transform your life. Ask the Lord to give you a relationship with him that's infinitely bigger and better.

PRAY IT

God, I want more of you. I want to experience your vast love for me. Do even more in and through me than I can dream.

day268 september 25

READ IT

Isaiah 47:1–49:7, Ephesians 4:1–16, Proverbs 23:19–28

"For I knew how stubborn you were; your neck muscles were iron, your forehead was bronze."

Isaiah 48:4

LIVE IT

You might hit the gym to get muscles as solid as iron. Think of the boards you could break with a forehead as hard as bronze. But that kind of toughness is out of line when it comes to you getting along with God.

The book of Isaiah communicates blunt warnings from the Lord mixed with assurances of his nonstop care for his people. In Isaiah 48 the Lord blasts their stubborn resistance to him.

God notes that his people happily use his name to pray and make solemn pledges. They're glad to call themselves citizens of Jerusalem, and they claim they rely on him. But when the people see their world shake, they interpret it as proof of their false gods' power, giving credit to their wooden and metal idols. That's why the Lord calls them stubborn. He vows to announce his mighty acts ahead of time so that no one doubts they come from him.

The Lord doesn't stop with those warnings. He goes on to remind Israel of his tenderness, and in Isaiah 49:1–7 a "servant song" divulges more about his plan to send a messenger to show off his splendor and make the whole world bow.

There's always a better choice than stubbornness. If you pay attention to him and keep his commands, his peace will refresh you like a river rushing through a desert (48:18).

PRAY IT

God, talk to me when I'm stubborn. Catch my attention when I ignore you. I want to follow you from the heart.

READ IT

Isaiah 49:8–51:16, Ephesians 4:17–5:7, Psalm 112:1–10

> *"You were taught, with regard to your former way of life, to put off your old self, which is being corrupted by its deceitful desires."*
>
> Ephesians 4:22

LIVE IT

Forgiveness seems like a sweet excuse to do wrong. If God wipes away your sins as soon as you confess them, why not keep breaking his rules?

The apostle Paul has nothing nice to say about that attitude. It's futile, darkened, ignorant, and insensitive (Ephesians 4:17–19). It's the way people think when they are cut off from God. It doesn't fit "the truth that is in Jesus" (v. 21). People who trust the Lord have caught a better outlook.

When you believe in Jesus, you get rid of old habits that come from evil desires, as if you're peeling off filthy clothes. God wants to refresh your mind, teaching you to think differently. He's begun a new life inside you, so you can build fresh habits. The Lord is remaking you to be just like him, full of his goodness and holiness.

That's the "way of life you learned when you heard about Christ" (vv. 20–21). If you want to know more of what that better life looks like, check out the rest of this book word by word. It gives details of practical ways the Lord plans to transform you.

God doesn't lay down rules for no reason. His commands aim to lead you to the best life ever. If you count on his death on the cross for your sins, then expect he has a new life in store for you.

PRAY IT

Lord, help me get rid of old habits that don't honor you. Train me to think the way you think and act the way you act.

day270 september 27

READ IT

Isaiah 51:17–54:17, Ephesians 5:9–33, Psalm 113:1–9

> *"But he was pierced for our transgressions, he was crushed for our iniquities; the punishment that brought us peace was on him, and by his wounds we are healed."*
>
> Isaiah 53:5

LIVE IT

If you snip Isaiah 52:13–53:12 from your Bible, place it in front of an assortment of people, and ask them who the passage is about, many will say "Jesus." Yet these Old Testament words were spoken hundreds of years before he came on the scene. Amazing!

This passage is the last of four "servant songs" in Isaiah, although other sections in the book also point to Christ. Isaiah 7:14 predicts that a virgin will give birth to a son called "God with us" (Matthew 1:23). Isaiah 61:1–2 records the striking words quoted by Jesus in his hometown near the start of his ministry (Luke 4:14–21). This passage gives deep insights into Jesus's death on the cross.

Isaiah foretells some of the details of that death, like the fact that the Lord's servant will be beaten to the point of being disfigured (Isaiah 52:14, Matthew 27:30) and that he will suffer without complaint (Isaiah 53:7, Mark 14:61). Even more importantly, it explains what the servant will accomplish on the cross. His body is pierced for our sins. God lets him suffer for our rebellion. His punishment brings us peace.

Jesus's death wasn't just another bloody execution inflicted by a potent ancient empire. When he went to the cross, he carried out God's own plan, paying the penalty for the world's sins. Do you believe he died for you?

PRAY IT

Lord, you went to the cross for me. You willingly suffered the punishment I deserve. Thank you for your incredible love.

READ IT

Isaiah 55:1–57:13, Ephesians 6:1–24, Psalm 114:1–8

"Finally, be strong in the Lord and in his mighty power. Put on the full armor of God, so that you can take your stand against the devil's schemes."

EPHESIANS 6:10–11

LIVE IT

Even if you have a bully living next door, he's not the worst of your worries. Your real enemy is the unseen "spiritual forces of evil in the heavenly realms" (Ephesians 6:12). At the head of those forces is the devil, who "prowls around like a roaring lion looking for someone to devour" (1 Peter 5:8).

Getting the Lord's own power is the only way you become strong enough to survive Satan's schemes. God provides you with armor as effective as the combat gear worn by Roman soldiers. You start by girding yourself in a "belt of truth," a habit of integrity that protects you in situations where your reputation may be challenged. Your real-life proven character forms a "breastplate of righteousness" that guards your body front and back. Tough studded shoes let you run fast and far with the good news about Jesus. Your trust in God deflects the devil's fiery darts like a shield. A "helmet of salvation" protects your mind with the real facts of your friendship with God. And the "sword of the Spirit" is your grip on the Bible, useful both to defend yourself and to go on the attack against the devil.

Once you put on this spiritual armor, you can stand your ground and survive any threat. God knows precisely what weapons you need to win. Don't even think about fighting without putting on every piece of your equipment.

PRAY IT

Lord, give me your lifesaving protection against Satan's schemes. Help me put on the gear I need to get ready for his attacks. Keep me strong and safe.

day272 september 29

READ IT

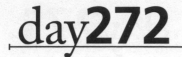

Isaiah 57:14–59:21, Philippians 1:1–26, Proverbs 23:29–24:4

"Do not gaze at wine when it is red, when it sparkles in the cup, when it goes down smoothly! In the end it bites like a snake and poisons like a viper."

PROVERBS 23:31–32

LIVE IT

Either you control alcohol, or it controls you. There's not much middle ground.

Proverbs declares that all kinds of terrible effects track back to excessive drinking. Proverbs 23:29–30 says it brings "woe," a deep grief or affliction. It causes "sorrow," extreme sadness and the total opposite of joy. When people get drunk, they spout "complaints," they sport "needless bruises," and they greet the world with "bloodshot eyes."

That's just the start. People who drink too much "see strange sights" and their brains "imagine confusing things" (v. 33). Even when they lie down to rest, their bodies heave "like one sleeping on the high seas," strung up high in a sailing ship's rigging (v. 34). They get thrashed but feel no pain, so they keep going back for more. All they can think about is finding another drink (v. 35).

The Bible doesn't ban all alcohol consumption, but this passage makes it clear that drunkenness stings like the bite of a poisonous snake. The problem starts when people don't see any further than alcohol's sparkle and smooth taste.

Your parents and other mentors can teach you the best ways to deal with alcohol when you're of age. But for now it's out of bounds, usually illegal and surely against what God wants for you. Don't miss the main point of this passage: alcohol isn't the giant party everyone says it is.

PRAY IT

God, I commit to not using alcohol now and not abusing it ever. Convince me of the problems it can cause.

september 30 day273

READ IT

Isaiah 60:1–62:12, Philippians 1:27–2:11, Psalm 115:1–11

> *"Do nothing out of selfish ambition or vain conceit. Rather, in humility value others above yourselves, not looking to your own interests but each of you to the interests of the others."*
>
> PHILIPPIANS 2:3–4

LIVE IT

You know you're supposed to watch out for other people, making sure you don't run them over literally or in any other way. God aims to turn that duty from a "should do" into a "want to."

You have to pay attention to detail to catch the situation behind this letter from the apostle Paul to his good friends in Philippi. He writes about deep joy and peaceful contentment, even though he's in prison awaiting trial (Philippians 1:7). And late in the book he challenges two women, Euodia and Syntyche, to quit quarreling (4:2). Their fight must have been severe for Paul to correct them publicly by name.

With that in the background, Paul tells everyone to put each other first, lay aside selfishness, and serve each other more than their own personal happiness. He challenges them to get the attitude of Jesus, who set aside the privileges of heaven to serve the human race, even to the point of dying on the cross.

But Paul doesn't just command you to serve. He tells you how. He encourages you to pass along all the good things you get from God—closeness to Jesus, comfort from his love, togetherness in the Holy Spirit, tenderness, and compassion (2:1). When you realize everything the Lord has done for you, suddenly it's not so hard to serve others.

PRAY IT

Lord, because you serve me I can serve others. Teach me to recognize all the care you give me so I can care for them.

day274 october 1

READ IT

Isaiah 63:1–65:16, Philippians 2:12–30, Psalm 115:12–18

> *"Oh, that you would rend the heavens and come down, that the mountains would tremble before you!"*
>
> Isaiah 64:1

LIVE IT

When the prophet Isaiah begs the Lord to rip open the heavens and come to earth, he's hoping for more than a dose of excitement to break up his day. He wants to see the earth tremble. Just as a match can set twigs ablaze to make a pot boil, the Lord's arrival will make the world quake.

Isaiah remembers awesome and unexpected things the Lord did in the past, instances where he shook mountains. He no doubt recalls the Lord's thundering appearance at Mount Sinai, where he gave Moses the Ten Commandments (Exodus 19:16–18).

There's a catch if you invite the Lord to show up and smash evil. It's tough to ask him to step in and halt sin if you're part of the problem. Even though you want God to act at once, you aren't so happy if he's quick to correct your own wrongdoing. Isaiah admits that the Lord's people have broken his commands. No one struggles to know God, and even their best actions are just filthy rags (Isaiah 64:6).

The good news is that we don't have to be in fear of God's instant wrath for our sin. The apostle Paul said it like this: "God demonstrates his own love for us in this: While we were still sinners, Christ died for us" (Romans 5:8). That's not an excuse to sin; it's an opportunity for you to turn to him.

PRAY IT

God, thanks for loving me even though I'm not perfect. Your kindness makes me want to follow you more.

october 2 day275

READ IT

Isaiah 65:17–66:24, Philippians 3:1–4:1, Psalm 116:1–11

> *"But whatever were gains to me I now consider loss for the sake of Christ. What is more, I consider everything a loss because of the surpassing worth of knowing Christ Jesus my Lord."*
>
> Philippians 3:7–8

LIVE IT

The apostle Paul had a stack of reasons to take pride in his spiritual heritage. He kept the strict rules of the Pharisees, the most rigorous Jewish faction. His faith was so intense that he hunted Christians to imprison or kill them. He thought he followed the Lord's laws flawlessly.

Paul once believed those accomplishments would get him on God's good side. Now he considers them "loss," something damaged and useless (Philippians 3:7). They're no more impressive to God than disgusting and worthless "garbage" (v. 8). Compared to the greatness of knowing Jesus, they're nothing.

That sounds so spiritual you could easily assume Paul never fails at following Jesus. But he hasn't arrived at his final destination. Like everyone else, he falls down. Yet he keeps getting up. He grabs hold of Jesus, "forgetting what is behind and straining toward what is ahead" (v. 13).

You can be done trying to prove yourself to God by keeping rules. You can quit trying to impress God with spiritual accomplishments. What really counts with the Lord is being accepted because of what Jesus did on the cross. Faith in him is the only way you get right with God. Trust in him is what motivates you to follow him all the way to heaven. When you fall down, ask for forgiveness, get up, and go on.

PRAY IT

Lord, all the things I think will impress you are like garbage. I'm acceptable to you because Jesus died for me. Knowing you is the greatest thing ever.

day276 october 3

READ IT

Jeremiah 1:1 – 2:30, Philippians 4:2 – 23, Proverbs 24:5 – 14

"Before I formed you in the womb I knew you, before you were born I set you apart; I appointed you as a prophet to the nations."

Jeremiah 1:5

LIVE IT

God doesn't make you wait until you're old to serve him. He's thought hard about how he can move you into action. The apostle Paul wrote, "For we are God's handiwork, created in Christ Jesus to do good works, which God prepared in advance for us to do" (Ephesians 2:10).

The Lord had his eye on Jeremiah even before he was conceived. The fact that God "knew" Jeremiah wasn't merely a fuzzy awareness that he would someday be born. It means the Lord already had a relationship with Jeremiah and approved of him. No one knows exactly how old Jeremiah was when God commanded him to preach, but his ministry lasted forty years. He prophesied until the final days of the southern kingdom of Judah.

Jeremiah feels overwhelmed at the thought of taking the Lord's message to the world. First he argues he can't speak. Then he protests he's too young. God swats down both excuses. He promises to go with Jeremiah, to protect him, and to fully equip him for the task.

God has a plan to use you to do his work in the world. He says, "Get yourself ready!" (Jeremiah 1:17). He knows the unique opportunities he prepared for you long ago, and he commands you to be fearless as you accomplish whatever he has in store for you. When God sends you, he takes away your terror.

PRAY IT

God, show me how I can best serve you. Make me confident that your power works in and through me to influence my world for you.

READ IT

Jeremiah 2:31–4:9, Colossians 1:1–23, Psalm 116:12–19

"We continually ask God to fill you with the knowledge of his will through all the wisdom and understanding that the Spirit gives."

Colossians 1:9

LIVE IT

Figuring out what the Lord has in store for you can sound baffling. But the Lord promises to let you in on his plans.

The apostle Paul starts his letter to the Colossians thanking God for their solid faith in Jesus and love for the Lord's people. These believers know heaven awaits them because they trust God's good news. They live in God's grace, his kindness they can't do anything to earn.

Now Paul prays that God will fill their minds with a thorough knowledge of his "will," an understanding of how he wants them to live. Paul doesn't offer these Christians easy steps to follow. He instead hints they need to stay close to the Holy Spirit, counting on him for wisdom and insight.

Most of what the Lord has planned for you becomes clear in the commands of Scripture. He wants you to show love, to respect your parents, to live with honesty and purity, and much more. As you do these obvious things, his Spirit fills in the details so you can honor God and please him in every way. You will do good, know the Lord better, and live in his might.

You can't live for God if you don't know what he wants. So invite him to teach you. Whenever you lack wisdom, just ask (James 1:5). He's glad to show you your next steps.

PRAY IT

God, I want to please you in everything I do. Use the Bible to teach me your will. Show me the details as I stick close to you.

day278 october 5

READ IT

Jeremiah 4:10–5:31, Colossians 1:24–2:5, Psalm 117:1–2

> *"Oh, my anguish, my anguish! I writhe in pain. Oh, the agony of my heart! My heart pounds within me, I cannot keep silent."*
>
> Jeremiah 4:19

LIVE IT

Your chest thumps with compassion when you hear about hungry children. You get angry at the facts about human trafficking. You churn with frustration if your friends refuse to follow Jesus. Those are all signs you care about God and his goals for the world.

People call Jeremiah "the weeping prophet" because his heart breaks for the broken state of the Lord's people. The people of Judah had abandoned God and thrown themselves into sin (Jeremiah 1:16). They were once like a young bride devoted to the Lord (2:2) but now they act like a prostitute chasing other lovers (3:1). They seek military power from other nations instead of relying on God (2:18), and they worship the false god Baal (v. 23).

Jeremiah speaks the Lord's message, urging the people to come back to God and admit their guilt (4:1). But their refusal invites an attack from a distant army, and Jeremiah twists in pain as he announces sin's painful consequences for the nation. He feels their pain and won't quit caring.

Sometimes you might wish you could shut off your passion for God and not care about the world's troubles. But you can choose to be like Jeremiah. You can keep obeying God. You can continue doing the job he gives you. The Lord doesn't give up on the world, and neither should you.

PRAY IT

God, this broken world breaks my heart. Keep filling me with compassion for your world. I want to keep serving you.

october 6 **day279**

READ IT

Jeremiah 6:1 – 7:29, Colossians 2:6 – 23, Psalm 118:1 – 16

> *"The LORD is with me; I will not be afraid. What can mere mortals do to me? The LORD is with me; he is my helper."*
>
> PSALM 118:6 – 7

LIVE IT

There's no shortage of things "mere mortals" can do to hurt you. You don't need more than a few minutes to fill up a page with cruel things your peers do to you and each other. But with God on your side, you can live unafraid.

Times haven't been happy for the person who penned Psalm 118. He's surrounded on every side, with enemies swarming him like bees. He's pushed back on his heels and about to tip over. But the Lord rushes to his aid, intervening as his strong defense. No one can help this writer like the Lord. He's a far better refuge than either everyday people or powerful rulers.

This song likely tells the story of a king who trusts God for military victory. But this verse holds as true for you as it does for ancient royalty. The New Testament book of Hebrews quotes these words and instructs you to repeat them with confidence: "The Lord is my helper; I will not be afraid. What can mere mortals do to me?" (Hebrews 13:6).

Hebrews 13 also fills out the promise you hear in Psalm 118. It assures you of God's permanent presence in your life. He vows, "Never will I leave you; never will I forsake you" (Hebrews 13:5). Mortals won't suddenly get rid of their wicked tricks. But God is with you no matter what. Even when cruel people surround you, the Lord sticks close.

PRAY IT

Lord, stay close to me when I feel afraid. You're my helper. You're with me. You won't ever leave me.

day280 october 7

READ IT

Jeremiah 7:30–9:16, Colossians 3:1–4:1, Proverbs 24:15–22

"Since, then, you have been raised with Christ, set your hearts on things above, where Christ is, seated at the right hand of God."

COLOSSIANS 3:1

LIVE IT

Things scream for your attention. People beg you to notice them. Activities and experiences lure you to join in. Then God comes along, pointing in an entirely different direction. He commands you to set your heart on heaven.

The Bible declares that after Jesus rose, "he was taken up into heaven and he sat at the right hand of God" (Mark 16:19). By believing in Jesus, you not only have died with Jesus (Romans 6:3) but have also been raised with him (Ephesians 2:1–6). Your body lives on earth, but your spirit belongs above.

That fact should change how you think and act. It should nudge you to "set your mind on things above, not on earthly things" (Colossians 3:2). To "set your mind" means to want something so much you struggle for it. "On things above" means the best things of heaven. And instead of putting all your attention on the "earthly" here and now, you focus on things that last forever.

Nothing in this passage says you should quit having friends, cleaning your room, or working hard at school. But as a believer you do those things with a bigger point in mind. You focus on obeying God. You act in a way that shows off his love and character. And you get rid of bad habits of thinking and acting that don't have any part of heaven.

PRAY IT

God, heaven is my home. Help me act on that fact. I live on earth, but my heart is with you now and forever.

READ IT

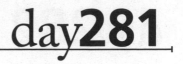

Jeremiah 9:17–11:17, Colossians 4:2–18, Psalm 118:17–29

> *"Let the one who boasts boast about this: that they have the understanding to know me."*
>
> Jeremiah 9:24

LIVE IT

Darkness was creeping across the land of Judah. As Jerusalem falls to the attacking Babylonian army, women who make a job out of loud public wailing take their place in the city's dramatic downfall (Jeremiah 9:17). The entire nation joins their cries for the ruined land. Death has climbed in the windows of homes and forts. Children and young people die in the streets (v. 21).

The nation flails, hoping for anything to save it. Some people think they're smart enough to escape the violence. Others say their strength will let them outrun their enemies. Still others trust their wealth to buy them peace. Then God sends a piercing message through the prophet Jeremiah. In his people's grim time of need, the Lord says, "Let not the wise boast of their wisdom or the strong boast of their strength or the rich boast of their riches" (v. 23). None of those things can rescue God's people. Only the Lord himself deserves their trust.

You might be bright, but that's not enough to save you from truly sticky situations. You might be buff, but the Lord possesses infinitely more power. You might be wealthy, but money can vanish in an instant. In your worst and best moments, there's only one thing worth bragging about — that you know and understand God. He's the one you can count on to always treat you with kindness, justice, and righteousness.

PRAY IT

God, I'm proud to be your friend. You're totally wise and strong. You have limitless riches. I trust you to take care of me.

day282 october 9

READ IT

Jeremiah 11:18–13:27, 1 Thessalonians 1:1–2:16, Psalm 119:1–8

"Our gospel came to you not simply with words but also with power, with the Holy Spirit and deep conviction."

1 Thessalonians 1:5

LIVE IT

It's easy to assume you're the fastest runner in the race until you meet someone who blows past you. So if you think you have a sweet relationship with God that couldn't get any better, challenge yourself with the example of the Thessalonian believers.

The apostle Paul started the church in Thessalonica, spending three weeks reasoning with them, proving that Jesus had to suffer and rise from the dead (Acts 17:1–9). He saw immediate evidence of the their authentic faith. They experienced the Holy Spirit's power and became completely convinced of the facts about Jesus. They strove to imitate both Paul and the Lord, and they joyfully endured fierce persecution for their faith from their non-Christian neighbors (1 Thessalonians 1:6, 2:14). The account of their faith spread throughout their nation as they became a model of how to turn from idols "to serve the living and true God" (1:9).

Being a Christian isn't a competition. But it never hurts to study other followers of Jesus so you get a picture what real maturity can look like. God wants to make astounding changes in your life, but that only happens when you let him take over your whole life and remake your every thought, word, and action.

The Thessalonians ran hard and fast after Jesus. If that's your goal, study their example. Let them set the pace.

PRAY IT

Lord, I don't want to play around with my relationship with you. Train me to run as fast and far as you want to take me.

READ IT

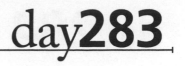

Jeremiah 14:1 – 15:21, 1 Thessalonians 2:17 – 3:13, Psalm 119:9 – 16

"I have hidden your word in my heart that I might not sin against you."

PSALM 119:11

LIVE IT

Maybe you remember Jesus doing battle with the devil in the wilderness (Luke 4:1 – 13). Each time the devil tempted him, Jesus jabbed back with a relevant Scripture. Your Lord was living out the truth of Psalm 119:11.

Psalm 119 is the longest chapter in the Bible. Each section of this song about the Lord's law begins with a sequential letter of the Hebrew alphabet, so that each line in Psalm 119:1 – 8 begins with "Aleph," each line of Psalm 119:9 – 16 begins with "Beth," and so on.

While the Bible contains other passages that pay tribute to the power of God's Word, Psalm 119 goes over the top about his "law," "word," "statutes," "commands," "decrees," "precepts," and "promises." Each term carries a slightly different meaning, but you quickly catch the overall theme that God's rules are beyond stupendous. They teach you the Lord's best way to navigate life.

Psalm 119:11 informs you that the Lord's words keep you from rebelling against him. That happens best when you deliberately insert them into the deepest part of yourself. If you memorize them and meditate on what they mean, the Lord can call them to mind at the right time to steer you away from sin. Whether you're defending yourself against temptation, getting comfort in pain, or making bold fresh moves for God, his words keep you close to him.

PRAY IT

God, help me get more of your words inside me so I don't sin against you. Use your Word to guide me in the best way to live.

day284 october 11

READ IT

Jeremiah 16:1–17:27, 1 Thessalonians 4:1–18, Proverbs 24:23–34

> *"It is God's will that you should be sanctified: that you should avoid sexual immorality."*
>
> 1 Thessalonians 4:3

LIVE IT

Plenty of people who don't claim to follow Jesus think the Bible is totally against sex. But they miss the point of one of God's most awesome inventions.

The Bible's teaching on sex goes all the way back to the Garden of Eden, where Adam and Eve find each other to be perfect mates, becoming "one flesh" without any shame (Genesis 2:23–25). One of the Lord's Ten Commandments is to stay away from adultery, sex with anyone other than your husband or wife (Exodus 20:14). Jesus said that ban on adultery also includes lust, sexually desiring something that isn't yours (Matthew 5:28).

The apostle Paul gets explicit when he says you should avoid "sexual immorality" (1 Thessalonians 4:3). That's a big term that includes any kind of sexual intimacy outside of marriage between a man and a woman, including before marriage.

All that Bible teaching clearly addresses the "no" of sex. But Paul also explains the positive side of staying sexually pure. When he says "each of you should learn to control your own body in a way that is holy and honorable" (v. 4), he's literally talking about how you "acquire" and "keep" a spouse. God says a giant yes to sex within marriage. To settle for anything less before or after you're married hurts everyone involved (v. 5).

God invites you to purity—and passion. But you only enjoy his best when you keep your Creator's commands.

PRAY IT

Lord, help me stay pure when people around me think sex is casual recreation. I trust that you always want my best.

october 12 **day285**

READ IT

Jeremiah 18:1–20:18, 1 Thessalonians 5:1–28, Psalm 119:17–24

"Open my eyes that I may see wonderful things in your law."

PSALM 119:18

LIVE IT

Suppose you disagree with God. You scan your Bible and you conclude he couldn't be more wrong about some random command. Maybe he bans an activity you think would be fun. Or he clearly tells you to do something you think is completely stupid. So what should you do?

Start by telling God what you're thinking, because he's big enough to deal with your objections. Then whatever your issue, pray the words of Psalm 119:18: "Open my eyes that I may see wonderful things in your law." Or say, "Teach me to see the wisdom of obeying you." Or pray, "Help me to see the upside of your rules."

If God's commands all seemed smart at first sight, no one would ever sin. Until you build new habits of thinking, you might need continual convincing the Lord knows best. That's a point the apostle Paul makes in Romans 12:2. He writes, "Do not conform to the pattern of this world, but be transformed by the renewing of your mind. Then you will be able to test and approve what God's will is—his good, pleasing and perfect will."

The world teaches you one way to think, and the Lord aims to teach you another. When you let him reason with you and transform your mind, his commands won't seem so farfetched. Soon you start to agree that his will is perfectly good.

PRAY IT

God, remake my mind so I think more like you. Teach me to see the value of your commands and to appreciate your total perfection.

day286 october 13

READ IT

Jeremiah 21:1 – 23:8, 2 Thessalonians 1:1 – 12, Psalm 119:25 – 32

> *"We ought always to thank God for you, brothers and sisters, and rightly so, because your faith is growing more and more, and the love all of you have for one another is increasing."*
>
> 2 THESSALONIANS 1:3

LIVE IT

Those Thessalonian Christians were models of faith, pacesetters in the long run to heaven. The apostle Paul wrote them not long after he founded their church (Acts 17:1 – 9). His first letter applauded their solid first steps in following Jesus. His second note tells them how to stay on track.

By the end of 1 Thessalonians Paul was already reminding his friends to keep doing what he had previously taught them. He says they know "how to live in order to please God, as in fact you are living," then he urges them to "do this more and more" (1 Thessalonians 4:1). Now in 2 Thessalonians he says their faith is growing "more and more" and their love for each other is steadily increasing (2 Thessalonians 1:3). It all sounds so basic.

You might wonder if the Thessalonians got tired of hearing the same old commands, as if a track coach were telling them over and over to keep putting one foot in front of the other. But they must have welcomed these reminders from Paul, who praised their perseverance even through violent persecution. Their step-by-step obedience signaled their faith was authentic and enduring.

Opening your Bible every day might not always wow you with surprises. A sermon or study might not communicate startling new information. But the Lord loves when you keep hearing and acting on his simplest reminders.

PRAY IT

God, I promise not to tune out things I think I already know from your Word. I want to pay attention to your every command.

READ IT

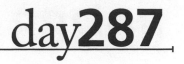

Jeremiah 23:9 – 25:14, 2 Thessalonians 2:1 – 17, Psalm 119:33 – 40

> *"Do not listen to what the prophets are prophesying to you; they fill you with false hopes. They speak visions from their own minds, not from the mouth of the Lord."*
>
> Jeremiah 23:16

LIVE IT

Ancient Judah was awash in people who claimed to speak for God. After all the tough messages Jeremiah brought from the Lord, it's no surprise that an assortment of preachers popped up who spoke happier words. As Jeremiah prophesied destruction, these false prophets uttered things like "You will have peace" and "No harm will come to you" (Jeremiah 23:17).

Jeremiah calls out these fake prophets. He points out that none of them has listened to God and heard his word (v. 18). The Lord hadn't sent them (v. 21). A genuine prophet turns people from their evil ways (v. 22). And the Lord himself wonders how long people will believe these delusions (v. 26).

Back in Deuteronomy 13:1 – 18 the Lord told his Old Testament people to get rid of false prophets who tempted them away from worshiping the one true God. As a New Testament believer it's not your job to stone people who disagree with the Lord. But often it's still wise to tune out a conversation, change a channel, or surf to another site. Unless you're teaming up with other believers to understand and defend your true faith, feeding on false ideas will pull you away from the Lord.

Like the days of Jeremiah, your world is awash with misguided people who speak lies about God. Look for real spokespeople whose words and actions point to the Lord, and listen closely to them.

PRAY IT

Lord, alert me when I listen to voices that lead me away from you. Teach me to know the difference between truth and lies.

day288 october 15

READ IT

Jeremiah 25:15–26:24, 2 Thessalonians 3:1–18, Proverbs 25:1–10

"Remove the dross from the silver, and a silversmith can produce a vessel."

PROVERBS 25:4

LIVE IT

"Dross" is the name for solids that rise to the surface of metal that has been blasted with heat to the point of melting. Skimming these floating impurities off the top results in pure metal ready to pour into a mold to make something useful or beautiful. Liquefying silver sounds amusing if you're experimenting in science or art class. It's not so happy if you're the stuff feeling the heat.

Impurities in a metal weaken a vessel and prevent it from performing up to its potential. They spoil the vessel's beauty. Impurities inside you keep you from accomplishing all the Lord has planned for you. Those flaws spoil your outward appearance as a believer or your inward devotion to God.

God puts every follower of Jesus through a process of purification. He aims to rid you of every little piece of crud that doesn't belong in your life. First he goes after obvious outward sins. But he doesn't miss hurtful secret habits or bad attitudes. And sometimes he turns up the heat to get rid of flaws you don't even know are there. God says in Isaiah 1:25, "I will thoroughly purge away your dross and remove all your impurities."

You never know what process the Lord will use to make you pure. But when he lets you feel the heat, you can be sure he's forging you into a stunning work of art.

PRAY IT

God, purify me of anything that gets in the way of my serving you. Get rid of my obvious sins and everything else that spoils my beauty.

READ IT

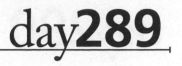

Jeremiah 27:1 – 29:23, 1 Timothy 1:1 – 20, Psalm 119:41 – 48

"Here is a trustworthy saying that deserves full acceptance: Christ Jesus came into the world to save sinners — of whom I am the worst."

1 Timothy 1:15

LIVE IT

The Lord didn't pick the apostle Paul to serve him because he was especially good. The Lord went out of his way to save Paul because he was particularly bad.

Paul isn't proud of the person he was before God laid him flat on the road to Damascus (Acts 9:1 – 19). But he isn't afraid to bring his dark side out into the open. He reminds his young friend Timothy that he was once a "blasphemer," someone who speaks against God. He was a "persecutor," a guy who hunted down believers to imprison or kill them. He was a "violent" man, a word that means rude and scornful of others.

God looked at that man and showed him mercy. He knew that Paul didn't understand what he was doing or whom he was hurting. The Lord didn't hold back. He poured out abundant grace on Paul, showering him with kindness he didn't deserve.

God did all of this to show off a fact that's indisputably true: Jesus arrived on this planet to save sinners, and by sparing Paul he showed off his immense power and patience. Anyone can believe in Jesus and receive eternal life, no matter who they are or what they have done.

You might feel like you have offended God so deeply that he can never accept you. But the Lord has mercy big enough for everyone.

PRAY IT

God, help me admit that I need your grace as much as Paul did. I'm grateful for your forgiveness. Let others see your greatness because you saved me.

day290 october 17

READ IT

Jeremiah 29:24–31:14, 1 Timothy 2:1–15, Psalm 119:49–56

> *"They will come with weeping; they will pray as I bring them back. I will lead them beside streams of water on a level path where they will not stumble."*
>
> Jeremiah 31:9

LIVE IT

Jeremiah's most painful message from God must have been his prediction that the Lord would send his people into captivity in a distant land (Jeremiah 5:19). That prophecy came to pass when waves of people were captured and led into exile in Babylon. Living as prisoners in a foreign land was like getting a long time-out as a consequence for sin.

But there was good news after the bad news. Jeremiah also predicts that after seventy years of captivity the Lord will bring his people back to the land he promised them long ago (Jeremiah 29:10). And God reassures his people of his unstoppable love. He says, "For I know the plans I have for you ... plans to prosper you and not to harm you, plans to give you hope and a future" (v. 11).

The Lord says his people will call on him ... come to him ... pray to him ... seek him ... and find him (v. 12). They will weep as they return to the land. He will lead them on a level path all the way home. Bubbling streams will quench their thirst along the way (31:9).

When you wander from God, you might worry he won't take you back. Yet he won't harm you. He has a fresh future in store for you. Don't wait any longer to come home.

PRAY IT

Lord, lead me back to you when I have sinned and feel far from you. I want to admit what I have done and come back to you right now.

READ IT

Jeremiah 31:15–32:25, 1 Timothy 3:1–16, Psalm 119:57–64

"I will make a new covenant with the people of Israel and with the people of Judah. It will not be like the covenant I made with their ancestors."

JEREMIAH 31:31–32

LIVE IT

The old "covenant" or "agreement" between God and people wasn't working. Nothing was wrong with the plan the Lord had laid out. He had grabbed his people by the hand and loosed them from slavery in Egypt. But as soon as the people had their freedom, they bowed to other gods.

God needed a bold new plan. The old covenant was a list of rules on tablets of stone, inscribed by God's finger and passed down through Moses (Exodus 31:18). Those laws came at people from the outside, telling people to obey but giving them no power to do good. But now the Lord promises to make a new and better agreement with his people. He says, "I will put my law in their minds and write it on their hearts" (Jeremiah 31:33). He will be their God, and they will be his people. Everyone will know him well, and he will totally forgive their evil ways.

The New Testament shows you that better agreement between God and people. It's a fresh plan for how they get along. It calls Jesus "the mediator of a new covenant" (Hebrews 12:24) begun at the cross.

As a Christian, you're part of that new covenant. Through Jesus, he provides a way for you to be forgiven. Through the Holy Spirit, he gives you all the power you need to obey. God wants you to get with his bold new plan.

PRAY IT

Lord, help me to live in your new promises. Thanks for your forgiveness. Remake me from the inside out.

day292 october 19

READ IT

Jeremiah 32:26–34:22, 1 Timothy 4:1–16, Proverbs 25:11–20

> *"Don't let anyone look down on you because you are young, but set an example for the believers in speech, in conduct, in love, in faith and in purity."*
>
> 1 Timothy 4:12

LIVE IT

Some salespeople stare you down like you're plotting to steal the store. Some teachers severely underestimate your abilities and aspirations. Some people don't bother to understand the marvelous things happening in your adolescent brain. But the Lord has a staggeringly high view of you. He never puts you down because of your age. He even gives you a way to silence people who glance at you sideways because you're not yet an adult.

Timothy was a young disciple when he met the apostle Paul, a man who would serve as his mentor and ministry partner as long as the apostle lived (Acts 16:1). Timothy joined Paul on his mission trips across the Mediterranean (v. 4). By the time Paul wrote him this letter, he was no longer a kid. In those days "young" (1 Timothy 4:12) was a word used to describe men as old as forty.

Timothy still has to prove himself to people who look down on him because of his age. So Paul tells his youngish friend to make his life a model for everyone to follow. He should set an example in his words and actions. He should display maturity in "love," his sacrifices for others; in "faith," his trust in God; and in "purity," his obedience to God's sexual standards in both actions and thoughts.

You can't control the fact that some adults look at you harshly. But you can challenge and change what they see.

PRAY IT

God, help me make my relationship with you a model for others. Thanks for believing in me.

october 20 **day293**

READ IT

Jeremiah 35:1–37:21, 1 Timothy 5:1–6:2, Psalm 119:65–72

> *"Whenever Jehudi had read three or four columns of the scroll, the king cut them off with a scribe's knife and threw them into the firepot."*
>
> Jeremiah 36:23

LIVE IT

Friends might ignore you when you try to tell them about Jesus. Or they might unmistakably signal you to shut up. But you haven't likely experienced the outrageous hostility the prophet Jeremiah faces from King Jehoiakim.

Jeremiah 36 shows the prophet listening carefully to every word the Lord speaks about the fate of Israel, Judah, and the surrounding nations. The Lord threatens disaster, hoping his people will turn from evil and seek forgiveness. Jeremiah dictates God's message to his scribe, Baruch, who reads the Lord's words in the temple. When royal officials hear these words, fear pierces their hearts. They insist the king hear the message.

As Jehudi, Jeremiah's secretary/assistant, reads the Lord's words, King Jehoiakim slices the scroll, tossing it column by column into the fire. The king and his attendants show no trepidation. They don't rip their clothing, an ancient sign of alarm and grief. Rather than turning from evil and seeking forgiveness, the king tries to silence Jeremiah and Baruch. He orders their arrest, and the Lord responds with a promise to carry out all his threats for Judah's destruction.

Your friends might not be eager to listen to God. But that shouldn't stop you from paying attention to the Lord's words and putting them into action—and respectfully sharing what he says.

PRAY IT

God, I promise to listen to your words and act on them. Help me know how to share them with friends who don't want to listen.

day294 october 21

READ IT

Jeremiah 38:1–40:6, 1 Timothy 6:3–21, Psalm 119:73–80

> *"But godliness with contentment is great gain. For we brought nothing into the world, and we can take nothing out of it."*
>
> 1 Timothy 6:6–7

LIVE IT

Maybe you have occasionally fallen into the trap of buying things you think will make you happy, but the appeal wears off as soon as you get them home from the store. That's when you feel a tug to buy more ... better ... bigger stuff. That inner anxiety is the exact opposite of contentment.

Timothy was serving as a pastor in Ephesus (1 Timothy 1:3) when he received this letter from the apostle Paul. Don't picture Timothy barely surviving in a backward village. Ephesus was a thriving seaport with an amphitheatre that seated twenty-five thousand people. Its temple to the goddess Artemis was one of the Seven Wonders of the Ancient World, built with 127 columns nearly two hundred feet high.

Ephesus was a prosperous and sophisticated place. So Timothy and his congregation would be as challenged as anyone in our culture by God's command to be happy with basics like food and clothing (1 Timothy 6:8). It isn't wrong to have and enjoy things beyond these real needs, because God is the source of every good gift (1 Timothy 4:4, James 1:17). But problems always arise when people rush to get rich. Their desire lures them away from their relationship with the Lord and causes them grief.

There's one cure for the discontentment our culture encourages. When you share with people who have little, you learn that you already have far more than you need (1 Timothy 6:17–19).

PRAY IT

Lord, train me to be happy with what I have. Teach me to share everything you have given me.

october 22 **day295**

READ IT

Jeremiah 40:7–42:22, 2 Timothy 1:1–18, Psalm 119:81–88

> *"Pray that the LORD your God will tell us where we should go and what we should do."*
>
> JEREMIAH 42:3

LIVE IT

In 586 BC the Lord's most dire threats against his people come true. King Nebuchadnezzar and the Babylonian army lay siege to Jerusalem. When they break through the city wall, King Zedekiah of Judah flees. Enemy soldiers catch the king and slaughter his sons and put out his eyes. The Babylonians burn the city and drag all but the poorest people back to Babylon (Jeremiah 39:1–10).

The Ammonites are another of Israel's enemies, and soon an Ammonite named Ishmael assassinates the land's new governor, Gedaliah. He takes scores of other Israelites captive, but they're freed by Johanan and other army officers (41:1–15).

That victory puts Johanan and his allies in a tough spot. They worry Nebuchadnezzar will wrongly strike back at them for Gedaliah's death. So they beg Jeremiah to ask the Lord what they should do. They pledge to obey God's instruction "whether it is favorable or unfavorable" (42:6). Days later the Lord replies that they shouldn't fear Nebuchadnezzar. He commands them to stay in Judah and warns that running away to Egypt will lead to their deaths. Johanan angrily rejects this message. He leads a mass escape of God's people south to Egypt, kidnapping Jeremiah and taking him along (43:1–7).

The lesson? Don't tell God you want to know what he thinks if you aren't ready to do what he says. He deserves your utter obedience, even in those tough times when you question his commands.

PRAY IT

God, help me listen to you even when I don't like what you say. I'm ready to obey as soon as you speak.

day296 october 23

READ IT

Jeremiah 43:1–45:5, 2 Timothy 2:1–26, Proverbs 25:21–26:2

> *"Flee the evil desires of youth and pursue righteousness, faith, love and peace, along with those who call on the Lord out of a pure heart."*
>
> 2 Timothy 2:22

LIVE IT

God knows you face pressure inside and out to go against his commands. So he reminds you to flee evil. Then he tells you why and how to do it.

Recall that Timothy is the apostle Paul's younger friend, his "true son in the faith" (1 Timothy 1:2). As Paul gets ready to die (2 Timothy 4:6–8), he wants to make sure his partner in ministry has the strength to press on. He reminds Timothy of his family's faith (1:3–5) and invites him to join him in serving and suffering for Jesus (vv. 1:6–12). Timothy will only be useful to God if he rids his life of wrongdoing (2:19–21).

That's why the Lord wants you to flee evil. He has a plan for you that requires you to think, speak, and act more and more like Jesus. God doesn't ever expect you to be perfect, but he needs you to be heading in the right direction, away from anything evil and toward everything good.

You can't just try to ditch evil desires. You truly escape when you make it your goal to grow in admirable qualities like righteousness, faith, love, and peace. And that happens best when you team up with others who aspire to follow God as much as you do. So don't try to go it alone in following God. Get together with others who chase him too.

PRAY IT

Lord, I want to pursue you with people who know and love you. Help me find friends who strive to follow you.

READ IT

Jeremiah 46:1–47:7, 2 Timothy 3:1–17, Psalm 119:89–96

> *"All Scripture is God-breathed and is useful for teaching, rebuking, correcting and training in righteousness, so that the servant of God may be thoroughly equipped for every good work."*
>
> 2 TIMOTHY 3:16–17

LIVE IT

The Bible is more than a thick human book. It's based on the reports of people who met God firsthand. They didn't concoct their messages from their own imaginations. They "spoke from God as they were carried along by the Holy Spirit" (2 Peter 1:20–21).

As the apostle Paul coaches his young friend Timothy, he fills out more of what you should know about Scripture. He explains what it is. It's a "God-breathed" document, meaning it was completely inspired by him. (In fact, our English word *inspired* comes from the same idea—"being breathed into.") Paul also details what the Bible does. It's "useful" or "profitable" in accomplishing several things in your life. "Teaching" means it conveys the truth you need about God. "Rebuking" says it convicts you when you mess up, demonstrating what you did wrong beyond any doubt. "Correcting" means the Bible sets you straight. And "training in righteousness" is a term for training a child.

The Lord wants his Word to do more than fill your head with information. He designed it to change your life, showing you how to become his friend and follow him. But unless you're convinced the Bible is more than a book made up by people, you won't take it seriously. You won't let its arguments persuade you or its commands direct your life.

The Bible gives you God's trustworthy words. It hands you everything you need to know to obey God. How are you letting it change you?

PRAY IT

God, you gave me your Word so I can know you. Use it to teach me how to live as your friend.

day298 october 25

READ IT

Jeremiah 48:1 – 49:6, 2 Timothy 4:1 – 22, Psalm 119:97 – 104

"I have more insight than all my teachers, for I meditate on your statutes."

Psalm 119:99

LIVE IT

God warns against thinking you're so smart you take it upon yourself to teach everyone else. The apostle James writes, "Not many of you should become teachers, my fellow believers, because you know that we who teach will be judged more strictly" (James 3:1). James makes a solid point. If you want your thoughts and your life picked apart, just stand up in front of a group and open your mouth.

James goes on to say that the world's smartest people prove their wisdom by their humble deeds. You can't mistake them for people who are all talk and no action. They get their wisdom straight from heaven, and the brains they display are "first of all pure; then peace-loving, considerate, submissive, full of mercy and good fruit, impartial and sincere" (v. 17).

Many people drift through their days never getting any wiser, but there's a way you can join the elite squad of the truly smart. The Lord invites you to "meditate" on his "statutes" (Psalm 119:99). To "meditate" comes from a word that means to "murmur," repeating things to quiet yourself. His "statutes" are the laws the Lord has decreed. You get wise when you continually think hard about the Lord and his ways.

You truly can be smarter than all of your teachers. But you have to know where to get real wisdom.

PRAY IT

God, I want to learn about everything you say. Make me smart as I think about your words and act on your wisdom.

READ IT

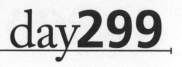

Jeremiah 49:7–50:10, Titus 1:1–16, Psalm 119:105–112

"Your word is a lamp for my feet, a light on my path."

Psalm 119:105

LIVE IT

Picture yourself trying to walk down a wilderness path through the inky blackness of ancient Israel. Once the sun sets, you're practically blind. There are no sprawling cities throwing off electric light for dozens of miles in every direction. A village in the distance is only a dim glow. When clouds roll in and cover the moon and stars, you can't see your hand in front of your face. You might be able to shuffle ahead a few feet, but you won't travel far or fast.

Inching your way through life without God's help can feel like that. Yet he gives you his Word to light the path where you need to go. His obvious commands teach you the right things to do. He teaches you the details you need step by step.

There's one point to remember about that ancient lamp. It's a simple oil-burning contraption that stays lit for a few hours, with technology limited to a wick and a carrying handle. God doesn't give you a modern megawatt searchlight to make your path blazingly bright for miles ahead. He gives you a little lamp to take you forward.

That's a good thing. The Lord uses his Word to lead you. But you can't run off into the distance without him. He tells you exactly what you need to know for the moment. He keeps you close.

PRAY IT

Lord, use your Word to lead me step by step. Light my path and show me where to go.

day300 october 27

READ IT

Jeremiah 50:11 – 51:14, Titus 2:1 – 15, Proverbs 26:3 – 12

> *"For the grace of God has appeared that offers salvation to all people. It teaches us to say 'No' to ungodliness and worldly passions, and to live self-controlled, upright and godly lives."*
>
> Titus 2:11 – 12

LIVE IT

Titus must have thought he was on the wrong end of a prank. The apostle Paul left this guy behind on the island of Crete, instructing him to put everything in order by organizing and pastoring a church eager to follow Jesus. But the people of the island were famous across the Mediterranean for their violent crudeness. The Cretan poet Epimenides even said his fellow islanders were "always liars, evil brutes, lazy gluttons" (Titus 1:12).

Against those odds, God has a plan to remake this island of pirates and thugs. Titus is to start by picking leaders who live up to Jesus's teaching. He should silence false teachers who are spreading lies. And he must deliver hard-hitting practical teaching to every kind of person in his church.

The Lord has reason to be confident the Cretans can be transformed. Out of his limitless kindness he offers to save anyone who believes, giving them a forever home in heaven. But his grace also teaches them to say no to cravings of people set against God. It changes them inwardly, so they have self-control; outwardly, so they act uprightly toward others; and upwardly, so their godly lives are totally committed to him.

God knows how to change even the most stubborn people. He rescues you from the ugliest bad habits and makes you eager to do what's good.

PRAY IT

Lord, thanks for your grace that reaches out to rescue me. Change the worst parts of me. Purify me so I'm happy to follow you.

READ IT

Jeremiah 51:15–64, Titus 3:1–15, Psalm 119:113–120

> *"Sustain me, my God, according to your promise, and I will live; do not let my hopes be dashed."*
>
> Psalm 119:116

LIVE IT

Bad days make you feel like you're deep underwater. Your lungs scream for air. You don't know if you will ever again break the surface and breathe. But then a hand reaches into the water, lifts you to the surface, and sets you on solid ground.

That's how God's promises work. They lift you up and keep you alive. Because the Lord never goes back on his word, they fill you with hope. And they aren't just nice-sounding words, because God always carries out what he says. Psalm 145:13 gives you his solid guarantee: "The Lord is trustworthy in all he promises and faithful in all he does."

God's relationship with humankind is built on his promises. He pledged to give Abraham a new land and make him a mighty nation (Genesis 12:1–2). He vowed to rescue his people from slavery in Egypt (Exodus 3:16–17). He swore he would send a Savior to rescue the human race (Luke 1:30–33). And he promises eternal life to everyone who believes in Jesus (John 3:16).

If you really want to grab hold of the Lord's promises, study Jesus. The apostle Paul wrote, "For no matter how many promises God has made, they are 'Yes' in Christ" (2 Corinthians 1:20). When you trust everything Jesus said and rely on everything he did, all of the Lord's promises to you come true.

PRAY IT

God, you never break your promises to me. I count on your words to lift me up and give me life.

day302 october 29

READ IT

Jeremiah 52:1–34, Philemon 1–25, Psalm 119:121–128

> *"I appeal to you for my son Onesimus, who became my son while I was in chains."*
>
> PHILEMON VERSE 10

LIVE IT

Philemon isn't the Bible's smallest book, but it's close, with just a few dozen more words than 3 John and 2 John. Yet don't overlook this tiny book's big message.

This letter gets its name from its recipient, a friend of the apostle Paul. Philemon is a resident of Colossae, a committed believer, and the owner of a slave named Onesimus. Onesimus might have sold himself to pay off a debt, becoming more like an indentured servant than a slave. Onesimus not only broke his agreement but stole from Philemon as he left.

Onesimus had become a Christian after meeting Paul, who is imprisoned in Rome. Paul encouraged this Onesimus to go home and make things right. But Paul pleaded for mercy. Philemon had the legal authority to beat, brand, or even kill his runaway slave. Paul gently pressured his friend to welcome Onesimus back as a sign of their brotherhood in Jesus.

Paul never says here whether slavery is right or wrong, but elsewhere he teaches that Jesus makes all people equal (Galatians 3:26–9), words that later inspired believers to fight to end slavery in England and America.

This brief personal letter shows you that your relationship with Jesus is bigger than any sin you commit or any wrong you suffer. Maybe you need to show that kind of compassion today. Or maybe you need to get it.

PRAY IT

God, teach me to receive your forgiveness when I do wrong. Help me give your grace when others wrong me.

READ IT

Lamentations 1:1–2:6, Hebrews 1:1–14, Psalm 119:129–136

"In the past God spoke to our ancestors through the prophets at many times and in various ways, but in these last days he has spoken to us by his Son."

HEBREWS 1:1–2

LIVE IT

If you struggle to see the connection between the Old Testament and the New Testament, Hebrews is your book. While you might occasionally get turned around as you wander its pages, this is the most detailed information ever for making sense of how Jesus perfectly fulfills everything you read in the front part of your Bible.

No one knows who wrote Hebrews, though for centuries scholars have suggested possible authors including Apollos (Acts 18:24), Priscilla (v. 2), and Barnabas (4:36). Although the book is anonymous, it's obvious the author doesn't want you to miss the fact that Jesus reveals the one real God.

The author begins with the news that the Lord spoke throughout history through the prophets "at many times and in various ways," but now "he has spoken to us by his Son" (Hebrews 1:1–2). The universe was made through Jesus, and he is "the radiance of God's glory and the exact representation of his being" (v. 3). His throne "will last for ever and ever" (v. 8).

That's just the start of this book's portrait of who Jesus is and what he accomplished. He's the one who "provided purification for sins" and "sat down at the right hand of the Majesty in heaven" (v. 3). If you want to learn more about the Jesus you strive to know and follow, press on into these pages.

PRAY IT

Lord, I want to understand deep things about you, but I need your help. Show me more of yourself in the pages of Scripture.

day304 october 31

READ IT

Lamentations 2:7–3:39, Hebrews 2:1–18, Proverbs 26:13–22

"Because of the LORD's great love we are not consumed, for his compassions never fail. They are new every morning; great is your faithfulness."

LAMENTATIONS 3:22–23

LIVE IT

Ancient Hebrews didn't grieve privately or quietly. When an individual died, relatives wailed. Neighbors ran to join the crying. Families even hired professional mourners to add to the volume of shrieks and sobs.

Don't expect to stumble upon much happiness in the book of Lamentations. Many scholars credit this book to the prophet Jeremiah, the "weeping prophet," but it expresses a whole nation's grief for the loss of its land, capital, and spiritual center. Each of the book's five chapters records a sad poem for the holy city of Jerusalem after the Babylonians burned it to the ground. These "laments" are dirges, songs meant to be sung at a funeral.

This book gives plenty of reasons to cry. It explains why God let his people be taken as prisoners to a distant nation. It describes the desolation of their home city. It announces the people's shame and anguish. It cries out in anguish for God to rush to rescue his people. Yet the book also shouts hope; the Lord's people remain alive because of his steady love. His compassion keeps showing up morning after morning. His faithfulness never stops. So his people can wait patiently for him.

Don't ever give up when you face a bad situation, even when sadness overwhelms you. The Lord can carry you through your worst circumstances and set you free from your darkest feelings. His care for you never fades or fails.

PRAY IT

Lord, reassure me of your love when I grieve. Fill me with hope when I feel sad. I trust you to never quit loving me.

READ IT

Lamentations 3:40–5:22, Hebrews 3:1–19, Psalm 119:137–144

"Your promises have been thoroughly tested, and your servant loves them."

Psalm 119:140

LIVE IT

Occasionally chairs snap, brakes fail, and roller coasters take flight. But you throw your weight on a chair because it's caught you a thousand times. You push on a brake pedal because it's never failed to halt your car. You dare to ride a roller coaster because it's always stayed on the tracks.

The Lord's words do even better. For thousands of years, millions of people have thoroughly tested them and found them flawless. Time after time his promises have proven trustworthy. They never break. That's good reason to fall in love with your Lord's words.

Jesus once invited his followers to test his words. He said, "If you hold to my teaching, you are really my disciples. Then you will know the truth, and the truth will set you free" (John 8:31–32). Every time you apply the Lord's words to a part of your life, you demonstrate that you're his follower. You get a chance to see if they're true. And you discover that you can count on every promise that comes from the Lord's lips. No one has to force you to trust him. You're free.

Even if countless throngs of people have tested God's promises, you still need to check them out for yourself. That isn't a mind game, an exercise you can do in your head. You need to dare to act on the Lord's promises. Then you can figure out for yourself that they're true.

PRAY IT

God, lots of people have tested your promises and found that you're trustworthy. I choose to rely on you too.

day306 november 2

READ IT

Ezekiel 1:1–3:27, Hebrews 4:1–13, Psalm 119:145–152

> *"In my thirtieth year, in the fourth month on the fifth day, while I was among the exiles by the Kebar River, the heavens were opened and I saw visions of God."*
>
> Ezekiel 1:1

LIVE IT

The book of Ezekiel doesn't make much sense if you don't understand its setting right from the start. The prophet Ezekiel is thirty years old (Ezekiel 1:1). Five years have passed since he and some of his fellow Israelites were dragged into captivity by the Babylonians (v. 2). He's hundreds of miles from home living with other exiles along Babylon's Kebar River.

That's when heaven splits open and Ezekiel experiences a wild vision of God. He sees strange angelic creatures high overhead. Wheels spin within wheels. God outshines everything else. It feels like Ezekiel doesn't have words to describe what he sees, so don't be surprised if his descriptions puzzle you too.

Ezekiel sees the Lord and falls on his face. Then God speaks, sending him to speak to his stubborn people. The rest of this book records the prophet's visions, words, and sometimes bizarre actions meant to help the captives come back to God.

You might not always track with the action of this dramatic book. But don't miss its main point: God never turns his back on his people. Even when you rebel against him, he never stops loving you. He never quits trying to win you back.

PRAY IT

God, I'm filled with awe when I see you. Show me how I can serve you. Teach me to let go of my stubbornness and live for you.

READ IT

Ezekiel 4:1–6:14, Hebrews 4:14–5:10, Psalm 119:153–160

> *"For we do not have a high priest who is unable to empathize with our weaknesses, but we have one who has been tempted in every way, just as we are—yet he did not sin."*
>
> HEBREWS 4:15

LIVE IT

Back in the days of Old Testament sacrifices, the high priest was the only person on earth who could enter the Lord's intense presence in the Most Holy Place. Once a year on the Day of Atonement he slipped into that small temple room and sprinkled blood on top of the ark of God, offering the required sacrifice on your behalf.

The high priest stood between you and the Lord. You could never enter that room and experience God for yourself.

It's tough to imagine going through another human being to get to God. It's even more difficult to picture getting close to God through a flawed person who might abuse that power. What if he constantly criticizes you? What will he say about your failures? Will he let you near the Lord or push you away?

Hebrews assures you that Jesus is the greatest of all high priests. Through his death on the cross, he throws open the path to God. He was tempted just like you, so he has sympathy for every pressure you feel. Because he refused to sin, he can teach you to obey.

Jesus is a high priest you don't have to fear. Like Hebrews says, "Let us then approach God's throne of grace with confidence, so that we may receive mercy and find grace to help us in our time of need" (Hebrews 4:16).

PRAY IT

Lord, you know what it's like to struggle against evil. I count on you for encouragement. Give me everything I need to help me grow.

day308 november 4

READ IT

Ezekiel 7:1–9:11, Hebrews 5:11–6:12, Proverbs 26:23–27:4

"But solid food is for the mature, who by constant use have trained themselves to distinguish good from evil."

HEBREWS 5:14

LIVE IT

When you were a baby, you did nothing but eat, sleep, mess your diaper—and look exceedingly cute. But you're not so adorable if you reach adolescence and still act like a baby. That's true of your spiritual life too. The author of Hebrews aims to help you grow up.

Hebrews teaches monumental ideas about the Lord. But they all make a practical point. The author begs you to pay attention so you don't drift from God (Hebrews 2:1). He urges you to believe God's truth so you don't end up hard-hearted (3:12–13). He tells you to run to Jesus so you get all the help you need (4:14–16).

Merely hearing those words doesn't make you mature. In fact, at the end of Hebrews 5 you catch some of the author's frustration. He has far more to teach, but his readers have given up trying to understand. They should be teachers, but they need to go back to school. They should eat meat, but they still sip milk.

It stings when someone you respect tells you to "Grow up!" But it supplies you with a reason to look at yourself and ask if you're making the most of all the opportunities God gives you to mature in the faith, like studying his Word, acting on what you know, and teaming with others to do big things. You're ready for grown-up food. Don't settle for baby mush.

PRAY IT

God, help me digest your Word and grow up. Make me strong and mature, grounded in your truth and living up to what I know.

november 5 **day309**

READ IT

Ezekiel 10:1 – 12:28, Hebrews 6:13 – 7:10, Psalm 119:161 – 168

> *"Then the glory of the LORD departed from over the threshold of the temple and stopped above the cherubim."*
>
> EZEKIEL 10:18

LIVE IT

Solomon was smart enough to know God didn't literally live in the temple, as if he had a physical body and needed a kitchen and bed in a back room. The king said to his friend Hiram about the Lord, "But who is able to build a temple for him, since the heavens, even the highest heavens, cannot contain him? Who then am I to build a temple for him, except as a place to burn sacrifices before him?" (2 Chronicles 2:6).

Nevertheless, the Lord had promised to make the temple the one and only place of his intense presence. Just as God dwelled in the old tabernacle (Exodus 40:34 – 36), he made the temple his new home. When Solomon finished praying to dedicate the temple, "fire came down from heaven and consumed the burnt offering and the sacrifices, and the glory of the LORD filled the temple" (2 Chronicles 7:1).

Those facts help you understand why it's such a colossal tragedy when the Lord's glory leaves the temple. Because of Israel's habitual idolatry and other sins, the Lord's presence up and exits. It's one of the most heart-wrenching scenes of the Old Testament.

Today *you* are the Lord's temple — through the Holy Spirit a part of God resides in you (1 Corinthians 6:19 – 20). Even though he promises to never leave you (Hebrews 13:5), sin makes him feel far away. So admit when you do wrong. Let him know you want his presence in every bit of your life.

PRAY IT

Lord, forgive me when I do wrong and push you away. I want to live close to you now and forever.

day310 november 6

READ IT

Ezekiel 13:1 – 15:8, Hebrews 7:11 – 7:28, Psalm 119:169 – 176

> *"Woe to the women who sew magic charms on all their wrists and make veils of various lengths for their heads in order to ensnare people."*
>
> Ezekiel 13:18

LIVE IT

God didn't drop the Bible into the world with a handy timeline to inform you when the action takes place. Even so, scholars use Scripture's hints to do the math and calculate the timing of significant events.

Obvious dates in the records of Ezekiel and Jeremiah make clear the two prophets preach at roughly the same time. Ezekiel is swept up and transported to Babylon with a group of exiles a decade before the fall of Jerusalem in 586 BC. Jeremiah remains in Judah until after the city's destruction, and he keeps preaching even after being abducted to Egypt (Jeremiah 43 – 44).

The messages of these guys separated by hundreds of miles frequently overlap. Jeremiah goes nose-to-nose with false prophets in Judah who claim to speak for God (Jeremiah 23:9 – 32). Ezekiel battles women who likewise speak false prophecies, inventing speeches in their own imaginations. Ezekiel confronts these false prophetesses for using sorcery to cast death spells. Their charms and veils are dark magic accessories that symbolize tying up victims to hunt them down. Apparently many people died as a result of the deception spread by these women.

You might wonder why God's people listened to these liars. Yet once people reject the truth of the Lord's real words, even the most obvious and destructive lies become believable. If you're not on guard, you can fall for anything.

PRAY IT

Lord, keep teaching me your truth so I know it well. Alert me when I fall for spiritual lies.

november 7 **day311**

READ IT

Ezekiel 16:1–63, Hebrews 8:1–13, Psalm 120:1–7

> *"Too long have I lived among those who hate peace. I am for peace; but when I speak, they are for war."*
>
> Psalm 120:6–7

LIVE IT

Psalm 120 doesn't name its author, but it introduces you to his neighbors, barbarians who hate peace and love war. This song even tells you their names.

The psalmist says he dwells "in Meshek" and "among the tents of Kedar" (v. 5), ancient tribes famed for their ferocity. The people of Meshek likely descended from a grandson of Noah (1 Chronicles 1:5). They grew into a clan of slave traders who spread terror wherever they went (Ezekiel 27:13, 32:26). The tribe of Kedar came from the line of Ishmael (1 Chronicles 1:29).

The author of this psalm has had enough of these lovers of war and their lying lips. He's lived among them far too long. When he wants peace, they go to war. He counts on the Lord to hear his cry and come to his rescue. He trusts the Lord to end their violent behavior.

Even if you don't know any actual Meshekites or Kedarians, you may be surrounded by deceitful people who love violence. They beat up their peers or inflict pain with their words. Even if you're not the target of their physical and verbal violence, there's something drastically wrong if their cruelty ever stops breaking your heart.

Jesus declared, "Blessed are the peacemakers, for they will be called children of God" (Matthew 5:9). If you claim to be on God's side, then step up. Make a habit of striving for peace.

PRAY IT

Lord, I see all kinds of violence everywhere I look. Stop me when I'm part of the problem. Train me to seek peace when others want war.

day312 november 8

READ IT

Ezekiel 17:1 – 18:32, Hebrews 9:1 – 15, Proverbs 27:5 – 14

> *"The prudent see danger and take refuge, but the simple keep going and pay the penalty."*
>
> Proverbs 27:12

LIVE IT

When you get behind the wheel of a car, nothing keeps you safer than gluing your eyes to the road. You can't often stop another driver from slamming you from behind. But as long as you stay alert, you can look ahead and steer around all kinds of accidents.

"Prudence" is a common Bible word for the skill, common sense, and good judgment you need to navigate life safely. It's not at all the same thing as running through life scared. Paranoid people see danger where it doesn't exist. They flee imaginary threats, and their insides churn with fear. But the prudent spot real danger even when others can't see it. They recognize genuine threats. They know when fear is appropriate, and prudence lets them walk through life with calm confidence.

The Lord aims to train you to be prudent. He wants to teach you the skill of looking down a road to avoid danger. Less attentive people plow right ahead, and they pay the price. The Bible calls them "simple." They lack sense and intelligence but abound in ignorance.

Prudence means choosing to be alert about what lies ahead and the harm it can cause you. So think through your day. What threatens to injure you spiritually, emotionally, or physically? Who wants to help you get closer to the Lord — and who wants to drag you away? What might destroy you if you don't pay attention?

PRAY IT

God, make me smart enough to get through today. Help me spot danger and steer around it.

READ IT

Ezekiel 19:1–20:44, Hebrews 9:16–28, Psalm 121:1–8

"Christ was sacrificed once to take away the sins of many."

Hebrews 9:28

LIVE IT

One bold act put an end to the countless sacrifices commanded in the Old Testament. Jesus arrived and died to take away human sin.

That doesn't mean all those offerings were pointless. The Lord ordered them repeated year after year as a reminder of sin (Hebrews 10:1). When sacrificial animals bled and died, it demonstrated in vivid color the awfulness of evil. As precious grain went up in smoke, it proved the high cost of human sin.

The old sacrifices did more than inform people about sin. They hinted that something better was on the way. All the requirements of the law were "only a shadow of the good things that are coming—not the realities themselves" (v. 1). Human sin needed a better solution, because "it is impossible for the blood of bulls and goats to take away sins" (v. 4).

Jesus came and offered himself as a sacrifice for sin. The high priest had always carried a goat's blood into the temple's Most Holy Place once a year, but Jesus took his own blood straight to heaven, appearing in God's presence as the perfect and complete sacrifice for sin (9:24).

The Bible says that "the wages of sin is death, but the gift of God is eternal life in Christ Jesus our Lord" (Romans 6:23). Sin earns death, but Jesus died in your place. His sacrifice was once and for all. He's all you need to get near to God.

PRAY IT

Lord, you sacrificed yourself for me. You took the punishment I deserved and paid for my sins completely. Thank you.

day314 november 10

READ IT

Ezekiel 20:45–22:22, Hebrews 10:1–18, Psalm 122:1–9

"I rejoiced with those who said to me, 'Let us go to the house of the LORD.'"

PSALM 122:1

LIVE IT

"A song of ascents" appears fifteen times in the titles of songs in the book of Psalms (Psalms 120–134). "Ascents" literally means "goings up." Believers sang these tunes while "going up" to Jerusalem to worship. Several times a year thousands of pilgrims traveled to the holy city from every direction to offer sacrifices and participate in religious festivals.

The book of Isaiah fills out that scene. It says, "And you will sing as on the night you celebrate a holy festival; your hearts will rejoice as when people playing pipes go up to the mountain of the LORD" (30:29).

The psalmist says he's gleefully happy when others invite him on a trip to the temple. He likes the crowded feel of the compact city. He recognizes Jerusalem not only as a place to praise the Lord but also as the home of government, "the thrones of the house of David" (Psalm 122:5). He unites with other worshipers who pray for God's peace to reign in the city and overflow with blessings to their family and friends.

You don't have to trek to Jerusalem to get that same rush of excitement. Every time you and your friends get together to worship, you're "going up" to God's holy home. Give each other an encouraging nudge to get moving. Then praise God together and experience his blessings.

PRAY IT

God, my friends and I want to worship you. We promise to invite each other to praise you. We will make a habit of getting together to worship.

READ IT

Ezekiel 22:23–23:49, Hebrews 10:19–39, Psalm 123:1–4

> *"Therefore, brothers and sisters, since we have confidence to enter the Most Holy Place by the blood of Jesus, by a new and living way opened for us through the curtain, that is, his body [. . .] let us draw near to God."*
>
> Hebrews 10:19–20, 22

LIVE IT

Bible writers often use the word "therefore" to signal that everything said so far is about to culminate in major point. Whenever you see the word "therefore," you need ask yourself what it's "there for."

"Therefore" in Hebrews 10:19 signals the start of one of the Bible's most amazing passages. So far the entire book of Hebrews has described who Jesus is and what he accomplished on earth. Because he fulfilled and did away with the Old Testament sacrificial system, you're no longer obligated to keep those ancient commands. And there's a practical point to all that. Because Jesus died for you, now you have confidence to approach God.

Jesus's body is like the temple curtain that covered the entrance to the Most Holy Place, and at his death that veil tore wide open (Matthew 27:51). You now have permanent access to God. You can get close to him anytime you want, with no doubt that he accepts you. He's cleansed you from everything you have ever done wrong. These truths give you and other believers a reason to make a regular habit of getting together to encourage each other to grow in love and good deeds.

Hebrews 10:19–25 sums up so much of what it means to live as a believer. Jesus died for you. So get close to God. Live tight with his people, and love everyone within reach.

PRAY IT

God, because of Jesus I can come close to you with total confidence. You accept me and let me be friends with you and your people

day316 november 12

READ IT

Ezekiel 24:1 – 25:17, Hebrews 11:1 – 16, Proverbs 27:15 – 22

"As iron sharpens iron, so one person sharpens another."

PROVERBS 27:17

LIVE IT

Old Jewish rabbis read Proverbs 27:17 and said it applied to those studying God's law. The arguments and insights each student puts forward make other students smarter. So if you want to get to know God's Word better, don't read it solo. Pull a group together and dig in.

That makes sense. But like all proverbs, this practical truth is bigger than just "spiritual" applications. You need helpers in every part of life. The Bible points this out in nearby passages like Ecclesiastes 4:9 – 10: "Two are better than one, because they have a good return for their labor: If either of them falls down, one can help the other up. But pity anyone who falls and has no one to help them up." Or Ecclesiastes 4:12: "Though one may be overpowered, two can defend themselves."

You and your friends will always be better together than you are on your own. You get more work done. You pick each other up and dust each other off. You stand together against all enemies.

It's one thing to have friends you like to hang out with. It's another to purposely scrape against each other to become better people. That's a process the Lord uses to make you into the person he wants you to be. So who are you helping to sharpen? Who do you allow to hone you to a razor edge?

PRAY IT

God, don't let me settle for friendships that never sharpen me. Bring others into my life that I can help sharpen.

READ IT

Ezekiel 26:1–27:36, Hebrews 11:17–40, Psalm 124:1–8

"By faith Moses ... chose to be mistreated along with the people of God rather than to enjoy the fleeting pleasures of sin."

HEBREWS 11:24–25

LIVE IT

Hebrews 11 presents the Bible's grand "Hall of Faith." It's a unique account of famous Old Testament believers and their bold trust in God.

This famous chapter starts by making sure you know exactly what faith is and how it works. Faith is a firm belief in the existence of things you can't see. As Hebrews 11:1 says, it's "confidence in what we hope for and assurance about what we do not see." You can't please the Lord without this certainty in his existence and promises. Hebrews 11:6 declares that "without faith it is impossible to please God, because anyone who comes to him must believe that he exists and that he rewards those who earnestly seek him."

The ancient saints who fill this chapter excelled at trusting God. By faith Noah built an ark long before floods rose. Abraham left his home for a new land he couldn't pinpoint on a map. Joseph foresaw that his family would one day head back home. Moses left Pharaoh's palace to lead the Israelites to freedom. Rahab welcomed spies. By faith some experienced victory and success. Others were mistreated, imprisoned, beaten, stoned, and sawed in half.

All of these people were "commended for their faith" (v. 39). They were applauded by the Lord for their trust in him. They're all models of how you can live for God.

PRAY IT

God, I want to live today with total faith in you. When I'm challenged to doubt you or your care for me, teach me to trust.

day318 november 14

READ IT

Ezekiel 28:1 – 29:21, Hebrews 12:1 – 13, Psalm 125:1 – 5

"Let us throw off everything that hinders and the sin that so easily entangles. And let us run with perseverance the race marked out for us."

HEBREWS 12:1

LIVE IT

You don't have to be a track star to know you shouldn't race in football gear. You don't run with your shoes laced together. To go as fast and far as possible, you want to lose everything that can possibly hold you back.

The author of Hebrews knew that ancient competitive runners would strip naked to win. So he encourages his readers to get rid of everything that "hinders" (Hebrews 12:1). That word refers to any kind of weight, whether excess body weight or unnecessary gear that keeps you from giving your best effort. Believers should also get rid of "sin that so easily entangles" (v. 1), because getting wrapped up in evil guarantees you will trip and fall.

Following the Lord is a race, but it's not a quick dash. It's a long run that requires true endurance, and the only way you cross the finish line is by looking at Jesus. "Fixing our eyes" (v. 3) means we look trustingly at him, making him our example and power. Your Lord has already finished his own race. He conquered the cross because he had a joyous goal in mind. He wanted to save you and everyone else he loves.

With Jesus as your model, you won't wear out in your efforts to run after him. You won't get discouraged and lose heart. You will overcome every obstacle. You will blast past any opposition.

PRAY IT

Lord, I want to persevere in chasing after you. Help me get rid of anything that holds me back. Let me run fast and far with you.

READ IT

Ezekiel 30:1–31:18, Hebrews 12:14–29, Psalm 126:1–6

> *"Our mouths were filled with laughter, our tongues with songs of joy. Then it was said among the nations, 'The LORD has done great things for them.'"*
>
> PSALM 126:2

LIVE IT

The Lord is better than any late night comic at filling you with laughter and belly-rocking joy. Yet that happiness comes from an unusual source. It's all because he does astonishing things for you.

Don't miss the fact that this song of ascent comes from the era after Israel's captivity in Babylon. It's a radical change from what you read in a passage like Psalm 137, which expresses the deep grief the exiles felt. They sat by the rivers in that distant place and wept as they remembered their homeland. They hung up their harps and refused to sing for their tormenters. But now the Lord has brought them home.

That news is so good that these believers wonder if they're dreaming. Their mouths once were full of the mournful funeral songs you read in the book of Lamentations, but now they spill over with laughter. They all recognize the great acts the Lord has done on their behalf. They're like starving people who go to the fields to plant seed and return home carrying bundles of grain.

God didn't stop doing stunning things back in the Bible. He sends you streams when you feel stuck in dry places. He feeds you when you feel like you're about to starve. He brings you home when you feel far away. Ask him to meet your needs in surprising ways. He will fill you with joy when he does great things.

PRAY IT

God, I'm desperate for your help. I'm stuck in a distant place. Bring me home and meet my every need.

day320 november 16

READ IT

Ezekiel 32:1–33:20, Hebrews 13:1–25, Proverbs 27:23–28:6

"Son of man, I have made you a watchman for the people of Israel; so hear the word I speak and give them warning from me."

EZEKIEL 33:7

LIVE IT

The Bible's first murder was no mystery. Cain and Abel each present an offering to the Lord. Older brother Cain fumes when God looks down on his sacrifice, then he kills his brother. When the Lord asks where Abel is, Cain gives a notorious response. "I don't know," he says. "Am I my brother's keeper?" (Genesis 4:9)

The Lord made the prophet Ezekiel his brothers' keeper and more. He serves as a "watchman" for the entire nation of Israel, standing guard like an army lookout, blowing a trumpet to warn the Lord's people of danger. If a watchman sounds the alarm and no one heeds the warning, the people have no one but themselves to blame for their own deaths. But if a watchman sees danger and fails to warn the people, the Lord holds the watchman accountable for their blood.

Ezekiel faces the daunting job as a spiritual watchman of trying to turn God's people from their evil habits. The Lord doesn't want the wicked to die. He wants them to turn from their sin and live. If Ezekiel fails to pass along this message, the Lord will hold him accountable.

You might not know it, but you're indeed your brothers' and sisters' keeper. You're appointed to stand guard over others within your reach. Show them the Lord's compassion. Sound the alarm when danger heads their way.

PRAY IT

God, give me wisdom to know when and how to speak up to people who live far from you. Teach me what to say.

READ IT

Ezekiel 33:21 – 35:15, James 1:1 – 27, Psalm 127:1 – 5

> *"Consider it pure joy, my brothers and sisters, whenever you face trials of many kinds, because you know that the testing of your faith produces perseverance."*
>
> JAMES 1:2 – 3

LIVE IT

Joy isn't the first thing you feel when you run headfirst into a wall. You spin, you see dazzling lights, and your noggin can feel bruised for weeks. What's there to smile about?

The distressed believers who received this letter from the apostle James probably had the same question. He writes to Jewish believers scattered outside their homeland. It appears that many are poor, possibly because they have been imprisoned and stripped of what little they owned. They face a variety of trials, difficult outward circumstances that test their trust in the Lord. James comes along and tells them to be joyful amidst these problems.

As crazy as it sounds, these believers actually have a solid reason to celebrate. The tests they endure will teach them to press on. Their perseverance will make them "mature," taking them all the way to their final destination. They will be "complete," which means "whole" (James 1:4).

Trials are never senseless. You learn lessons about God and yourself that you can't master any other way. Whether or not you successfully pass these tests depends on whether you bring faith to your tough circumstances. So keep trusting that the Lord cares for you. Believe that he will give you everything you need to survive. Then your trials will help you grow up spiritually. You will get even closer to God.

PRAY IT

God, I want to keep trusting you no matter what I face in life. Encourage me and give me the strength I need to press on.

day322 november 18

READ IT

Ezekiel 36:1–37:28, James 2:1–26, Psalm 128:1–6

> *"My brothers and sisters, believers in our glorious Lord Jesus Christ must not show favoritism."*
>
> JAMES 2:1

LIVE IT

The people who received this letter from the apostle James are deep into the drama of popularity and power. The grammar behind that phrase "must not show favoritism" (James 2:1) proves they already play favorites and need to stop.

"Favoritism" means giving special treatment to a person or group, and you need to look no further than your school lunchroom to spot favoritism in action. And it's everywhere. You see it among your peers, at school, on teams, at work, maybe even at home. Favoritism can leave you feeling left out. Or you might be the person who picks winners and losers, cozying up to the best and ditching the rest.

The readers of this letter dishonor people on the fringes of society, aggressively pushing them down and out of sight. Yet they welcome the same powerful people who mercilessly exploit them, take them to court, and slander their Lord. These believers are blind to their own bad habits. They don't notice evil patterns in how they think and act. They can't see their own sinful prejudices.

Playing favorites is so much a part of your world that you might not think twice about shunning people who seem to have less value. You might not notice when you try to earn the affection of other people just because they're popular. But don't brush this passage aside. God calls favoritism sin. He tells you to stop.

PRAY IT

Lord, help me see when I push some people aside and try to get close to others. You call me to love everyone as much as you love me.

READ IT

Ezekiel 38:1 – 39:29, James 3:1 – 18, Psalm 129:1 – 8

> *"This is what the Sovereign LORD says: I am against you, Gog, chief prince of Meshek and Tubal. I will turn you around, put hooks in your jaws and bring you out with your whole army."*
>
> EZEKIEL 38:3 – 4

LIVE IT

First the prophet Ezekiel sees a vision of the Lord making a valley of dry bones rattle back to life (Ezekiel 37:1 – 14). Then God promises to raise up an eternal king from the line of David (15 – 28), a clear prediction of Jesus's arrival on earth. And now God offers a glimpse into a mighty battle at the end of time (38:1 – 39:29).

This prophecy says many nations will join a ruler named Gog to invade Israel. These troops will "be like a cloud covering the land" (38:9), coming from the north to plunder the nation. But the Lord will arise with fiery wrath, shaking the land and overturning mountains. He will pour hailstones and burning sulfur on the invaders. All this will happen so the world will see that God is in control. He proclaims that everyone will see his greatness and holiness, and know he is Lord (v. 23).

This is an extraordinary battle. "After many days" and "in future years" (v. 8) are unusual terms that point to the final days of earth. At the end of the Bible, Gog shows up to march against God's people (Revelation 20:7 – 8). Though all the details aren't clear, this passage assures you of firm facts: At the end of time, God wins. Evil loses. So choose the right side.

PRAY IT

Lord, you control the present and the future. You promise to defeat evil completely. I choose to be on your side now and forever.

day324 november 20

READ IT

Ezekiel 40:1–49, James 4:1–17, Proverbs 28:7–17

> *"What causes fights and quarrels among you? Don't they come from your desires that battle within you?"*
>
> James 4:1

LIVE IT

God knows why you get into spats and fights. As tempting as it might be to blame others for your arguments and tiffs, the Lord puts his finger on something going on inside you.

The apostle James has just finished warning his readers that the world has two kinds of wisdom (James 3:13–18). There's a wisdom that comes straight from God in heaven. It shows up in qualities like peacefulness, mercy, submission, and consideration for others. There's another kind of wisdom that flows from a far different place. James calls this pattern of thinking "earthly, unspiritual, demonic" (v. 15). It shows up in disorder and all kinds of evil. It's driven by envy and selfish ambition.

That me-first attitude is what fuels conflict. James points out that all human beings have desires raging within. Those longings aren't just ordinary wants and needs; they're urges to get as much pleasure and personal happiness as possible. If you let those cravings run your life, you will try to destroy anything that stands in your way. You "covet," wanting what others have. You "quarrel," demanding you get your way. You "fight," even to the point of physical battles (4:2).

There's a solution to this inner war. Ask the Lord for what you want. But don't bother praying that prayer if you plan to keep his gifts all to yourself. He doesn't answer selfish requests.

PRAY IT

God, show me when my out-of-control desires push me to battle with others. Teach me to live unselfishly.

READ IT

Ezekiel 41:1–42:20, James 5:1–20, Psalm 130:1–8

> *"If you, LORD, kept a record of sins, Lord, who could stand? But with you there is forgiveness, so that we can, with reverence, serve you."*
>
> Psalm 130:3–4

LIVE IT

Imagine being confronted with a list of everything you have ever done wrong. The list spells out every big sin and every small mistake. It details deeds you did on purpose and wrongs you're not even aware of. It covers every mishap, whether thoughts, words, or actions.

How many trees would the Lord have to kill to put all your faults on paper? Maybe not a whole forest, but far more than a little twig. The sweet reality is that you can banish that imaginary list from your mind, because the Bible promises that the Lord doesn't keep a record of your sins.

You can run to God and get forgiveness whenever you need it. But the Lord doesn't forgive your wrongdoing so you can go and sin some more. If sin is bad enough for Jesus to die for, it's bad enough to get rid of from your life. This song informs you that the Lord throws away every record of your sin so you can serve him with reverence, living for him with utter respect.

Forgiveness seems like a prime excuse to purposely go on sinning over and over. But that would be an act of total contempt for your God, showing disrespect for "the riches of his kindness, forbearance and patience" (Romans 2:4). The Lord has wiped your record clean. Don't abuse his kindness.

PRAY IT

God, you forget my faults and get rid of every sin. I promise to live for you. I'm grateful for your love.

day326 november 22

READ IT

Ezekiel 43:1–44:31, 1 Peter 1:1–2:3, Psalm 131:1–3

> *"I saw the glory of the God of Israel coming from the east. His voice was like the roar of rushing waters, and the land was radiant with his glory."*
>
> Ezekiel 43:2

LIVE IT

The Lord's presence dramatically departed from the temple early in the book of Ezekiel. But now the prophet sees the Lord's bright shining glory come back. That's an immensely good thing. It's a sign that God is back in the house.

"Glory" comes from a word that means the "weight" or "heft" or "worthiness" of something. When "glory" is used in connection with God, it means his greatness and splendor. Back in the days when the Lord's people wandered in the desert, glory hung like a cloud over the mountain where God met with Moses. That cloud looked like fire (Exodus 24:15–17). During Ezekiel's first vision, the prophet reported that the Lord's glory looked like a rainbow (Ezekiel 1:28). God's glory had always filled the tabernacle and the temple, but Ezekiel watched it leave as a consequence of the people's nonstop idolatry (11:23).

When God's presence left the temple, it headed east over the Mount of Olives. Now it returns from the same direction, and Ezekiel knows exactly what to do when he experiences God's intense presence. He shows respect by falling on his face (43:3).

The Lord displays his glory every time he acts in your life—like when he sends Jesus to save you, provides food to feed you, and surrounds you with family, friends, and every good gift. So show your respect to him today. Bow down and give your life to him.

PRAY IT

Lord, I will bow to you today. I will live for you with all the respect I know how to give you.

november 23 **day327**

READ IT

Ezekiel 45:1–46:24, 1 Peter 2:4–25, Psalm 132:1–18

> *"But you are a chosen people, a royal priesthood, a holy nation, God's special possession, that you may declare the praises of him who called you out of darkness into his wonderful light."*
>
> 1 PETER 2:9

LIVE IT

Not everyone who meets Jesus gives him a friendly welcome. His best friend John declared that Jesus "came to that which was his own, but his own did not receive him" (John 1:11). Jesus cautioned his followers to expect to face the same treatment he does. He said, "If the world hates you, keep in mind that it hated me first" (15:18).

The world's hatred for believers sometimes turns deadly. The apostle Peter wrote this letter not long before he was killed for his faith around 65 CE. Tradition says he died under the Roman emperor Nero, crucified upside-down because he insisted he was unworthy to die right-side-up like his Master. With that violent persecution looming in the near future, Peter wanted his readers to know that even if the world rejects them, they are accepted and cherished by God.

You may be mocked for your faith at times, or even be told by some people that your faith is a lie. Maybe you'll even lose relationships or have to give up certain opportunities because of people's bias against Jesus. Following Jesus may not always be easy in this world. But whether the people around you applaud your faith or want to shut you out, the Lord's care for you never stops. Once you didn't belong to him, but now you do. Don't let anyone tell you anything different.

PRAY IT

God, I belong to you. You chose me as your own special treasure. I want to tell people everything you have done for me.

day328 november 24

READ IT

Ezekiel 47:1–48:35, 1 Peter 3:1–22, Proverbs 28:18–28

"The man brought me back to the entrance to the temple, and I saw water coming out from under the threshold of the temple toward the east."

EZEKIEL 47:1

LIVE IT

That guy who took Ezekiel on a tour of the new temple kept wading deeper and deeper into water that flowed from the temple. What started as a trickling stream grew knee-deep within a thousand cubits, about a third of a mile. Before long the water became a flood too deep for anyone to cross. And then Ezekiel's tour guide asks, "Son of man, do you see this?" That question forces you to notice a cool fact: God's river gives life.

As this water flows east, it empties into the Dead Sea, a forty-mile long lake so salty nothing survives in its water. God's fresh river makes that deadly waterhole suddenly swarm with fish. People toss their nets in the water. Trees spring up and never stop bearing fruit.

You can see that image of a life-giving river pop up from the front of the Bible to the back. Streams watered the garden of Eden (Genesis 2:8–10). Jesus shouted that thirsty people should all come to him, because anyone who believes in him will experience living water springing up inside (John 7:37–38). The book of Revelation ends with a river watering the tree of life (Revelation 22:2).

Do you see that? God's water gives life. If you're looking for refreshment, you get it from the Lord. He's a river of life. He's a gushing flood for you to dive in and enjoy.

PRAY IT

God, give me water when I feel dried up and dead. Make me swarm with life. Show me how to dive into you.

READ IT

Daniel 1:1 – 2:23, 1 Peter 4:1 – 19, Psalm 133:1 – 3

"How good and pleasant it is when God's people live together in unity!"

Psalm 133:1

LIVE IT

Psalm 133:1 might underwhelm you with the thought of God's people getting along. Unity that's merely "good" and "pleasant" sounds as unexciting as a tiny breeze on a blazing hot day when you really need a swimming pool, ice-cold drinks, and a hurricane of wind.

But unity is better than that. Those words in Psalm 133:1 really mean "great delight" and "good pleasure." If that doesn't entice you, catch the images that come next. Unity is like Aaron the priest getting the oil of God's blessing poured on his head. Instead of halting in his wild mop of hair, the oil gushes down his long beard and drenches his shoulders (v. 2). And the "dew of Hermon" is high-altitude moisture that keeps the top of Mount Hermon green all year long, even when the rest of the nation turns to dust (v. 3).

God intends for you and his people to enjoy unity, and it's not an abstract ideal or fuzzy feeling. The believers in this passage experience harmony as they trek to Jerusalem for worship. They come from every region and tribe in the nation, bumping elbows all the way to the temple. They're rich, poor, and middle-class, but they bow to God together.

If you never experience that togetherness with other believers, you're missing out on one of God's best blessings. Make a plan to bond with other Christians. Don't give up on unity until you get the real thing.

PRAY IT

God, I want to find other believers intent on knowing you and each other. Help us experience the deep unity you want us to enjoy.

day330 november 26

READ IT

Daniel 2:24–3:12, 1 Peter 5:1–14, Psalm 134:1–3

> *"Be alert and of sober mind. Your enemy the devil prowls around like a roaring lion looking for someone to devour."*
>
> 1 PETER 5:8

LIVE IT

You wouldn't mindlessly wander outside if a lion were prowling nearby. Before you put a foot out the door, you would arm yourself with real tactics for not becoming that hungry beast's next meal.

In 1 Peter 5:8 the apostle Peter tells you to be "alert," watching for danger and avoiding obvious traps, and to be "of sober mind," disciplining yourself and thinking straight. Then Peter says why this matters. You have an enemy who never stops hunting you down. The devil aims to trouble you and test your faith until it breaks. He's a lion on the prowl, both sly and deadly. And he's looking for something to eat.

Peter knows how it feels to get caught and chewed up by the devil. Just before his crucifixion, Jesus warned his disciples that Satan was going to shake and beat them all like kernels of wheat. Peter swore he would go to prison or die for Jesus, but the Lord retorted that his friend would soon deny even knowing him. Peter thought he was too tough to become the devil's next victim, but he was wrong (Luke 22:31–38, 54–62). Peter denied Jesus not once but three times before weeping bitterly about what he had done.

Only God can make you smart enough to resist the devil and stay strong in your faith. You won't be alone in your suffering, because other believers face the same test you do. But before long, that lion will go looking for a different meal.

PRAY IT

God, teach me to be alert to the devil's attacks. I'm not smart enough or strong enough to defend myself without your help.

READ IT

Daniel 3:13–4:18, 2 Peter 1:1–12, Psalm 135:1–12

> *"If we are thrown into the blazing furnace, the God we serve is able to deliver us from it.... But even if he does not... we will not serve your gods or worship the image of gold you have set up."*
>
> Daniel 3:17–18

LIVE IT

The book of Daniel oozes drama. The adventure starts when a conquering king seizes the best and brightest Israelites he can find, transporting them from Judah to Babylon to serve in his kingdom.

King Nebuchadnezzar tries to win over Daniel and his friends Shadrach, Meshach, and Abednego by giving them a royal education and spoiling them with rich food. When they choose to stick to a simple Jewish diet, their Babylonian trainers discover these guys aren't pushovers. The four young men end up healthier and smarter than all their peers (Daniel 1:1–21).

The real clash comes when Shadrach, Meshach, and Abednego refuse to bow to a gigantic gold idol, and Nebuchadnezzar threatens to throw them in a blistering furnace. When the young men won't worship the image, they're tied up and tossed in. Moments later the king sees them walking around unharmed in the fire—and there's a fourth person with them, someone who looks like "a son of the gods," a bodily manifestation of the Lord (3:25). The king orders Daniel's friends out of the furnace, praising their God for sparing them.

Those three guys were determined to stand up for the Lord. They hoped he would rescue them, but they decided to obey him whether or not he helped them. They wouldn't stop worshiping the one real God.

Your Lord is worth whatever it costs to serve him. When you're forced to choose between him and anything else, choose God.

PRAY IT

Lord, make me bold when others want me to serve their gods. I choose to honor you no matter what it costs me.

day332 november 28

READ IT

Daniel 4:19–5:16, 2 Peter 2:1–22, Proverbs 29:1–9

> *"Whoever remains stiff-necked after many rebukes will suddenly be destroyed—without remedy."*
>
> Proverbs 29:1

LIVE IT

There's something that happens in the back of your head before you choose to do wrong. It's not as obvious as a cartoon devil popping up on your shoulder, but a little voice whispers that "it's okay ... it doesn't hurt anyone ... nothing will happen ... you won't get caught."

But the truth is it's not okay ... it does hurt someone ... something will happen ... and you will get caught. You just never know when the consequences of sin will kick in.

That's the point of Proverbs 29:1. A "rebuke" is a sharp correction. The person described here is literally "a man of rebukes," someone corrected so often it's as if "rebuke" is now part of his name. To be "stiff-necked" means the opposite of physically bending your neck, a sign of submission. This stubborn person doesn't see destruction coming, and when it does arrive, there will be no way to put him back together again.

You're smart enough not to do wildly stupid things like driving drunk, knowing that sooner or later you will maim or kill yourself or someone else. When you can foresee the consequences of all sins, it's a sign you're starting to think clearly. Sure, you might *think* you'll get away with sin sometimes. But there are usually consequences. Maybe your sin will become a habit that will hook you forever. Or it will cause destruction you can't avoid forever. So get smart. When the Lord corrects you, don't ignore him.

PRAY IT

Lord, teach me not to fight your correction. I want to get rid of every bit of stubbornness and submit to you.

READ IT

Daniel 5:17–6:28, 2 Peter 3:1–18, Psalm 135:13–21

> *"The Lord is not slow in keeping his promise, as some understand slowness. Instead he is patient with you, not wanting anyone to perish, but everyone to come to repentance."*
>
> 2 PETER 3:9

LIVE IT

People in Peter's day were laughing out loud. After all, the Old Testament predicted a "day of the LORD" when God would strike earth and put an end to evil (Amos 5:18–20). So where was he? And Jesus vowed to return to earth riding the clouds in phenomenal power and glory to judge the world (Matthew 24:30). Why wasn't he here?

The apostle Peter says the Lord has a good reason for what humans perceive as a delay. First, the Lord doesn't count time the way humans do. "With the Lord a day is like a thousand years," he wrote, "and a thousand years are like a day" (2 Peter 3:8). Second, God is slow to show up because he doesn't want anyone to die. He's giving everyone time to repent—to quit sinning and turn to him.

That doesn't mean Jesus will never come back. The day of the Lord will surprise the world like a thief, yet no one will miss when the sky and earth melt with fire.

Then Peter asks a crucial question. "Since everything will be destroyed in this way, what kind of people ought you to be?" (2 Peter 3:11). There's a clear answer. You look forward and strive to be holy, committing yourself completely to the Lord as you anticipate his stupendous arrival.

Jesus said you can't predict when he will come back (Matthew 24:36). But whenever he shows up, you can be ready.

PRAY IT

Lord, I look forward to the day when you come back. Help me live for you right now.

day334 november 30

READ IT

Daniel 7:1–8:14, 1 John 1:1–2:11, Psalm 136:1–12

> *"If we confess our sins, he is faithful and just and will forgive us our sins and purify us from all unrighteousness."*
>
> 1 John 1:9

LIVE IT

You're fooling yourself if you think you never mess up. It's tough to dig into the commands of the Bible—all the do's and don'ts—and miss the point that you fall short of God's expectations. In case you're persuaded that you're perfect, 1 John 1:8 sets you straight. It says, "If we claim to be without sin, we deceive ourselves and the truth is not in us."

That's difficult to hear, until you get to the next verse, 1 John 1:9. It teaches, "If we confess our sins, he is faithful and just and will forgive us our sins and purify us from all unrighteousness." If you roll those two verses together, you get one of the Bible's most crucial messages. We all fall down. But God picks us back up.

The literal meaning of the verb "to sin" is "to miss the mark," like shooting an arrow and failing to hit the bullseye. It doesn't matter whether you miss by a little or a lot. It's still sin. But you're a truly bad shot if you claim you hit the target when you don't.

God has a simple requirement. He wants you to "confess" or "acknowledge" your sins to him, agreeing with him about what you did wrong. When you admit your failings, God has an equally simple reaction. He forgives you and cleanses you from every wrong.

PRAY IT

God, I admit my sins to you. I won't ignore them or hide them. I admit them to you one by one. Thanks for your forgiveness.

december 1 **day335**

READ IT

Daniel 8:15–9:19, 1 John 2:12–27, Psalm 136:13–26

"Give thanks to the God of heaven. His love endures forever."

PSALM 136:26

LIVE IT

People know what to expect when you open your mouth. You have signature words or comic lines everyone knows. You might have jokes you constantly repeat or lyrics you sing in your sleep. If you move your lips, you have phrases you say over and over.

Psalm 136 contains an obvious repeated refrain: *His love endures forever.* This song starts by telling you to "Give thanks to the LORD, for he is good" (v. 1) and ends the same way (v. 26). The lines between start and finish recite good things the Lord has done, concrete things the psalmist is grateful for. Some describe God's stunning acts of creation. Others come from ancient Israelite history. Still others sound straight out of your life. But every line illustrates that obvious theme: *His love endures forever.*

That "love" is the Lord's "mercy" or "loyal love," and it's the Psalms' most significant description of God. It's the kind of love that leads the Lord to help people in misery. It's a love that lasts forever. It's part of his unchanging eternal character.

If you want to add a new line to your vocabulary of most-used words, this is a good one. No matter what God gives you, *his love endures forever.* Whenever he leads you through a rough patch, *his love endures forever.* Don't let a day slip by without inserting that line into your life.

PRAY IT

Lord, I have countless reasons to praise you, and I will name them one by one. Your love endures forever.

day336 december 2

READ IT

Daniel 9:20–11:1, 1 John 2:28–3:10, Proverbs 29:10–18

"Do not be afraid, Daniel. Since the first day that you set your mind to gain understanding and to humble yourself before your God, your words were heard, and I have come in response to them."

DANIEL 10:12

LIVE IT

You know Daniel as the guy who survived the lion's den (Daniel 6:1–28), a punishment he received for continuing to pray to the one real God despite a ban by the Babylonian ruler, King Darius. But there's more to his story.

In Daniel 9 this much-loved guy is still praying. He pours out a potent mixture of worship and confession, praising his awesome God and admitting the sins of his whole nation. He pleads to the Lord who rescued his people from Egypt to stop being furious with Jerusalem. He throws himself on God's mercy. Then he wraps up his prayer, saying, "Lord, listen! Lord, forgive! Lord, hear and act! For your sake, my God, do not delay, because your city and your people bear your Name" (v. 19).

In the middle of Daniel 9 this much-respected guy is still praying. He admits sins. He makes requests. Then suddenly God sends a reply through the angel Gabriel. The answer was a long time coming, but the Lord had heard Daniel's words all along (10:12).

If you keep at prayer like Daniel did, it might seem like a long time before you ever hear back from God. You might wonder if it's worth your breath to continue talking. Yet the Lord sends his answers at the right time. And some of his answers are sure to surprise you.

PRAY IT

Lord, teach me to keep praying. I'm not trying to impress you. I just want to stick close to you. I will worship you and tell you what I need.

READ IT

Daniel 11:2–35, 1 John 3:11–4:6, Psalm 137:1–9

> *"By the rivers of Babylon we sat and wept when we remembered Zion."*
>
> Psalm 137:1

LIVE IT

The Bible repeatedly offers up details about the "exile," the period of captivity when God's people were led away to distant Babylon. You learn about this desperate era not only in the history books of 2 Kings and 2 Chronicles but also in prophetic writings like Jeremiah and Ezekiel.

Psalm 137 gives you more than bare facts. Like the book of Lamentations, it lets you feel the pain of people struggling to exist a foreign land. It's easy to picture the Lord's people sitting by a river hundreds of miles from home, weeping as they remember their old city. They can't shake the image of their temple in ruins and their homes and shops burning to the ground. When their captors taunt them with demands that they burst into joyful songs from back home, they hang up their harps and weep some more.

These displaced people wonder how they can worship God so far away from the land where he swore he would dwell with them. They vow never to forget their holy city, and they ask God to strike back at the enemies causing them such horrible anguish.

Some days you might feel like the Lord has left you. But your intense pain doesn't mean God isn't present. It's just one more reason to reach out to him. Even if you don't feel him nearby, he's always with you. He will never abandon you (Deuteronomy 31:6).

PRAY IT

God, you're present even when I worry you're not. You're with me even when I can't feel you.

day338 december 4

READ IT

Daniel 11:36–12:13, 1 John 4:7–21, Psalm 138:1–8

> *"Dear friends, let us love one another, for love comes from God. Everyone who loves has been born of God and knows God."*
>
> 1 John 4:7

LIVE IT

A man named John wrote this letter to close friends to announce that looking at Jesus is how you understand the meaning of real love. He says, "This is how we know what love is: Jesus Christ laid down his life for us. And we ought to lay down our lives for our brothers and sisters" (1 John 3:16).

Jesus gave up his life for you, so you should give up your life for others. It sounds so simple. It also sounds so impossible. Yet the Lord doesn't just command you to love; he gives you the power to do it.

Laying down your life for others definitely doesn't mean you hang on a cross for the world's sins. It doesn't even mean you're doomed to die on someone else's behalf. It does mean you live sacrificially. There's a problem if you talk about love or even feel love but never act in love. Like John says, "Dear children, let us not love with words or speech but with actions and in truth" (v. 18).

Showing others that deep love becomes possible only when you rely on one fact: God is love. Since he's the source of all love, he gives you every bit of the care he expects you to give others. As John says, "We love because he first loved us" (4:19). Once you experience God's love firsthand, your love for others never runs out.

PRAY IT

Lord, help me understand and experience your love for me. When I have your love, I can love others.

READ IT

Hosea 1:1–2:23, 1 John 5:1–21, Psalm 139:1–10

> *"I will betroth you to me forever; I will betroth you in righteousness and justice, in love and compassion."*
>
> Hosea 2:19

LIVE IT

The book of Hosea should come with a warning label: "Don't try this at home." The Lord commands Hosea to do an outrageous deed, instructing him to marry a prostitute and have children with her. It's a true-life illustration showing how Israel acts toward God like an unfaithful spouse.

This book doesn't say whether Hosea and his wife, Gomer, ever laughed and enjoyed happy days together. The couple soon gives birth to three children, assigning them painful names like "Not-Loved" and "Not-My-People" (Hosea 1:6, 9). A couple chapters later you learn that Gomer is living with another man, having become not only his lover but also his property. Hosea can't simply persuade his wife to come home. He has to buy her back with fifteen shekels of silver as well as over four hundred pounds of barley, the price of a female slave (3:1–2). This time he insists she stay faithful to him (v. 3).

Hosea loves his wife despite her adulterous behavior. Obeying God's command had to be as tough for the prophet as it would be for any other rejected husband. Yet his love for Gomer illustrates the Lord's intense passion for his people.

This story's explicit language helps you sense the Lord's pain. He feels betrayed by his people as they chase other gods. This book isn't easy to read. But it shows how God feels when his people choose to leave him.

PRAY IT

Lord, you feel pain when I make anything a false god, letting it become more important than you. Call me home to you when I run away.

day340 december 6

READ IT

Hosea 3:1 – 5:15, 2 John 1 – 13, Proverbs 29:19 – 27

> *"And now, dear lady, I am not writing you a new command but one we have had from the beginning. I ask that we love one another."*
>
> 2 John verse 5

LIVE IT

This letter isn't any longer than a short bit of homework, yet it offers a glimpse into the real struggles of early Christians. Make sure you read 2 John alongside 3 John, because each note tackles the same problem from a different angle.

John wrote in his first letter about the Lord's command to love each other (1 John 3:23). This time around he doesn't apologize for repeating the same instruction (2 John v. 5). But it sounds like his readers have taken love in the wrong direction. John needs to warn them that the world is full of deceivers who teach that Jesus didn't have a real body. They make the Lord nothing more than a spirit, and a Savior without a physical body can't pay the price for human sin.

John tells his readers to shut out these false teachers. Welcoming them into their homes is sharing in their sin (2 John v. 11). John's third letter shows his readers have taken that warning to heart, but now they're slamming the door on genuine preachers. John tells his readers they should welcome these messengers of truth (3 John v. 8).

This trio of letters points out that the right way to love isn't always obvious. The Bible is your first and greatest source of wisdom. But don't be afraid to get input from experienced, trustworthy leaders. Whatever your situation, they can help you figure out the right way to act.

PRAY IT

Lord, I want to obey you but I'm not always sure what that means. Teach me from your Word, and give me leaders who help me choose best.

december 7 **day341**

READ IT

Hosea 6:1–7:16, 3 John 1–14, Psalm 139:11–16

> *"I praise you because I am fearfully and wonderfully made; your works are wonderful, I know that full well."*
>
> Psalm 139:14

LIVE IT

If Psalm 139 doesn't make you feel special, read it again. Plenty of Bible passages praise the Lord's incredible deeds. This one highlights one of his best pieces of work: You.

King David starts these lyrics with the news that the Lord perceives everything. God knows his moves before he makes them, his thoughts before he thinks them, his words before he says them. This insight overwhelms the human mind (vv. 1–6).

David also recognizes there's nowhere he can run where the Lord can't find him. Whether he flies to heaven or tunnels underground, God is there (vv. 7–12). The Lord knows David's intricate uniqueness because he assembled the king inside his mother's womb, making him "fearful and wonderful." But this kind of fear is more magnificent than scary. David is an awesome wonder (vv. 13–18).

This song tells the truth about you and every human being. The Lord knows you inside and out, because he handcrafted you. You're one of his most amazing creations.

David isn't scared to let the Lord see right through him. He even invites the Lord to study him and fix anything wrong. When you understand how much the Lord cares for you as his special creation, you don't fear him. He's your most powerful friend ever. He leads you "in the way everlasting" (v. 24).

PRAY IT

God, I'm not scared that you know me so well. Help me to see why you value me so highly. You made me your one-of-a-kind creation.

day342 december 8

READ IT

Hosea 8:1–9:17, Jude 1–25, Psalm 139:17–24

> *"I felt compelled to write and urge you to contend for the faith that was once for all entrusted to God's holy people."*
>
> JUDE VERSE 3

LIVE IT

"Standing up for your faith" can sound obnoxious, but it's not. It's all about wisely communicating truth to people who need it most.

Jude gets right to his point. He meant to write about salvation, maybe a longer and more complicated explanation of how God rescues us. But instead he shouts a brief immediate warning. False teachers lurk among true believers.

Jude tells his readers to "contend for the faith that was once for all entrusted to God's holy people" (Jude v. 3). To "contend" means to "agonize," the intense effort expended in a wrestling match. It's not a one-time effort but a continuous struggle. And "the faith" is the body of facts about Jesus communicated by God and well known among believers.

This note details the lies of these teachers, but all the issues aren't clear to us a couple thousand years later. We do know these liars turn God's forgiveness into an excuse to keep sinning. They reject Christ's authority to rule their lives as King and Lord. Their arrogance has let them fall prey to evil.

Jude doesn't tell you to use the same tactics on everyone who doesn't agree with the facts about Jesus. He urges a sharp response to false teachers, but he commands you to show mercy to the confused. Helping doubters understand the truth is like "snatching them from the fire" (v. 23).

PRAY IT

God, show me how to respond to people who disagree with your truth. Show me who needs correction—and who needs compassion.

READ IT

Hosea 10:1 – 11:11, Revelation 1:1 – 20, Psalm 140:1 – 5

> *"The revelation from Jesus Christ, which God gave him to show his servants what must soon take place. He made it known by sending his angel to his servant John, who testifies to everything he saw."*
>
> Revelation 1:1 – 2

LIVE IT

The apostle John must have jumped when he heard the blast of a voice behind him. Sentenced to the prison island of Patmos for speaking up about his Lord, this elderly follower of Jesus is praying one Sunday morning when a loud voice tells him to take down a message for seven churches in modern Turkey.

That's the start of a stunning vision that stretches from John's day until the end of time. It's a message from God about what will "soon take place" (Revelation 1:1).

When John turns around, he sees his friend Jesus like never before. He appears as one like the "son of man," a title used in Daniel 7:13 and often used by Jesus as a name for himself, like in Matthew 24:30. Jesus shines with heavenly glory, and he announces he's back from the dead and alive forever and ever.

Revelation means "unveiling" or "disclosure," and the message of this book comes in the form of apocalyptic literature, a popular ancient genre that uses vivid yet sometimes cryptic symbols to portray the clash between good and evil.

You won't catch the meaning of every image of this book. You can still read to catch the main points, which are blazingly clear. Evil meets a bitter end. God triumphs. And believers live forever with him. You're blessed if you accept and act on what God says, "because the time is near" (Revelation 1:3).

PRAY IT

Lord, I look forward to the day you come back to earth. Thanks for helping me understand what lies ahead.

day344 december 10

READ IT

Hosea 11:12 – 14:9, Revelation 2:1 – 17, Proverbs 30:1 – 10

"Give me neither poverty nor riches, but give me only my daily bread."

PROVERBS 30:8

LIVE IT

Money is a double-edged knife. It brings you grief whether you have too much or too little. When you have exactly enough you can wield it as a highly useful tool.

Plenty of people in your world don't have basics like food, clothing, and shelter. Some people experience lack because of their own laziness, as in Proverbs 10:4, which says, "Lazy hands make for poverty, but diligent hands bring wealth." Yet poverty usually comes from complex causes, and the needy are never far from God's heart. Deuteronomy 10:18 says, "He defends the cause of the fatherless and the widow, and loves the foreigner residing among you, giving them food and clothing."

Wealth brings its own set of problems. The writer Agur recognizes a grim danger when he begs God not to give him more than what he needs each day. "Otherwise," he says, "I may have too much and disown you and say, 'Who is the LORD?' " (Proverbs 30:9). The Bible warns that wealth makes it easy to forget God (Deuteronomy 8:10 – 20). Wanting to get rich pulls you away from him (1 Timothy 6:6 – 10).

Money finds its right place when you keep God in the top spot of your life. If you chase money like most people do, you misplace the Lord. But if you work to know him above everything else, he's never out of your sight.

PRAY IT

God, I don't want to make money my biggest priority. You give me everything I need and more. Don't let any of it distract me from following you.

READ IT

Joel 1:1–2:17, Revelation 2:18–3:6, Psalm 140:6–13

> *"Blow the trumpet in Zion; sound the alarm on my holy hill. Let all who live in the land tremble, for the day of the* LORD *is coming."*
>
> JOEL 2:1

LIVE IT

The people of Israel awoke one morning to see swarms of locusts choking the air and covering their fields. The invasion was as deadly as any enemy army. A single swarm of these supersized grasshoppers eats enough food in a day to feed forty thousand people for a year.

The prophet Joel's first words detail the devastation caused by millions of ravaging locusts. The nation's farmers despair. Priests mourn. With fields and fruit trees empty, starvation looms. Joel tells the nation to tear their clothes in grief. He pleads to the Lord for the sake of cattle and wild animals, whose food supplies have vanished. All joy is gone.

Joel sees the locust invasion as a sign of a coming day of the Lord when God will strike the earth and put an end to evil, calling it "a day of darkness and gloom, a day of clouds and blackness" (Joel 2:2). He envisions a fiery army leaping over mountains (vv. 3–5), an image some Bible readers interpret as a picture of nuclear war.

God tells you the right response to his warnings. He says, "Return to the LORD your God, for he is gracious and compassionate, slow to anger and abounding in love, and he relents from sending calamity" (v. 13). Your God never quits being compassionate. When you realize you're headed in the wrong direction, stop. Run back to him.

PRAY IT

Lord, you hate evil. But you love the human beings you made. Teach me to flee sin and come back to you. I can count on your grace.

day346 december 12

READ IT

Joel 2:18–3:21, Revelation 3:7–22, Psalm 141:1–10

> *"Here I am! I stand at the door and knock. If anyone hears my voice and opens the door, I will come in and eat with that person, and they with me."*
>
> Revelation 3:20

LIVE IT

After Jesus announces himself to John at the start of the book of Revelation, he speaks short, hard-hitting messages to seven churches. The Lord knows his people inside and out. He encourages and corrects specific attitudes and actions to help them be "victorious," overcoming evil and enduring all kinds of trials.

These prophetic words read like other New Testament letters. They address issues unique to believers in a specific location, but they contain lessons that matter for every follower of Jesus. And there are famous words in Revelation 3:20 that go straight to your heart.

That verse pictures Jesus standing at a door, knocking to get inside. But this isn't any ordinary door. It's the gateway to your life. Jesus wants you to pay attention to his words and welcome him in. If you or anyone else answers his knocking, he will "come in and eat with that person," and they with him.

"Eat" refers to the main meal of the Middle Eastern day, a long-lasting time of community and enjoyment with your closest friends. So Jesus isn't hankering for a quick bite. He wants to spend time with you, and he offers you deep fellowship with him.

You welcome Jesus into your life the first time you believe in him. But you also invite him in whenever you interact with him. He's always available to meet. You can do that right now.

PRAY IT

Lord, you offer me a one-of-a-kind relationship with you. I want you to be part of every minute of my life.

READ IT

Amos 1:1 – 2:16, Revelation 4:1 – 11, Psalm 142:1 – 7

> *"This is what the LORD says: 'For three sins of Israel, even for four, I will not relent.' "*
>
> Amos 2:6

LIVE IT

God is fed up with his people's constant wrongdoing. You can hear him burst with anger as he speaks through the prophet Amos.

Amos thunders against Israel (the northern kingdom) even though he comes from Judah (the southern kingdom). The Bible mentions his hometown, Tekoa (Amos 1:1), a village a few miles south of Jerusalem. Amos comes on the scene "two years before the earthquake" (v. 1), an event historians can't precisely date.

This real-life guy never planned on becoming the Lord's spokesperson. He wasn't born to a line of prophets, priests, or other religious workers. When pressed for his credentials, he explains, "I was neither a prophet nor the son of a prophet, but I was a shepherd, and I also took care of sycamore-fig trees" (7:14). Yet the Lord compels him to speak up. As Amos puts it, "The LORD took me from tending the flock and said to me, 'Go, prophesy to my people Israel' " (v. 15).

This prophet speaks against Israel's neighbors before turning to the sins of God's people. He rebukes them for abandoning God's laws and following false gods. He repeatedly denounces Israel's treatment of the poor, a key theme of his preaching.

Amos illustrates that God can pluck you out of your everyday life and send you to places you never expected, doing things you could never foresee. Tell him you're willing to serve him wherever and however he wants.

PRAY IT

God, I want to serve you in whatever way you think is best. Prepare me to work for you and launch me into ministry.

day348 december 14

READ IT

Amos 3:1–4:13, Revelation 5:1–14, Proverbs 30:11–23

> *"Worthy is the Lamb, who was slain, to receive power and wealth and wisdom and strength and honor and glory and praise!"*
>
> Revelation 5:12

LIVE IT

You might have heard the details of the cross so many times that you quit listening when the old story comes up. Yet your faith has seriously fizzled if you ever stop being astonished by your Lord's death and resurrection on your behalf. After all, heaven will sing forever about what Jesus did for you.

Right after the Lord dictates messages for seven ancient churches, he props open the door to heaven and lets John peer inside (Revelation 4:1). The Spirit sweeps John up and he stands before God's jewel-crusted throne. The creatures around the Lord all bow and cast their own crowns at the base of the throne. They sing that he deserves worship for creating the world (v. 11).

A powerful angel next wonders aloud who can open "the scroll," a document with seven seals that unleashes the next events of history. Out of all the beings in the universe, only the Lamb has earned the right to break the seals. He's worthy because he died for the world, bringing to God people "from every tribe and language and people and nation" (5:9).

Jesus's death for all humankind makes him worthy of worship. His blood set you free and transformed you into an eager servant of God. So don't take what he did for granted. Open your mouth and worship him. Hand over your life to him and serve him.

PRAY IT

Lord, I won't ever forget what you have done for me. I won't ever stop worshiping you. You deserve everything I can give you.

READ IT

Amos 5:1–27, Revelation 6:1–27, Psalm 143:1–12

"But let justice roll on like a river, righteousness like a never-failing stream!"

AMOS 5:24

LIVE IT

You never have to wonder what the prophet Amos is thinking. As soon as he opens his mouth you discover he has a message burning inside. He aims to rescue the poor and oppressed.

Amos points out the obvious idolatry and immorality of God's people. But right from the start the prophet attacks people who mistreat the weakest members of society. He says the Israelites "sell the innocent for silver, and the needy for a pair of sandals" (Amos 2:6), forcing neighbors into slavery and selling them for the price of cheap flip-flops. When the Israelites go to court, "they trample on the heads of the poor as on the dust of the ground and deny justice to the oppressed" (v. 7).

The prophet compares rich women to well-fed cows who force their husbands to crush the needy (4:1). Even though the wealthy have money to build stone mansions, the poor are taxed to the point of starvation (5:11). Merchants cheat the poor with dishonest scales (8:5).

There's no evidence that Israel ever listened to Amos, and a few decades later the kingdom fell to invading Assyrians. But even now the words of Amos push you to work to overcome injustice. For example, around the world, thousands of people are working in sweatshops to create the clothes we buy, and you can affect change by being aware of where your clothing and other products are made. People are living with day-to-day starvation, and you can find an organization that helps meet their needs. Like the prophet said, "Let justice roll on like a river, righteousness like a never-failing stream!" (5:24).

PRAY IT

God, show me where I take advantage of the needy, whether they are people nearby or far away. Show me how to work for justice in my world.

day350 december 16

READ IT

Amos 6:1 – 7:17, Revelation 7:1 – 17, Psalm 144:1 – 8

> *"Part your heavens, LORD, and come down; touch the mountains, so that they smoke. Send forth lightning and scatter the enemy."*
>
> PSALM 144:5 – 6

LIVE IT

David doesn't want small favors from God. He begs the Lord to rip open heaven. He urges God to stretch out his hand and make mountains smoke. He wants bolts of lighting to send his enemies running. And those are just a few of the items on his list of prayer requests.

David needs an unusual brand of divine assistance to help him rule Israel. His enemies pursue him with deadly swords (Psalm 144:10). He fends off foreigners spewing lies (v. 8). He worries about enemies breaking through city walls, and he hopes he never hears cries of distress rise from the streets (v. 14). So he asks the Lord for military victory. He praises God for training him to win at war. He counts on God to make entire peoples submit to him (vv. 1 – 2).

As David watches over the nation, he looks for God's blessings not just for him but for every person under his care. He wants young women and men to grow up like well-fed plants (v. 12). He prays for barns full of crops and fields covered with flocks (v. 13).

David's requests for military triumph might not resemble what you need from God. But you can make your own bold requests of the Lord, asking him to meet your real needs. He knows you're a mere mortal. Your life is but a breath. But because he is your God, you can count on his care.

PRAY IT

Lord, you know my unique problems. No one else can meet my needs. I trust you to bless me.

december 17 **day351**

READ IT

Amos 8:1–9:15, Revelation 8:1–9:12, Psalm 144:9–15

> *"'In that day,' declares the Sovereign LORD, 'the songs in the temple will turn to wailing. Many, many bodies—flung everywhere! Silence!'"*
>
> AMOS 8:3

LIVE IT

Amaziah the priest must have thought Amos was a country boy who was easy to push around. He tattles on the prophet to his boss, King Jeroboam. He accuses Amos of conspiring against the king. Then he orders Amos to go home to Judah and do his prophesying there (Amos 7:10–12). Instead of backing down, Amos utters an intense prophecy against the priest. He says that Amaziah's wife will become a prostitute, and his children will die in war (v. 17).

Amos rages at Israel's religious system. He sees people bring sacrifices to the illegal worship center they had erected then go home bragging about their offerings (4:4–5). God's people sing in the temple, but they trample the needy and kill off the poor (8:4). They celebrate the New Moon festival and refrain from working on the Sabbath, but they can't wait to get back to their business of cheating the poor and selling slaves (vv. 5–6).

When God can't take any more of their hypocrisy, he promises to fling dead bodies everywhere. And the Lord has another, even darker threat. Because his people refuse to listen to him, he will send a famine—not of food or water, but a famine of his word (v. 11).

Bad things happen when God's people rebel against him. When they stop listening to him, sometimes he stops speaking.

PRAY IT

God, warn me when I act like a hypocrite. I want my relationship with you to be real. I promise to listen to everything you say to me.

day352 december 18

READ IT

Obadiah 1–21, Revelation 9:13–10:11, Proverbs 30:24–33

> *"The rest of mankind who were not killed by these plagues still did not repent of the work of their hands."*
>
> Revelation 9:20

LIVE IT

Revelation shows off ultimate human stubbornness. From the instant the Lamb opens the first of seven seals on a heavenly scroll (Revelation 6:1), God starts to pour judgment on the earth. Yet some humans refuse to quit sinning.

Revelation paints vivid pictures of destruction ranging from war to famine to plagues. Earthquakes rock the earth. The sun turns black, and the moon goes red. Stars drop from the sky, and the heavens roll up like a scroll. Everyone from rulers to regular people scurry to hide from the Lord's anger. "For the great day of their wrath has come," they say, "and who can withstand it?" (v. 17).

This last book of the Bible shows slain believers patiently waiting for their deaths to be avenged (vv. 9–11) and others killed during the great tribulation (7:14). Then seven trumpets signal more destruction. Humans die in vast numbers.

Some people survive these plagues. Despite having seen evil punished on an immense scale, they refuse to repent—to quit sinning and turn to God. They continue worshiping idols, practicing dark arts, and committing sexual sin.

It's tough to imagine how these people living at the end of time can see the harsh consequences of sin and continue doing evil. Yet refusing to follow the Lord here and now is like imitating their stubbornness. And no matter when or where you live, that's not a smart move.

PRAY IT

God, help me see the wrong things I do and turn away from them. I want to get rid of my stubbornness and obey you completely.

READ IT

Jonah 1:1–4:11, Revelation 11:1–19, Psalm 145:1–7

> *"Now the LORD provided a huge fish to swallow Jonah, and Jonah was in the belly of the fish three days and three nights."*
>
> JONAH 1:17

LIVE IT

Bible critics say the book of Jonah is nothing more than a big fish story. But Jesus seemed to accept this account as literal history, using Jonah's three days in a fish belly to make a point about his own death and resurrection (Matthew 12:40). Despite this debate, the book's lesson is obvious: Your God longs to show mercy.

The Lord tells Jonah to preach to the hated enemy city of Nineveh, capital of the Assyrian empire, a kingdom famous for rampant sin and brutal military tactics. The Assyrians had overrun Israel and conquered it, so you can imagine they weren't Jonah's favorite people. Jonah runs from the Lord, boarding a ship and heading as far and fast as he can in the opposite direction. God whips up a storm, and Jonah's shipmates toss him overboard to save their own lives.

When the Lord sends a huge fish to swallow Jonah, it might seem like he's lashing out. But that fish actually rescues the prophet from drowning. As soon as Jonah admits his foolishness, the fish vomits him onto land (Jonah 2:10).

The Ninevites surprise Jonah by believing God's message. Even the king gets rid of his royal clothes and mourns. Because they turn from their evil ways, God doesn't destroy them.

You might not like that God wants to show kindness to your enemies. It's especially aggravating that he uses you to demonstrate his love. But the Lord always longs to give mercy. He gave it to you, so pass it along.

PRAY IT

Lord, I don't love my enemies like you do. Give me your concern for them. Teach me how to show them your mercy.

day354 december 20

READ IT

Micah 1:1–4:13, Revelation 12:1–13:1a, Psalm 145:8–13a

> *"The accuser of our brothers and sisters, who accuses them before our God day and night, has been hurled down."*
>
> Revelation 12:10

LIVE IT

There's a dazzling woman who gives birth in Revelation 12:2. Readers of this book disagree whether the woman is Israel, the church, or the Virgin Mary. But there's no doubt about the newborn. That baby boy is Jesus.

As the woman goes into labor, a dragon stands ready to catch the baby Jesus, who "will rule all the nations with an iron scepter" (v. 5). Jesus escapes when he is snatched up to heaven, a reference to his ascension (Acts 1:9).

After the baby's birth, war breaks out in heaven. The archangel Michael hurls the dragon to earth. The dragon is the "ancient serpent called the devil, or Satan, who leads the whole world astray" (Revelation 12:9). The real powers behind the dragon's demise are events happening on earth. He's defeated by "the blood of the Lamb," Christ's death on the cross. He's beaten by "the word of their testimony," believers who speak up about Jesus even to the point of dying for their faith (v. 11). The dragon once continually accused God's people of sin. The cross means your guilt is gone, so he has no more power to condemn you.

The dragon doesn't go down without a fight. Two beasts soon emerge as his allies, including one known by the number 666 (13:18). Yet you have nothing to fear from dragons, beasts, or any other supernatural force of evil. Just wait. Their final defeat is coming.

PRAY IT

Lord, you protect me from evil beings who cause chaos in my world. Because of Jesus's death, evil is going down.

december 21

day355

READ IT

Micah 5:1 – 7:20, Revelation 13:1b – 18, Psalm 145:13b – 21

> *"He has shown you, O mortal, what is good. And what does the* LORD *require of you? To act justly and to love mercy and to walk humbly with your God."*
>
> MICAH 6:8

LIVE IT

You can get all wrapped up in flashy religious activities, but the Lord calls you to a faith that's simple and real. He wants you to act justly, love mercy, and do life full of humble respect for him.

Micah spoke for God about the same time as the prophet Isaiah, during the reigns of kings including Hezekiah. He came from a country town in southern Judah, Moresheth (Micah 1:1), and he railed against all kinds of corruption from the top to the bottom of his society.

Micah announces that the Lord has a case against his people. God had rescued them from slavery in Egypt and commanded them to worship only him (Exodus 20:1 – 6). Micah asks these fellow worshipers how they should approach God, hitting them with intentionally absurd questions. Does God need thousands of rams or ten thousand rivers of olive oil? Does he require them to kill their firstborn children as payment for sin?

No! God expects a better response. He's already told them what's good. To "act justly" means to live with fairness to all. To "love mercy" is to happily show kindness to others. To "walk humbly with your God" means to stay continually connected to him, recognizing that he's infinitely high above you.

Outward acts of worship aren't totally worthless, but they mean nothing without a loving heart. So don't do anything for show. Do everything to live rightly with God.

PRAY IT

God, alert me when my faith has become an outward act. I want to act justly, love mercy, and walk humbly with you.

day356 december 22

READ IT

Nahum 1:1 – 3:19, Revelation 14:1 – 13, Proverbs 31:1 – 9

> *"If anyone worships the beast and its image and receives its mark on their forehead or on their hand, they, too, will drink the wine of God's fury."*
>
> Revelation 14:9 – 10

LIVE IT

You met the beast back in Revelation 13, where he emerges from the sea to fill everyone with awe and wage war against God's people. He ultimately gains control of anyone who hasn't trusted in Jesus and had their names inscribed in the Lamb's book of life (Revelation 13:7 – 8).

A second beast emerges from the sea to promote the first beast. This deceiver forces everyone on earth to receive a mark on their right hand or forehead necessary to buy or sell anything. The "number" or "name" of the first beast is 666. That name identifies him as the most dominant man ever, a ruler John calls "the antichrist" (1 John 2:18).

Revelation 14 shows a crowd of people with a different mark. These 144,000 wear the names of the Lamb and his Father on their foreheads, and they sing a fresh song. After that pause three angels take wing to proclaim the gospel to the world and warn that anyone who worships the beast and receives his mark will face God's fury.

All of these details are baffling. But the Bible tells you how you should respond to these things now and forever. It says, "This calls for patient endurance on the part of the people of God who keep his commands and remain faithful to Jesus" (Revelation 14:12). Keep obeying God, count on his love, and let him take care of your future.

PRAY IT

God, keep me obedient to you. You're the only God I will ever worship. I know your love carries me through life.

READ IT

Habakkuk 1:1 – 3:19, Revelation 14:14 – 15:8, Psalm 146:1 – 10

> *"Though there are no sheep in the pen and no cattle in the stalls, yet I will rejoice in the LORD, I will be joyful in God my Savior."*
>
> HABAKKUK 3:17 – 18

LIVE IT

The prophet Habakkuk doesn't make speeches to the people around him. His book is a question-and-answer session with the Lord. He lodges a complaint, then waits for an answer. Once God replies, he unleashes another objection.

Habakkuk sounds desperate. He cries, "How long, LORD, must I call for help, but you do not listen?" (Habakkuk 1:2). He sees violence everywhere, and he can't understand why the Lord doesn't put an end to injustice. God replies that he's raising up the Babylonians, a cruel and impulsive people, to sweep across the earth and punish the people of Judah.

The prophet isn't completely pleased with that solution. In a second complaint he reminds the Lord of his holiness. God is too pure to tolerate evil. He doesn't put up with wrongdoing. So how can the Lord use the evil Babylonians to do his work? The Lord again replies. He tells Habakkuk to wait for the end of the story. One day God will destroy Babylon, paying back their plunderings and killings.

You can be like Habakkuk and ask God bold questions. His answers might make your heart pound and your lips quiver. But you can settle in and wait for the Lord to act, being happy about your God no matter what happens. Even when life leaves you confused, the Lord makes you strong. He lets your feet dance on mountaintops.

PRAY IT

God, thanks that you welcome my questions. Help me hear your answers. Put me at ease as I trust in you.

day358 december 24

READ IT

Zephaniah 1:1–3:20, Revelation 16:1–21, Psalm 147:1–11

> *"Praise the LORD. How good it is to sing praises to our God, how pleasant and fitting to praise him!"*
>
> PSALM 147:1

LIVE IT

Maybe you pray at the dinner table, reciting words you learned as a toddler. Or you listen to Christian music, then mouth the lyrics all day long. And when you show up at church, you sing a hymn or whatever pops up on a screen. There's nothing wrong with using any of these scripts to praise the Lord. But how often do use your own words to worship?

God deserves praise. He commands it. It also happens to be a good thing to do, both "pleasant and fitting" (Psalm 147:1). You can scan this psalm and many others to discover reasons to praise God. He's good to his people, fixing their hurts (v. 3). He's mighty over creation, calling out each star by name (v. 4). His intelligence knows no limits (v. 5). He upholds everyone who depends on him (v. 6).

You have far more to praise God for than you might realize. Think about everything he does for you morning, noon, and night. Ponder how he helps you at home, school, work, and with friends, sports, and hobbies. Think of reasons to be thankful for the past and hopeful for the future.

You can worship God through speaking or writing a prayer, by making up a song, or creating art that expresses what you think and feel. You can get creative on your own or with friends. Whatever you do, let your own words flow. It's pleasant and fitting to praise God.

PRAY IT

God, you give me countless reasons to praise you. Teach me to worship you from my heart using my own words.

december 25 **day359**

READ IT

Haggai 1:1 – 2:23, Revelation 17:1 – 18, Psalm 147:12 – 20

> *"Then the word of the* Lord *came through the prophet Haggai: 'Is it a time for you yourselves to be living in your paneled houses, while this house remains a ruin?'"*
>
> Haggai 1:3 – 4

LIVE IT

The Jews arrived home from exile in Babylon nearly two decades before the start of this book. Immediately after their return, they erect an altar for burnt offerings and begin to rebuild the temple. When the foundation is complete, they celebrate and praise God. But opposition and their own concerns soon distract them, and the work halts (Ezra 4:24).

The prophet Haggai comes on the scene and confronts God's people. The Lord has noticed they live in houses with fine wood paneling while his own home remains a heap of rocks. The Lord commands his people to head to the mountains and bring back enough timber to finally finish the temple.

People who remembered the first temple aren't impressed by this new house of worship. But the Lord tells his people to be strong. He promises to help Zerubbabel the governor and Joshua the high priest. He will make this house even more glorious than the first.

This ancient scene shows how easy it is to pay attention to your own interests and forget about the Lord and his concerns. But God repeats a caution that can help you keep your priorities straight. He says, "Give careful thought to your ways" (Haggai 1:5, 7; 2:15, 18). If you think hard about how you live, you will know what it means to put God first.

PRAY IT

God, I choose to put you first in everything I do. Show me when I'm not living up to that goal. Help me keep you as my top priority.

day360 december 26

READ IT

Zechariah 1:1 – 4:14, Revelation 18:1 – 17a, Proverbs 31:10 – 20

"Charm is deceptive, and beauty is fleeting; but a woman who fears the LORD is to be praised."

PROVERBS 31:30

LIVE IT

No one knows for sure who King Lemuel is (Proverbs 31:1). Early rabbis believed "Lemuel" was a nickname for King Solomon or King Hezekiah. Or it could be the name of an Arabian prince. Whoever Lemuel is, he has a smart mom.

Lemuel's mother cautions her son not to waste his strength on women, avoiding the bad habit of kings who used their power to collect sizeable harems. She warns that alcohol will make the king forget his pronouncements and mistreat the oppressed. She instructs him to speak up for citizens too poor and powerless to speak for themselves (vv. 1 – 9).

Lemuel's mom then tells him what to look for in a wife. He should aim for a woman of "noble character" (v. 10). This "Proverbs 31 woman" embodies all the wisdom contained in this book. She works hard at business and provides for her family. She labors into the evening not to get wealthy but to give to the poor. She keeps her family well-dressed and warm. No one can accuse her of weakness or embarrassing behavior. She faces the future without fear, and her whole family calls her "blessed" (v. 28).

Most important of all, this woman lives for God with utter respect. Whether you're a guy or a girl, that's solid advice. Commit yourself completely to the Lord. And when you hunt a date or a mate, put that quality at the top of your list.

PRAY IT

Lord, make me a person of deep character. Help me live for you and seek a spouse who follows you completely.

december 27 **day361**

READ IT

Zechariah 5:1 – 8:23, Revelation 18:17b – 19:10, Psalm 148:1 – 6

"Praise him, sun and moon; praise him, all you shining stars."

PSALM 148:3

LIVE IT

When you worship the Lord, you join a cosmic choir that includes more than human beings. Psalm 19:1 says, "The heavens declare the glory of God; the skies proclaim the work of his hands." And the sky isn't the only thing in the universe that opens its mouth wide to praise God.

Psalm 148 shows every part of the Lord's creation bowing in worship. Praise starts in the heavens, "the heights above" (Psalm 148:1). It rings out among the angels, the Lord's heavenly army. It echoes from the sun, moon, and stars to the farthest reaches of space. All of these examples of the Lord's handiwork praise him because his command created them. He spoke and they sprang into existence (Genesis 1:3 – 14).

The Lord's earth-bound creation joins the song. Sea creatures and fish swimming the ocean depths sing. The weather waves its praise. Mountains large and small are joined by all kinds of trees. Wild and domestic beasts on land and in the air can't help but worship. Rulers from every part of the world worship the Lord along with men and women of every age (Psalm 148:7 – 12)

Only God deserves this kind of intense worship. His splendor rises above the entire universe (v. 13). When you praise God, you might think you're the only one singing. But the whole world joins with you. Praise the Lord!

PRAY IT

God, teach me to praise you nonstop. You're the only thing in the universe that deserves that kind of applause. Your greatness inspires me to worship you.

day362 december 28

READ IT

Zechariah 9:1 – 11:17, Revelation 19:11 – 21, Psalm 148:7 – 14

> *"On his robe and on his thigh he has this name written: KING OF KINGS AND LORD OF LORDS."*
>
> REVELATION 19:16

LIVE IT

Sometimes it doesn't look like Jesus is boss of your world. Evil runs rampant. Violent people get away with murder and more. Politicians lie, businesses cheat, and peers do wrong without ever getting in trouble. How can anyone think the Lord controls the world?

God made the world, so he owns it (Psalm 24:1 – 2). Yet his creation has lived in all-out rebellion since Adam and Eve disobeyed the Lord (Genesis 3:1 – 24). The world doesn't submit to Jesus now, but one day it will. The Bible declares that one day every human being will admit that Jesus Christ is Lord (Philippians 2:10 – 11).

The book of Revelation alerts you to facts about the future, but sometimes it also flashes back to the past. And there was a monumental moment in Revelation 11. Heaven shouted because at that moment "the kingdom of the world" became "the kingdom of our Lord and of his Messiah" and "he will reign for ever and ever" (Revelation 11:15). Jesus took his enormous power and began to rule (v. 17).

The arrival of that kingdom commenced when Jesus came to earth to live, die, and rise. But his reign won't be complete until he comes back as King of Kings and Lord of Lords. So you can bow to him now and live for him. If you don't, you will still bow to him later.

PRAY IT

Lord, I will live with you as my King even when others don't submit to your reign. You're in charge of my world and my life.

READ IT

Zechariah 12:1 – 14:21, Revelation 20:1 – 15, Psalm 149:1 – 9

> *"They will look on me, the one they have pierced, and they will mourn for him as one mourns for an only child, and grieve bitterly for him as one grieves for a firstborn son."*
>
> ZECHARIAH 12:10

LIVE IT

You can find Jesus all over the pages of the book of Zechariah. The man behind this book started prophesying as a young guy (Zechariah 2:4), a couple of months after Haggai wrapped up his preaching, and both men call the nation back from its selfishness to finish rebuilding the temple. But Zechariah preaches about more than God's house. He highlights the greatness of the Messiah promised by the Lord.

Zechariah describes this coming Savior as "the Branch" (Zechariah 3:8) who would serve as both king and priest (6:12 – 13). That's an exact description of Jesus's role on earth (Hebrews 1:1 – 4).

Details of the story of Palm Sunday show up here (Zechariah 9:9) hundreds of years before Jesus rides a donkey into Jerusalem (Matthew 21:1 – 9). His arrival on such a humble animal shows he's a king who comes in peace.

You catch facts about Judas's betrayal of Jesus both here (Zechariah 11:12 – 13) and in the New Testament (Matthew 26:15). And the prediction that Jerusalem's people will grieve for one they pierce (Zechariah 12:10) comes to pass as Jesus hangs on the cross (John 19:34, 37).

God had a plan from the very beginning to save you through Jesus. He laid out the details long in advance so you could recognize the Savior when he showed up on earth. It's all a sign of his one-of-a-kind care for you.

PRAY IT

God, you had a plan to rescue me. You show me how to recognize the Savior. Thanks for your astounding love.

day364 december 30

READ IT

Malachi 1:1 – 2:16, Revelation 21:1 – 27, Proverbs 31:21 – 31

" 'I have loved you,' says the LORD. 'But you ask, "How have you loved us?" ' "

MALACHI 1:2

LIVE IT

The Israelites felt so far from God that they started to doubt God's love. When he said, "I love you," they said, "Really? Why should we believe that?"

God always adored his chosen people. He didn't pick Israel because they were the best among the nations. He simply made a choice to love them (Deuteronomy 7:7). He saw their plight as slaves and plucked them from death. He would never quit loving them.

That didn't mean God wouldn't set consequences for sin, any more than good parents quit setting boundaries for their children. And it didn't mean Israel would never feel distant from him. But when they felt far away, it wasn't his fault. It was their doing.

The Lord reminds the people that they aren't giving him their all. They bring imperfect animals for sacrifices, like handing a best friend a broken gift (Malachi 1:6 – 14). Priests fail to teach truth (2:1 – 9). Husbands and wives break God's commands against divorce (vv. 10 – 16). Everyone acts unjustly (2:17 – 3:5) and they don't bring the offerings due him (3:6 – 12).

When you don't give the Lord your best, it's no surprise he seems distant. You can't live far from God and expect to feel like he's your tight friend. Pull close to him, and he pulls close to you (James 4:8).

PRAY IT

God, you choose to love me even when I don't deserve it. When you seem far away it's because I have wandered away. Help me live for you from now on.

READ IT

Malachi 2:17–4:6, Revelation 22:1–21, Psalm 150:1–6

"The throne of God and of the Lamb will be in the city, and his servants will serve him. They will see his face, and his name will be on their foreheads."

Revelation 22:3–4

LIVE IT

The Bible is a rare book where it's okay to peek at the final pages to see how it ends. The Lord wants you to be sure not only about the future of your planet and everything you call home but also about your own eternal destiny.

After all the seals and trumpets and bowls of Revelation, the book describes God's new city descending from heaven. It shines with God's glory, a crystal-clear brilliance. The city is constructed of pure gold, built on foundations bedazzled with every kind of precious stone. Each of the city's twelve gates is carved from a gigantic pearl (Revelation 21:9–21).

But the stunning appearance of this fresh construction isn't what matters most. The best part of heaven is God himself. He now lives with believers forever and ever. The Bible declares that "they will be his people, and God himself will be with them and be their God" (v. 3). And the Lord will "wipe every tear from their eyes. There will be no more death or mourning or crying or pain, for the old order of things has passed away" (v. 4).

This book—and the Bible—wrap up with the truth that Jesus is coming soon (22:20). He invites you to come and drink of his free water of eternal life (v. 17). The Lord himself is the only thing that can quench your thirst now and forever.

PRAY IT

God, I look forward to living with you forever in heaven. Keep my trust in you strong as I live for you right now.

Check out this bonus excerpt from the *NIV Once-A-Day Bible for Teens*

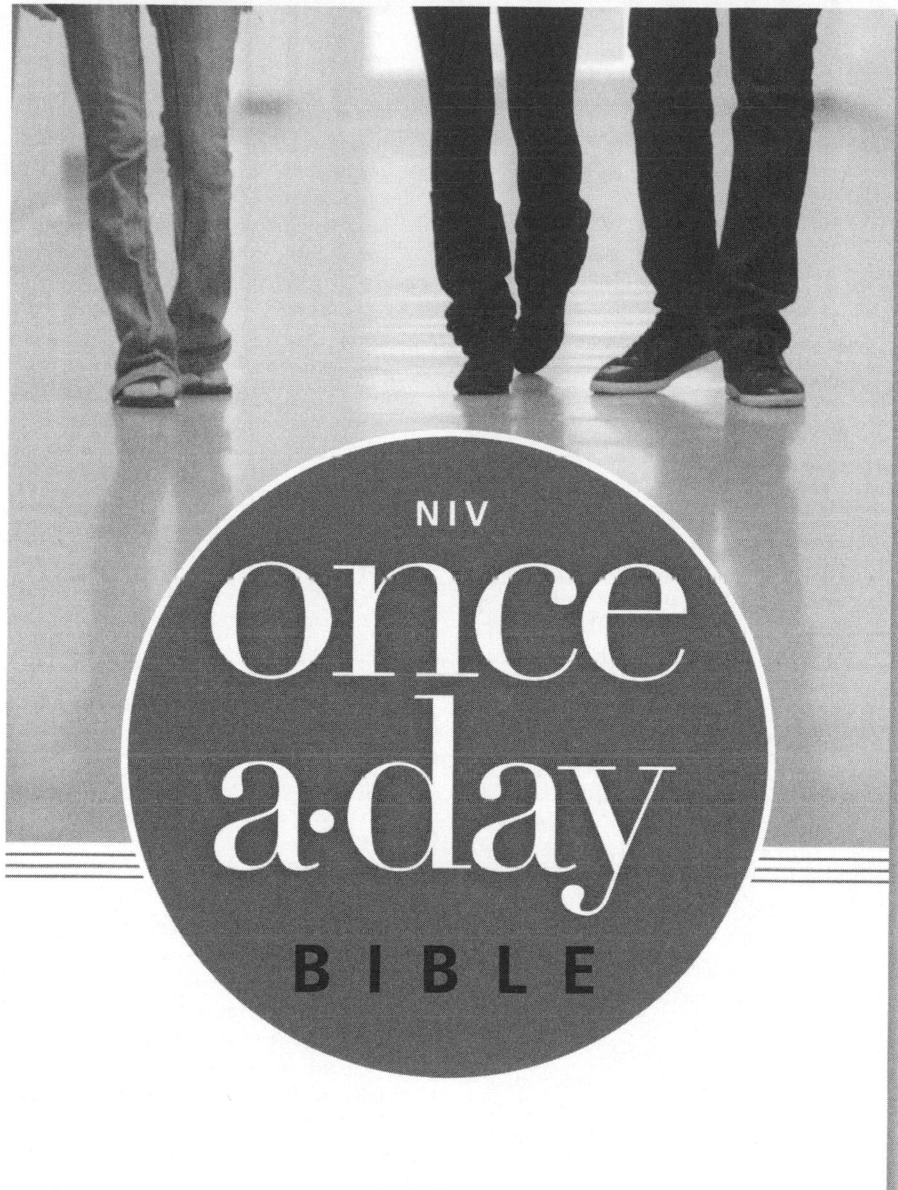

day 1

GENESIS 1:1—2:17

The Beginning

1 In the beginning God created the
heavens and the earth. [2]Now the earth
was formless and empty, darkness was
over the surface of the deep, and the Spirit of God was hovering over the waters.

[3]And God said, "Let there be light," and
there was light. [4]God saw that the light
was good, and he separated the light
from the darkness. [5]God called the
light "day," and the darkness he called
"night." And there was evening, and
there was morning—the first day.

[6]And God said, "Let there be a vault between the waters to separate water from
water." [7]So God made the vault and separated the water under the vault from
the water above it. And it was so. [8]God
called the vault "sky." And there was evening, and there was morning—the second day.

[9]And God said, "Let the water under the
sky be gathered to one place, and let dry
ground appear." And it was so. [10]God
called the dry ground "land," and the
gathered waters he called "seas." And
God saw that it was good.

[11]Then God said, "Let the land produce vegetation: seed-bearing plants and
trees on the land that bear fruit with seed
in it, according to their various kinds."
And it was so. [12]The land produced vegetation: plants bearing seed according to
their kinds and trees bearing fruit with
seed in it according to their kinds. And
God saw that it was good. [13]And there
was evening, and there was morning—
the third day.

[14]And God said, "Let there be lights in the
vault of the sky to separate the day from
the night, and let them serve as signs to
mark sacred times, and days and years,
[15]and let them be lights in the vault of
the sky to give light on the earth." And it
was so. [16]God made two great lights—
the greater light to govern the day and
the lesser light to govern the night. He
also made the stars. [17]God set them in
the vault of the sky to give light on the
earth, [18]to govern the day and the night,
and to separate light from darkness. And
God saw that it was good. [19]And there
was evening, and there was morning—
the fourth day.

[20]And God said, "Let the water teem with
living creatures, and let birds fly above
the earth across the vault of the sky."
[21]So God created the great creatures
of the sea and every living thing with
which the water teems and that moves
about in it, according to their kinds, and
every winged bird according to its kind.
And God saw that it was good. [22]God
blessed them and said, "Be fruitful and
increase in number and fill the water in
the seas, and let the birds increase on the
earth." [23]And there was evening, and
there was morning—the fifth day.

[24]And God said, "Let the land produce living
creatures according to their kinds: the
livestock, the creatures that move along
the ground, and the wild animals, each
according to its kind." And it was so.
[25]God made the wild animals according to their kinds, the livestock according to their kinds, and all the creatures
that move along the ground according
to their kinds. And God saw that it was
good.

[26]Then God said, "Let us make mankind in our image, in our likeness, so
that they may rule over the fish in the
sea and the birds in the sky, over the
livestock and all the wild animals,[a] and
over all the creatures that move along the
ground."

[27]So God created mankind in his own
image,
in the image of God he created them;
male and female he created them.

[a] *26* Probable reading of the original Hebrew text (see Syriac); Masoretic Text *the earth*

28 God blessed them and said to them,
"Be fruitful and increase in number; fill
the earth and subdue it. Rule over the
fish in the sea and the birds in the sky
and over every living creature that moves
on the ground."
29 Then God said, "I give you every
seed-bearing plant on the face of the
whole earth and every tree that has fruit
with seed in it. They will be yours for
food. 30 And to all the beasts of the earth
and all the birds in the sky and all the
creatures that move along the ground—
everything that has the breath of life in
it—I give every green plant for food."
And it was so.
31 God saw all that he had made, and
it was very good. And there was evening,
and there was morning—the sixth day.

2 Thus the heavens and the earth were
completed in all their vast array.

2 By the seventh day God had finished the
work he had been doing; so on the seventh day he rested from all his work.
3 Then God blessed the seventh day and
made it holy, because on it he rested from
all the work of creating that he had done.

Adam and Eve

4 This is the account of the heavens and the
earth when they were created, when the LORD
God made the earth and the heavens.

5 Now no shrub had yet appeared on the
earth[a] and no plant had yet sprung up, for the
LORD God had not sent rain on the earth and
there was no one to work the ground, 6 but
streams[b] came up from the earth and watered
the whole surface of the ground. 7 Then the
LORD God formed a man[c] from the dust of the
ground and breathed into his nostrils the breath
of life, and the man became a living being.
8 Now the LORD God had planted a garden in the east, in Eden; and there he put the
man he had formed. 9 The LORD God made
all kinds of trees grow out of the ground—
trees that were pleasing to the eye and good
for food. In the middle of the garden were the
tree of life and the tree of the knowledge of
good and evil.
10 A river watering the garden flowed from
Eden; from there it was separated into four
headwaters. 11 The name of the first is the
Pishon; it winds through the entire land of
Havilah, where there is gold. 12 (The gold of
that land is good; aromatic resin[d] and onyx are
also there.) 13 The name of the second river is
the Gihon; it winds through the entire land of
Cush.[e] 14 The name of the third river is the Ti-
gris; it runs along the east side of Ashur. And
the fourth river is the Euphrates.
15 The LORD God took the man and put
him in the Garden of Eden to work it and take
care of it. 16 And the LORD God commanded
the man, "You are free to eat from any tree in
the garden; 17 but you must not eat from the
tree of the knowledge of good and evil, for
when you eat from it you will certainly die."

MATTHEW 1:1—1:25

The Genealogy of Jesus the Messiah

1 This is the genealogy[f] of Jesus the Messiah[g] the son of David, the son of Abraham:

2 Abraham was the father of Isaac,
Isaac the father of Jacob,
Jacob the father of Judah and his brothers,
3 Judah the father of Perez and Zerah, whose mother was Tamar,
Perez the father of Hezron,
Hezron the father of Ram,
4 Ram the father of Amminadab,
Amminadab the father of Nahshon,
Nahshon the father of Salmon,
5 Salmon the father of Boaz, whose mother was Rahab,
Boaz the father of Obed, whose mother was Ruth,
Obed the father of Jesse,
6 and Jesse the father of King David.

[a] *5* Or *land*; also in verse 6 [b] *6* Or *mist* [c] *7* The Hebrew for *man (adam)* sounds like and may be related to the Hebrew for *ground (adamah)*; it is also the name *Adam* (see verse 20). [d] *12* Or *good; pearls* [e] *13* Possibly southeast Mesopotamia [f] *1* Or *is an account of the origin* [g] *1* Or *Jesus Christ. Messiah* (Hebrew) and *Christ* (Greek) both mean *Anointed One*; also in verse 18.

David was the father of Solomon, whose
mother had been Uriah's wife,
7 Solomon the father of Rehoboam,
Rehoboam the father of Abijah,
Abijah the father of Asa,
8 Asa the father of Jehoshaphat,
Jehoshaphat the father of Jehoram,
Jehoram the father of Uzziah,
9 Uzziah the father of Jotham,
Jotham the father of Ahaz,
Ahaz the father of Hezekiah,
10 Hezekiah the father of Manasseh,
Manasseh the father of Amon,
Amon the father of Josiah,
11 and Josiah the father of Jeconiah[a] and
his brothers at the time of the exile
to Babylon.

12 After the exile to Babylon:
Jeconiah was the father of Shealtiel,
Shealtiel the father of Zerubbabel,
13 Zerubbabel the father of Abihud,
Abihud the father of Eliakim,
Eliakim the father of Azor,
14 Azor the father of Zadok,
Zadok the father of Akim,
Akim the father of Elihud,
15 Elihud the father of Eleazar,
Eleazar the father of Matthan,
Matthan the father of Jacob,
16 and Jacob the father of Joseph, the
husband of Mary, and Mary was
the mother of Jesus who is called
the Messiah.

17 Thus there were fourteen generations in all from Abraham to David, fourteen from David to the exile to Babylon, and fourteen from the exile to the Messiah.

Joseph Accepts Jesus as His Son

18 This is how the birth of Jesus the Messiah came about[b]: His mother Mary was pledged to be married to Joseph, but before they came together, she was found to be pregnant through the Holy Spirit.
19 Because Joseph her husband was faithful to the law, and yet[c] did not want to expose her to public disgrace, he had in mind to divorce her quietly.

20 But after he had considered this, an angel of the Lord appeared to him in a dream and said, "Joseph son of David, do not be afraid to take Mary home as your wife, because what is conceived in her is from the Holy Spirit.
21 She will give birth to a son, and you are to give him the name Jesus,[d] because he will save his people from their sins."

22 All this took place to fulfill what the Lord had said through the prophet:
23 "The virgin will conceive and give birth to a son, and they will call him Immanuel"[e] (which means "God with us").

24 When Joseph woke up, he did what the angel of the Lord had commanded him and took Mary home as his wife.
25 But he did not consummate their marriage until she gave birth to a son. And he gave him the name Jesus.

PSALM 1:1—1:6

Psalm 1

1 Blessed is the one
who does not walk in step with the
wicked
or stand in the way that sinners take
or sit in the company of mockers,
2 but whose delight is in the law of the
LORD,
and who meditates on his law day and
night.
3 That person is like a tree planted by
streams of water,
which yields its fruit in season
and whose leaf does not wither—
whatever they do prospers.

4 Not so the wicked!
They are like chaff
that the wind blows away.
5 Therefore the wicked will not stand in the
judgment,
nor sinners in the assembly of the
righteous.

6 For the LORD watches over the way of the
righteous,
but the way of the wicked leads to
destruction.

[a] *11* That is, Jehoiachin; also in verse 12 [b] *18* Or *The origin of Jesus the Messiah was like this* [c] *19* Or *was a righteous man and* [d] *21* *Jesus* is the Greek form of *Joshua,* which means *the LORD saves.* [e] *23* Isaiah 7:14

REWIND

Genesis 1:1–2:17; Matthew 1; Psalm 1

IT'S ALL ABOUT BEGINNINGS.

Genesis 1–2 describes the origination of the universe, from nothingness to God's creation of everything you see. The story moves from the beginning of space and time to the start of every plant, animal, and person on earth. Matthew 1 traces Jesus' roots from Abraham to Joseph, his earthly father, and tells of his miraculous birth to a virgin, Mary. And Psalm 1 explains how you can make your first moves toward a life close to God. ✣

day2

GENESIS 2:18—4:16

18 The LORD God said, "It is not good for
the man to be alone. I will make a helper suitable for him."
19 Now the LORD God had formed out of
the ground all the wild animals and all the
birds in the sky. He brought them to the man
to see what he would name them; and whatever the man called each living creature, that
was its name. 20 So the man gave names to all
the livestock, the birds in the sky and all the
wild animals.
But for Adam[a] no suitable helper was found.
21 So the LORD God caused the man to fall
into a deep sleep; and while he was sleeping,
he took one of the man's ribs[b] and then closed
up the place with flesh. 22 Then the LORD God
made a woman from the rib[c] he had taken out
of the man, and he brought her to the man.
23 The man said,

"This is now bone of my bones
  and flesh of my flesh;
she shall be called 'woman,'
  for she was taken out of man."

24 That is why a man leaves his father and
mother and is united to his wife, and they become one flesh.
25 Adam and his wife were both naked, and
they felt no shame.

The Fall

3 Now the serpent was more crafty than
any of the wild animals the LORD God
had made. He said to the woman, "Did God
really say, 'You must not eat from any tree in
the garden'?"
2 The woman said to the serpent, "We may
eat fruit from the trees in the garden, 3 but
God did say, 'You must not eat fruit from the
tree that is in the middle of the garden, and
you must not touch it, or you will die.'"
4 "You will not certainly die," the serpent
said to the woman. 5 "For God knows that
when you eat from it your eyes will be opened,
and you will be like God, knowing good and
evil."
6 When the woman saw that the fruit of the
tree was good for food and pleasing to the eye,
and also desirable for gaining wisdom, she
took some and ate it. She also gave some to
her husband, who was with her, and he ate it.
7 Then the eyes of both of them were opened,
and they realized they were naked; so they
sewed fig leaves together and made coverings
for themselves.
8 Then the man and his wife heard the
sound of the LORD God as he was walking
in the garden in the cool of the day, and they
hid from the LORD God among the trees of
the garden. 9 But the LORD God called to the
man, "Where are you?"
10 He answered, "I heard you in the garden, and I was afraid because I was naked; so
I hid."
11 And he said, "Who told you that you
were naked? Have you eaten from the tree that
I commanded you not to eat from?"

[a] 20 Or *the man* [b] 21 Or *took part of the man's side* [c] 22 Or *part*

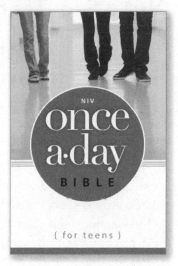

Not a Fan: Teen Edition

What does it mean to really follow Jesus?

Kyle Idleman

If someone asked, "Are you a fan of Jesus?", how would you answer?

You attend every movie featuring a certain actor, you know the stats of your sports hero, and you can recite lyrics from your favorite songs. In short, you're a huge fan. But are you treating Jesus the same as the other people you admire? The truth is Jesus wants more than the church attendance, occasional prayer, and the ability to recite Scripture—the fan response. He's looking for people who are actually willing to sacrifice in order to follow him. In this teen edition of *Not a Fan*, Kyle Idleman uses humor, personal stories, and biblical truth as he challenges you to look at what it means to call yourself a Christian and follow the radical call Jesus presents. So, will you be a fan, or a follower?

Available in stores and online!

ZONDERVAN®
.com

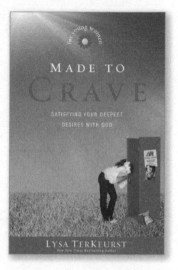